WITHDRAWN

T H E
BOND
FUND
ADVISOR

UNDERSTANDING THE RISKS AND REWARDS

Werner Renberg

Dearborn
Financial Publishing, Inc.

To Dalia, Dan and Gil and to Ken.

While a great deal of care has been taken to provide accurate and current information, the ideas, suggestions, general principles and conclusions presented in this book are subject to local, state and federal laws and regulations, court cases and any revisions of same. The reader is thus urged to consult legal counsel regarding any points of law—this publication should not be used as a substitute for competent legal advice.

Publisher: Kathleen A. Welton
Project Editors: Ellen Allen and Linda S. Miller
Cover Design: Salvatore Concialdi

©1990 by Werner Renberg

Published by Dearborn Financial Publishing, Inc.

Printed in the United States of America

90 91 92 10 9 8 7 6 5 4 3 2 1

Library of Congress Cataloging-in-Publication Data

Renberg, Werner.
   The bond fund advisor: understanding the risks and rewards /
by Werner Renberg.
     p. cm.
   ISBN 0-88462-912-0
   1. Bond funds. I. Title.
   HG4651.R46 1990
   332.63′27—dc20
                                  89-48628
                                    CIP

TABLE OF CONTENTS

PREFACE

Few developments on the U.S. investment scene in the 1980s were as significant as the evolution and sudden burst of growth of bond mutual funds. In just five years, the number of shareholder accounts more than quadrupled to over 15 million (of which about one-fourth are individual retirement accounts). The number of funds more than tripled to well over 1,000 and assets more than quintupled to over $300 billion, pushing bond funds ahead of stock funds.

If the sales pitches of fund sponsors and brokers have led you to think about whether you *should* invest in a bond fund, this book is for you. If in recent years you bought shares of a fund that turned out to be unsuitable and you now want to switch, this book is also for you. And, if you've owned shares in a bond fund for many years but wondered whether your current goals or circumstances might call for putting money into a second one, this book is for you, too.

Many who were enticed by sales pitches and invested their money were impressed by the explicit or implicit—but misleading—promise of perennial double-digit yields or by the presumed—but unwarranted—assurance that the U.S. government stood behind government bond funds. Those who wanted regular cash distributions from the funds, instead of reinvesting dividends in additional shares, were gladdened by the prospect of getting monthly checks. Bond fund ads didn't always say whether any risks were involved, and investors didn't always remember to ask. It wasn't until later—when prices of bonds fell (regardless of whether they were high-quality or high-yield securities)—that investors became aware of other facets of bond fund investing.

Clearly, there is more to bond funds than the expectation of monthly dividend checks, the assurance of governmental backing for a fund portfolio's securities (in the case of government bond funds) or the avoidance of taxes on income (in the case of tax-exempt bond funds). As some investors have unfortunately learned the hard way, bond funds are not like savings accounts or money market funds. They involve risks as well as rewards. So long as the risks incurred are known and acceptable, bond fund shares can be appropriate investments for many.

Because I found no existing book devoted exclusively to providing comprehensive background and guidance to bond fund investors, I decided to write this book. It should help you to understand:

- whether *any* category of bond fund is for you;
- if so, which category (or categories); and
- within each category, how to identify the funds that are likely to be the most suitable for you.

Learning how to invest in bond funds isn't as simple as you may have assumed or been led to believe. Nor is it terribly complicated. Bond fund investing has certain elements in common with stock fund investing—such as the importance of matching investments with your investment objectives, knowing your risk tolerance and taking a long-term view. However, it also requires assimilation of different factors and concepts. Unless your situation is highly unusual, you can master what you really need to know with relatively little time and effort.

As you will see, the large number of bond funds in operation today differ widely in investment objectives and policies, acceptance of risks, results, age and costs to shareholders. Although the great and growing variety of choices that they offer may seem confusing at first, you'll soon realize that that makes it all the more likely that you'll find a fund (or two) with the combination of characteristics appropriate for you.

The book begins with a review of the explosion in governmental and corporate debt and the proliferation of debt securities in the United States. Chapter 1 looks at the issuers (borrowers): federal, state and local governments and corporations.

Chapter 2 focuses on the purchasers (lenders): you and I, wearing our different hats as direct investors and as indirect investors via mutual funds, 401(k) and other savings plans, pension plans, financial corporations in which we may have directly or indirectly invested and so forth.

Chapter 3 reviews the growth in bond mutual funds, which has accompanied the growth in corporate and government debt, and the pervasiveness of bond fund share ownership. ("Bond funds" is the term used throughout this book to refer to mutual funds that primarily own one or more types of debt securities—including debentures, notes, mortgage-backed securities and others not literally called bonds. The term is generally synonymous with "fixed-income funds" or "income funds," although the first may also be invested in preferred stocks and the second in high-yielding common stocks.)

Chapter 4 discusses the classification of taxable and tax-exempt bond funds and describes the characteristics of the various categories.

In Chapter 5 you will see how well or poorly bond funds have performed and why. Past performance does not automatically guarantee that future performance will be the same, whether good or bad. But it should give us some idea of what we may expect of a fund, so long as its investment objectives, policies and portfolio manager remain the same.

Chapter 6 helps you to look at your circumstances and goals so that you can decide whether debt securities are appropriate for you and, if so, whether you would be better off investing in them directly or indirectly through bond funds.

If you've concluded that you should invest in one or more bond funds, Chapter 7 offers help in choosing the one(s) likely to help you achieve your investment objectives. It also suggests how to put your money to work—and how to watch it.

For ordering the prospectuses, annual reports and other information from the funds you're considering, you'll find addresses and telephone numbers in the Appendices for funds that have track records of five years or longer. (Some funds that have been in business for shorter periods may be worth considering if sponsored by well-regarded fund families that also offer older bond funds or if managed by portfolio managers whose relevant long-term performance records you can check.)

Bond funds should be most rewarding when they are used as long-term investments to provide portfolio diversification and to provide generous income consistent with measured risk of principal. They are less likely to be rewarding when used as vehicles for short-term speculation on interest rates or for generation of maximum cash distributions while exposing principal to excessive risk.

In offering guidelines for your fund selection, I have stressed historic performance data on the assumption that, when you find funds that have done well over the long run under various economic and market conditions, you probably will have spotted funds that, similarly managed, could do well in the years ahead. Historic data are not an infallible indicator of future performance but, given the scarcity of prophets (if not of prophecy), they can be useful. Bond fund investment advisers and portfolio managers who have not yet had to deal with tough challenges, such as exceptional interest rate volatility, record downgrading of corporate bonds and increased globalization of credit markets, may not be sufficiently experienced to handle your hard-earned cash.

To save you money—or to enhance the return on money you choose to commit to any bond fund—I have emphasized the rationality of investing in leading performers whose shares you can buy or sell without paying "loads" and whose annual expenses are low. After you're familiar with categories and funds, you'll realize that you can be self-reliant. You don't need to pay brokers and dealers as much as 8.5 percent commission to sell you shares of a bond fund or 5 percent to redeem your shares. Except for a firm's forecast of interest rates, which is unlikely to be superior to those you can read for yourself, a salesperson can't give you any vital information regarding a fund that you can't get on your own by reading its prospectus and shareholder report or by phoning the fund.

Once your money is pooled with that of other investors and used to buy securities for a fund's portfolio, you want as little as possible subtracted from income for annual operating expenses so that you'll receive more cash dividends or be credited with more shares. Naturally, the portfolio manager and others who make the fund tick deserve reasonable compensation. But don't forget that you, too, deserve adequate compensation for the risk you've taken.

ACKNOWLEDGMENTS

To produce a work of this scope and detail would not have been possible without cooperation of many in the fund industry, other financial services businesses and government who helped in various ways—from providing resource materials and historic information to discussing fund policies and investment strategies. With my deepest appreciation, I would like to acknowledge their contributions. Most helpful were: (in alphabetical order) Donald E. Farrar, Jane Ginsburg and John S. Schniedwind, Jr., Benham; Larry Mayewski, A.M. Best; Peter Langer and Isabelle V. Lindskoog, Capital Research and Management; Tom Regan, Colonial; W. Timothy Ryan, Dodge & Cox; Daniel C. Maclean III, Dreyfus; Dick Miller and Mark S. Venezia, Eaton Vance; Stephen A. Lumpkin, Patrick I. Mahoney, Robert Reewald, Laura S. Rubin, David P. Simon, John F. Wilson and Judith A. Ziobro, Federal Reserve System; Michael Guzzi, Federated; Robert Beckwitt, Larry Dwyer, Domenic Gaeta and James Wolfson, Fidelity; William W. Veronda, Financial Programs; Jerry R. Eubank and Liz Zazecki, First Investors; Lynn Closway, IDS; Margaret (Peg) A. Corwin, Ibbotson Associates; Jacob S. Dreyer, Matthew P. Fink, Betty K. Hart, L. Erick Kanter, C. Richard Pogue and Anne M. Schaffer, Investment Company Institute; William C. Hisey, Jones & Babson; William R. Buecking, Robert J. Butler and Steve Radis, Kemper; Nancy J. Finnerty, Keystone; Donald A. Petrie, Lazard Freres; A. Michael Lipper and Henry Shilling, Lipper Analytical Services; John B. Jamieson and

John F. Reilly, Massachusetts Financial Services; Kenneth A. Jacob and Dennis Reems, Merrill Lynch; Harold H. Goldberg and John Lonski, Moody's Investors Service; Larry M. Pence, Mutual of Omaha; Paul W. Boltz, Peter J.D. Gordon, Steven E. Norwitz and Charles P. Smith, T. Rowe Price; Lisbeth W. Chapman, Putnam; Carol A. Russo and David Torchia, Salomon Bros.; Donald C. Carleton, Olga Hadji, Donna M. Murtha, James Smith, Davia Temin and Samuel Thorne, Jr., Scudder; Joleen Jasinski, Standard & Poor's; Terri L. Berg, Stein Roe; Henry Wulf, U.S. Bureau of the Census; Jack Flynn, Albert J. Fulner, Jr. and Robert P. Kalish, U.S. Department of Housing and Urban Development; Robert W. Kilpatrick, U.S. Office of Management and Budget, Executive Office of the President; Joseph J. Doyle, Lawrence Friend, Gene A. Gohlke, Stanley Judd, Mary M. McCue and Kathryn B. McGrath, U.S. Securities and Exchange Commission; Peter Hollenbach, Carl M. Locken, Jr. and Carolyn Lynch, U.S. Department of the Treasury; William F. Hostler, Ian A. MacKinnon, Brian S. Mattes, Tami Wise and John S. Woerth, Vanguard; Andrew P. Ferretti, Peter B. Sholley and Robert A. Warren, retired Keystone executives; and last, but not least, Walter L. Morgan, chairman emeritus of the Wellington Fund, who founded it in 1928.

I am especially grateful to Lipper Analytical Services for generously permitting the extensive use of their data and to those men and women of the SEC's Division of Investment Management who, despite heavy workloads, always managed to squeeze in the time to return phone calls— even after hours—to answer questions.

Of all my debts of gratitude, however, none exceeds that owed to my wife, Dalia, and our sons, Dan and Gil, for their cheerful support as well as for their understanding during the months when this book project demanded most of my time.

April 1990   WERNER RENBERG

CHAPTER 1

The Debt Explosion

It is self-evident that neither bonds nor bond mutual funds would be available for investment if Polonius' advice to his son, Laertes, in *Hamlet* were heeded:

> Neither a borrower nor a lender be;
> For loan oft loses both itself and friend,
> And borrowing dulls the edge of husbandry.

Happily for lenders—or investors—there has not been a shortage of borrowers in the United States since the nation's birth. Happily for borrowers—from individuals building homes or businesses to the national government itself—there has rarely been a shortage of lenders, provided the interest rates and other terms were acceptable.

In a 1781 letter to Robert Morris, Alexander Hamilton said, "A national debt, if it isn't excessive, will be to us a national blessing." Since our public and private debt now exceeds $12 trillion, our first Secretary of the Treasury might consider the debt accumulated in recent decades too much of a blessing.

In this book we will concern ourselves with the types of debt instruments in which mutual funds invest and with the funds themselves. We will discuss securities accounting for more than $5 trillion, or slightly less than one-half of the credit market debt outstanding at the end of 1988. Included are U.S. government paper of various types, securities issued by state and local governments and others whose interest is exempt from federal income tax, and the fully taxable long-term debt securities of U.S. corporations. Table 1-1 shows how federal, state and local governments and U.S. corporations have increased their outstanding debt securities over the last quarter of a century. (Market values of outstanding

1

Table 1-1   U.S. Credit Market Debt Outstanding at End of Select Years 1963–1988 (in trillions of dollars)

Type of Debt	1963	1968	1973	1978	1983	1988
U.S. government securities	$0.3	$0.3	$0.4	$0.8	$1.6	$ 3.3
Tax-exempt obligations*	0.1	0.1	0.2	0.3	0.5	0.8
Corporate bonds	0.1	0.2	0.2	0.4	0.5	1.3
Mortgages and other debt**	0.5	0.8	1.3	2.3	3.7	6.2
Total	$1.0	$1.4	$2.2	$3.8	$6.3	$11.5
Corporate equities excluding shares of mutual funds	*$0.6*	*$1.0*	*$0.9*	*$1.0*	*$2.0*	*$ 3.1*

*Includes industrial revenue bonds.
**Principally consumer credit, bank loans and open-market paper.

Totals may not add due to rounding.

Source: Flow of Funds Section, Board of Governors of the Federal Reserve System.

corporate equities are shown in italics to permit comparison with corporate bonds.)

Whether called bonds, debentures, certificates of indebtedness or something else, all will be collectively referred to as bonds. No matter how varied their issuers or their merit as investments, all have essential elements in common: they are debt instruments promising lenders periodic payments of interest and eventual repayment of principal.

THE FEDERAL GOVERNMENT AS BORROWER

The Early Years

For two centuries, the federal government itself has set an example not only of borrowing continuously but also of paying interest and repaying principal on schedule. Its record of trustworthiness owes much to Hamilton, who set the standards with his Report on Public Credit, which he submitted to Congress in 1790, a few months after it had appointed him.

Hamilton reasoned that to promote the development of the economy as well as to conduct its operations, the federal government would have to be able to borrow money from time to time at home and abroad. To do that, it was essential that the infant government first establish its creditworthiness. This, he said in the face of strong opposition from other Founding Fathers, would justify assuming the Continental Congress' deeply discounted bonds at face value—even if that meant windfall profits for speculators who might have bought them for 25¢ on the dollar. Establishing creditworthiness also would warrant assumption of the debts that states incurred in fighting the War of Independence—although there was no legal obligation to do so.

The central government also would have to generate its own revenues by levying taxes instead of asking the state governments for contributions—and waiting, often in vain, for the money. In other words, the new Congress would have to exercise the "Power To lay and collect Taxes, Duties, Imposes and Excises" given it by the recently ratified Constitution. Thus, Hamilton persuaded Congress to impose duties on imports and excise taxes at levels sufficient to service the government's debts and pay its operating expenses. (Not until 1913 would the Sixteenth Amendment to the Constitution permanently empower Congress to tax individual and business income.)

Launched with a debt estimated by Hamilton at $77 million—about one-third of it inherited from the states—the federal government managed to reduce that amount slightly until the War of 1812. Then, with taxes inadequate to sustain the fight with the British while maintaining regular programs, the government had to step up its borrowing; by 1815 it owed twice as much as it had before the war.

Over the next two decades, the government was able to run surpluses despite outlays for such items as canals and veterans' pensions. Under a determined President Andrew Jackson, who did not regard a national debt as a blessing, the United States was able to redeem all of its outstanding interest-bearing bonds by 1835.

"An unprecedented spectacle," the Secretary of the Treasury, Levi Woodbury, proclaimed—"a government...virtually without any debt." He was the first secretary who could make such a statement about the U.S. government—and he may have been the last.

Wars and Recessions

Jackson had barely been succeeded by Martin Van Buren before the depression of 1837 occurred and deficits returned. The 1846 war with Mexico and the 1857 Panic led to a debt of $65 million by 1860. The magnitudes of federal expenditures and revenue needs rose exponentially soon thereafter with the outbreak of the Civil War, and the debt rose above the $2 billion mark.

During the 50 years following the Civil War, as the nation healed its wounds, settled the West and built its industry, the federal government was able to produce surpluses sufficient to halve its debt. It accomplished this even though it was enlarging its payroll as it expanded services and undertook more costly projects, such as the Panama Canal.

Then came World War I, with its enormous cost in lives—and capital. Although on entering the war the Wilson Administration had hoped to borrow only 50 percent of its cost, estimated at over $30 billion, by the end of 1919, the national debt had swollen to $25 billion.

Happier times—"normalcy"—returned in the 1920s. As the economy flourished, producing goods and services for a nation once again at peace, the government was able not only to reduce expenditures and taxes but also to operate at a surplus and bring the debt back down to $17 billion. It was too good to last. Joy gave way to gloom and despair as the Great Depression gripped the country. By the end of fiscal 1933, with income tax receipts from individuals and corporations the lowest in a decade or more and President Herbert Hoover having launched public works and welfare programs to employ the jobless and feed the hungry, the debt was back to $23 billion.

That was only the beginning. Under President Franklin Delano Roosevelt, such programs were greatly expanded, and the rate of spending was accelerated while tax collections from individuals and corporations rose only gradually. By the end of fiscal 1940, the federal debt had more than doubled to $51 billion.

The Japanese attack on Pearl Harbor and our consequent entry into World War II in December 1941, overwhelmed the debate about government spending and borrowing. With friendly nations overrun or imperiled and the security of the United States itself at stake, the financial cost of defeating the Axis Powers was not a consideration. Winning the war became the primary—and unifying—concern.

The dollar cost of achieving that goal, it turned out, would be an estimated $323 billion. Despite the increase of marginal income tax rates to as much as 53 percent for corporations and 94 percent for individuals for certain levels of corporate and individual income (and the introduction of payroll withholding), the government had to borrow as much as $211 billion for the war effort. By 1946 the outstanding federal debt had soared to $271 billion. It was staggering not only in absolute terms but also in relative terms, even exceeding the gross national product (GNP) by a significant margin.

In the postwar years expenditures receded, with the diminished need for military personnel and purchases, while personal and corporate incomes rose, thus raising tax collections even though tax rates were permitted to drop. From fiscal 1947 through 1949, the Truman Administration even managed to run small surpluses, the first since 1930, and to shave the federal debt. But prewar levels would never be seen again.

Rearming for the Cold War with the Soviet Union and for hostilities in Korea led national defense expenditures to soar again. By fiscal 1953

Table 1-2   Deficits and the Gross Federal Debt—1965-1989 (in billions of dollars)

Fiscal Year	Surplus (deficit) at Year-End	Gross Federal Debt	Fiscal Year	Surplus (deficit) at Year-End	Gross Federal Debt
1965	$ (1.4)	$ 322.3	1978	(59.2)	776.6
1966	(3.7)	328.5	1979	(40.2)	828.9
1967	(8.6)	340.4	1980	(73.8)	908.5
1968	(25.2)	368.7	1981	(78.9)	994.3
1969	3.2	365.8	1982	(127.9)	1,136.8
1970	(2.8)	380.9	1983	(207.8)	1,371.2
1971	(23.0)	408.2	1984	(185.3)	1,564.1
1972	(23.4)	435.9	1985	(212.3)	1,817.0
1973	(14.9)	466.3	1986	(221.2)	2,120.1
1974	(6.1)	483.9	1987	(149.7)	2,345.6
1975	(53.2)	541.9	1988	(155.2)	2,600.8
1976	(88.5)*	643.6*	1989	(152.1)	2,881.1
1977	(53.6)	706.4			

*Totals include the "transitional" July–September quarter of 1976, resulting from a change in the fiscal year's end from June to September.

Source: 1965–88, *Budget of the United States Government, Fiscal Year 1990* and *Special Analyses, Budget of the United States Government, Fiscal Year 1990;* Office of Management and Budget, Executive Office of the President; 1989, Department of the Treasury.

they were back to $50 billion, highest since World War II's last fiscal year. Owing to higher expenditures and two recessions (1953–54 and 1957–58), the debt climbed gradually but persistently through most of the Eisenhower years. It reached $290 billion by the end of fiscal 1960, a new high but a smaller percent of GNP thanks to the economy's growth.

Guns and Butter

With the election of John F. Kennedy in 1960 and his succession by Lyndon B. Johnson, the federal government expanded, undertaking social programs at an accelerating pace. At the same time, it became increasingly involved in a war in Vietnam. The combined costs of both domestic and defense programs were too much for the government to absorb on a current basis, leading to increased deficits (Table 1-2), increased inflation and an era of higher interest rates.

A large income tax cut enacted in February 1964, inhibited growth in revenues as the long expansion of the 1960s got under way. As the war escalated and national defense expenditures rose, many urged Johnson to raise taxes because the nation could not afford "guns and butter" at the same time. Johnson was not persuaded. By the time he proposed and

Congress enacted a temporary tax surcharge in 1968, the deficit had grown to $25 billion—by far the largest since World War II. While the surcharge produced a surplus in fiscal 1969—the last the country has known—the 1960s ended with the debt at $366 billion, $78 billion higher than it had been at the beginning of the period.

Nor did the $366 billion include all the debt instruments issued as a result of federal activities or programs. It did not include the billions of loans guaranteed or securities sold outside the budget by federal or federally sponsored credit agencies to raise capital for housing, agriculture, education and other purposes.

After the Federal Reserve restrained monetary growth in 1965 to cope with inflationary pressures resulting from the growing deficit, Johnson and Congress took the first of several new initiatives to help housing—and added to the supply of federally sponsored securities. First, in 1966 they authorized the Federal National Mortgage Association (Fannie Mae) to package Federal Housing Administration (FHA) and Veterans Administration (VA) mortgage loans, bought from banks and savings and loan institutions, in "pools" and sell "pass-through" certificates of participation in the pools to investors. ("Pass-through" applies to the interest and principal payments made by the borrowers, which are periodically passed through to the certificate holders.) Although money was tight, Fannie Mae could generate additional capital for mortgages from investors who found the certificates attractive.

While this activity increased the volume of federally sponsored securities, it did not raise the federal debt by one cent. Nor was the federal government's risk of loss raised; the government had been exposed to loss from borrowers defaulting on the mortgages that collateralized the certificates from the moment the FHA and VA had agreed to make the loans good.

In 1968, when interest rates rose as inflation reached its highest level since the Korean War, the government enhanced its efforts to generate funds for housing. It split Fannie Mae into two new organizations. One, retaining the name and functions of Fannie Mae, was converted into a stockholder-owned corporation under federal sponsorship. The other, a government agency named Government National Mortgage Association (Ginnie Mae), was authorized not only to buy FHA and VA mortgages from their originators and package them into pools but also to stamp its certification with the government's guarantee.

The election in 1968 of a conservative Republican, Richard M. Nixon, who promised to end the war in Vietnam, may have led some to expect that federal deficits and the federal debt *finally* would be reduced after the war's end and the freezing of Great Society programs. As things turned out, debt reduction was not to be. Spending for the war was dropping, to be sure, and the tax surcharge was extended, keeping the deficit under control through fiscal 1970. It was the calm before the storm.

The Turbulent 1970s

Inflationary pressures gained new strength in the 1970s, exacerbated at home by excessive fiscal and monetary ease and abroad by severe oil price increases initiated by the cartel of exporting nations. When the Federal Reserve acted, alone, to fight inflation by dampening the economy, interest rates soared to record levels. The high rates produced painful recessions, which led to greater federal non-defense spending—and Treasury borrowing—under three presidents, but inflation remained.

As the 1970s dawned, tightened fiscal and monetary policies ended the expansion that had lasted nearly nine years, threw the country into a recession, but were only moderately successful in combating inflation. Despite lingering inflation, monetary and fiscal policies were eased again: the tax surcharge was eliminated and spending for welfare and other non-defense programs was increased. By December 1970, a new expansion was under way.

Not surprisingly, an increase in outlays and drop in receipts led to a $23 billion deficit in fiscal 1971, causing the Treasury again to become a major borrower. It was joined in the credit markets by a new private but federally sponsored issuer of mortgage-backed securities, the Federal Home Loan Mortgage Corporation (Freddie Mac), created by the Emergency Home Finance Act of 1970 to strengthen the secondary market for conventional mortgages.

The expansion continued through 1971 and 1972, nourished by stimulative fiscal and monetary policies that were maintained in the face of persistent inflation. Instead of reversing course, President Nixon announced in August 1971, a new strategy to deal with inflation: the nation's first peacetime wage and price controls.

By mid-January 1973 the Fed realized that a different policy was in order, in part because the expansion was straining the nation's industrial capacity. Controls were proving to be less than effective—price controls may even have exacerbated inflation by creating shortages—and the federal government was continuing to spend more than it took in from a growing economy. The Fed invoked all of its weapons to slow down the growth of the money supply; among other things, it raised the discount rate seven times by mid-August.

This was the environment when in autumn 1973, the Organization of Petroleum Exporting Countries (OPEC), without forewarning, sharply increased the prices at which members would sell their crude oil.

To make matters worse, OPEC's Arab members imposed an embargo on shipments to the United States.

Although a recession had begun before the year was out, partly as a result of oil shortages, the Fed continued its policy of restraint through most of 1974. Interest rates soared; stock prices plunged, as did those of bonds. (In addition to economic problems, investors observed an unfolding political crisis: the threatened impeachment and eventual resignation in August of President Nixon.) U.S. inflation, nonetheless, reached levels unprecedented in peacetime, with the consumer price index (CPI) running at an annual rate of 12 percent. In September, believing its pressure on the money supply would exact the predictable toll with the unpredictable lag, the Fed began to ease. By year's end, the recession had indeed become more painful; industrial production was plunging and unemployment was rising sharply. The nation experienced the worst of both worlds: recession and inflation, running concurrently.

Recovery began in spring 1975, owing to continued monetary and fiscal stimulation, but unemployment became worse—reaching postwar peaks—before improving. With increases in transfer payments leading the way, federal outlays roared ahead under Gerald Ford, resulting in a deficit of $53.2 billion for Fiscal 1975, more than eight times as large as 1974's and only slightly below the record of $54.6 billion set in wartime 1943. Despite the new expansion, this mark was shattered in fiscal 1976, bringing the federal debt to above $600 billion. Inflation receded from double-digit levels, but it remained high.

Jimmy Carter kept fiscal policy on a similar course, despite the economic expansion that continued for three of the four years of his presidency. Expenditures rose faster than receipts, producing deficits ranging from $40 to over $70 billion and adding more than $250 billion to the Treasury's outstanding debt issues.

Inflation, subdued but not conquered in 1977, heated up again in 1978 as industrial production approached plant capacity, and the Fed once more raised interest rates in stages. In 1979 conditions deteriorated, in several ways paralleling 1973–74. Domestic inflationary pressures again were compounded by pressures from abroad as the world suffered the second "oil price shock": a virtual doubling of OPEC's export price in the wake of supply disruptions caused by Iran's revolution. By the end of the year, the CPI approached an annual rate of 13 percent, exceeding 1974.

Recognizing that more forceful monetary actions were required, the Fed in October launched a new approach: in addition to raising the discount rate to a record 12 percent, it decided to place greater emphasis on controlling bank reserves and less emphasis on the rate of federal funds (the rate at which banks lend money to one another). Interest rates soared again; by November the prime rate hit 15¾ percent.

As was later recognized, a new recession had begun in January 1980, while the CPI hit a rate of 17 percent. Before the cyclical trough was identified, however, the Fed kept the screws on, lifting the discount rate to 13 percent in February and taking appropriate actions in the money market. The bond market, meantime, was in disarray as investors watched bond prices drop and feared making new commitments. The Treasury, forced to borrow and to pay whatever the market demanded, continued to issue securities while other borrowers deferred floating new issues.

Economic activity fell as the rate of credit extension was impacted not only by a slower rate of monetary growth but also by direct controls on credit invoked by President Carter. After six months, the recession was over—the shortest on record.

The Reagan Years

With the gross federal debt above $900 billion and still rising—and extreme inflation making borrowing appear to be more sensible than lending—Ronald Reagan campaigned for and won the presidency, promising to cut non-defense spending and *finally* balance the federal budget.

In his first State of the Union address a month after his inauguration, he illustrated just how large a debt of $1 trillion would be: "...a stack of $1,000 bills 67 miles high." The debt reached the trillion-dollar level on October 22, 1981, according to an announcement by the Treasury's Bureau of the Public Debt, but it did *not* stop climbing.

In fact, the deficits of Reagan's two terms exceeded those of any predecessor, ranging as high as $221 billion in fiscal 1986, and they led to a tripling of the debt (Table 1-2).

The Reagan years were filled with irony and paradox, observed in the context of an economic expansion that was nourished by debt but unaccompanied, for the most part, by the experience or expectation of serious inflation. It was during these years of unimaginable growth in the issuance of debt securities that bond funds began to flourish, and, therefore, the highlights of the period are worth recalling.

By July 1981—a half-year after Reagan took office—the nation had slipped back into recession. To ease the hardship brought about by the 1980 recession, the Fed apparently had eased too soon; the economy had bounced back too fast in 1981's first quarter. With the CPI stuck at an annual rate of increase of around 10 percent, inflationary pressures had not been eliminated from the economy, and, thus, the Fed had decided in early 1981 to act again—and to persevere.

It restrained monetary growth more than before. By May the yield on three-month Treasury bills hit 16.3 percent. The unemployment rate rose, topping 9 percent—a level not seen since 1975—by April 1982.

Meantime, in August, Congress passed the Economic Recovery Tax Act of 1981 (ERTA), containing Reagan's proposals for $749 billion of cuts in individual and business income taxes to be spread over five years beginning October 1981. The hope was to encourage private-sector spending and investment. ERTA complicated the Fed's efforts to squelch inflation. It also increased the cost of issuing billions of additional Treasury securities because investors, apprehensive about the presumed inflationary implications of greater deficits, had to be offered higher interest rates. However, as the economy slowed down and credit demand weakened, short-run interest rates fell and long-term rates began to drift lower.

It was mid-July 1982, before the Fed's Federal Open Market Committee (FOMC) concluded that it had achieved its objective, could accept a higher rate of monetary growth, and acted accordingly.

Disclosure of this important decision was contained in a report to the Senate Banking Committee by Paul Volcker, the Fed's chairman, on July 20. Some astute observers of Fed chairmen and money markets quickly perceived what he had said. Others realized it a little later. But it took even longer for people to *believe* what he had said. Having learned to be skeptical of the idea that any president, Congress or the Federal Reserve could dampen the inflation that for so long had been factored into decision making by households and businesses, investors did not readily believe that things would be different this time.

Gradually, however, they did believe. Watching a steady drop in short-term interest rates, which supported the interpretation that the Fed was becoming less restrictive, investors turned at first to bonds, bidding up their prices and bringing long-term interest rates down more steeply. Then, in mid-August, they turned to stocks, igniting the great bull market of the 1980s. Financial assets—including, of course, mutual fund shares—had become desirable again. By November 1982, economic expansion was under way.

Euphoria dominated the bond and stock markets, with occasional interruption, until 1987 even though fiscal policy appeared to be essentially out of control. There had been so much slack in the economy that the CPI rose only moderately as idle human and plant resources were put to work.

After a dip in fiscal 1983, federal revenues continued to grow, benefiting from the boom as well as from occasional, select tax increases and elimination of "loopholes" in tax laws. But outlays, increased by defense spending and interest payments on those billions of new Treasury securities, rose even faster.

Table 1-3   Publicly Held Federal and Federally Related Debt*
1979-1988 (in billions of dollars)

Year End	Treasury Issues Excluding Savings Bonds	Savings Bonds	Federally Sponsored Mortgage Pool Securities**	Federally Sponsored Credit Agency Issues***	Total
1979	$ 578.1	$ 79.9	$ 94.8	$135.5	$ 888.3
1980	665.2	72.5	114.0	159.9	1,011.6
1981	757.4	68.2	129.0	190.4	1,145.0
1982	919.4	68.3	178.5	205.4	1,371.6
1983	1,102.9	71.5	244.9	206.8	1,626.1
1984	1,298.9	74.5	289.0	237.2	1,899.6
1985	1,517.3	79.8	368.9	257.8	2,223.8
1986	1,718.4	93.3	565.4	273.0	2,650.1
1987	1,854.0	101.1	718.3	303.2	2,976.6
1988	1,985.6	109.6	810.9	348.1	3,254.2

*Excludes Treasury securities issued to the Social Security and other federal trust funds and agencies, which are included in gross federal debt.
**GNMA, FNMA, FHLMC and Farmers Home Administration pools.
***Primarily FNMA, FHLMC, FHLBS, Farm Credit System, Student Loan Marketing Association.

Source: Flow of Funds Section, Board of Governors of the Federal Reserve System.

When Reagan turned over the reins to George Bush in January 1989, the debt was approaching $3 trillion. Reagan had estimated in his last budget (for fiscal 1990) that there would be at least two additional years of deficits, totaling $100 billion, before the government could show a tiny surplus in fiscal 1993. Bush hasn't changed the projection. No investor needed to worry that there would soon be a shortage of Treasury securities.

Nor, you'll recall, does the debt attributable to federal government activities consist exclusively of Treasury securities. As Table 1-3 shows, securities of federal or federally sponsored agencies were issued by the hundreds of billions in the 1980s, rising from about 25 percent to about 35 percent of the total of federal and federally related debt.

If presidents and Congress have lived up to the expectations of Polonius—their ability to borrow having dulled "the edge of husbandry"—they also have lived up to at least one of Hamilton's expectations: that the debts of the federal government always would be repaid on time, even if the Treasury had to borrow to do it.

STATE AND LOCAL GOVERNMENT BORROWING

The constitutions or statutes of all states except Vermont require—albeit, in different ways—that state governments' operating budgets be essentially balanced annually or biennially. However, they also permit, in different ways, capital outlays to be funded with long-term borrowing through the sale of general obligation bonds that are backed by their tax bases. Similar budget and debt requirements apply to those state offspring—counties, municipalities, townships, school districts and about 40 percent of special district governments—that have the authority to levy taxes.

Of the 83,236 state and local government entities counted by the Census Bureau in 1987, 65,871 units have the power to tax and to pledge future tax collections in support of their bonds. When these state and local governments issue long-term bonds, it is usually to finance construction and other capital projects. Some taxing bodies, administered imprudently or hit by adverse economic conditions, occasionally also issue bonds for current expenditures.

The remaining 17,365 special district governments build, own and operate utilities, turnpikes, ports, airports, sewage treatment plants, transportation systems and other public-purpose facilities for which they generally collect user fees. Lacking the power to tax, these government units must finance their general and capital expenditures essentially out of revenues generated by fees and borrowings. Most operate on a small scale and, according to the Census Bureau, over 40 percent have no debt at all. When the others undertake capital projects, they sell long-term bonds backed by the revenues from their operations, giving rise to the term "revenue bonds." Revenue bonds involve greater risk for investors than full-faith and credit bonds and, therefore, are likely to pay higher interest rates.

Public-purpose revenue bonds are not to be confused with private-purpose revenue bonds, which also have been issued by state and local governments—but for which they are not necessarily liable. Funds from these bonds have been used to build housing, industrial and commercial facilities and hospitals or to make student loans.

Of private-purpose revenue bonds, perhaps the most widely publicized are "industrial development bonds" (IDBs). These have been sold to finance the development of industrial and commercial projects of profit-making corporations, which pay the interest and repay the principal, and thus can take advantage of the lower interest rates at which tax-exempt securities are sold.

Thus, by one means or another—budgets balanced or not, liable or not—state and local governments have managed to issue a considerable volume of debt securities. Although Table 1–4 indicates that a large share of their outstanding debt at the end of 1988 consisted of securities sold during the 1980s, they have a long tradition of borrowing.

**Table 1–4   Tax-Exempt Obligations Outstanding at End of Select Years
1963–1988 (in billions of dollars)**

Type of Securities	1963	1968	1973	1978	1983	1988
State & local governments	$86.9	$122.1	$189.9	$253.5	$344.1	$564.5
Industrial revenue bonds	—	—	2.4	25.0	83.9	116.3
Households & non-profits	—	—	0.4	10.7	41.0	79.0
Total	$86.9	$122.1	$192.7	$289.2	$469.0	$759.8

Source: Flow of Funds Section, Board of Governors of the Federal Reserve System.

An Early Start

Having unloaded their War of Independence obligations on the federal government at its creation, the states went back into debt when they began to sell bonds for the development of canals, railroads, roads and other improvements in the ensuing decades. By 1835, when the federal debt was paid off, the states' combined debt was back over $45 million. Following the Panic of 1837, by which time the states' debt had soared to $175 million, some couldn't meet interest or principal payments and defaulted. Over the next three decades, despite the spread of debt limits and other reforms, there were two more cycles of addition to debt followed by defaults.

Concurrently with the development of states, cities and towns had begun to make major expenditures for waterworks, sewer systems, streets and schools, which required even greater borrowing. Before long, the outstanding debt of local governments exceeded that of the states and federal government combined, a situation that prevailed until World War I.

Comparing the Governments

Unlike the federal government, which has maintained its reputation for prompt payment of debts, state and local governments have periodically defaulted on their bonds. Such events were numerous during the Great Depression, but they also have occurred—or almost occurred—more recently, as illustrated by New York City's close call in 1975 and by the Washington (State) Public Power Supply System's actual default in 1983 on revenue bonds for two nuclear power plants.

While increases in population, living standards and the role of government have been among major underlying factors common to the increases in outstanding debt of all three levels, major differences have arisen from their different functions and revenue sources. Local governments spend more on construction than the federal and state governments combined. New public schools, streets, sewerage, water supply, electric power and public housing facilities account for most of this money. States' construction spending goes primarily for highways. Excluding receipts from the federal and state governments, property taxes are the principal source of revenue for local governments. They are not as responsive to economic expansion as individual and corporation income taxes, which are the federal government's main sources, and sales taxes, which states rely on the most. By the same token, property tax bills are less likely to drop during recessions.

Postwar Years

During the first 25 years following World War II, state and local governments' total expenditures rose more rapidly than revenues, largely due to capital outlays for new construction. Long-term borrowings, on which the governments rely heavily for funding, began to soar.

With the economy producing consumer goods again and an enlarged labor force enjoying increased income and spending it to raise its living standards, wartime shortages receded into memory and pent-up demand could be satisfied. Millions of new homes in cities and new suburbs required new streets, water mains, sewage systems, schools, police stations, fire stations and so on. Existing local facilities had to be modernized and expanded, as did state universities and colleges. Increased automobile and truck ownership and usage led in 1956 to Eisenhower's program to expand and improve the interstate highway system, triggering state outlays to be supplemented by federal grants.

Slowdown in the 1970s

After their constant dollar volume peaked in 1968, state and local governments' construction expenditures rose more slowly or remained essentially flat for many of the next 15 years or so—a period plagued by recessions and inflation, high borrowing costs and tight money.

Some states that had increased taxes and cut spending to balance budgets found themselves with surpluses they were able to enjoy all too briefly. The surpluses were large enough to invite taxpayer criticism, and governors and legislatures responded by cutting taxes. Before long, recessions and cuts in federal aid brought deficits back even though spending did not rise significantly.

Table 1–5   Growth in State and Local Governments' Outstanding Long-Term Debt by Type 1977–1987

Government Level	Full Faith and Credit (billions)		Change (%)	Non-guaranteed (billions)		Change (%)
	1977	1987		1977	1987	
State	$ 42.9	$ 66.8	55.7	$ 44.3	$197.3	345.5
County	15.3	27.0	76.5	6.2	69.8	1,025.8
Municipal	39.1	57.1	46.0	28.1	118.4	321.4
Town	3.2	4.7	46.9	0.2	2.1	950.0
School District	27.3	33.4	22.3	—	—	—
Special District	8.6	12.4	44.2	31.7	113.8	259.0
Total	136.4	201.4	47.7	110.5	501.4	354.2

Source: Bureau of the Census, *1982 Census of Governments* and *Government Finances.*

Growing Debt

In this environment, the outstanding long-term, full-faith and credit debt of these governments also rose more slowly, but non-guaranteed debt presented a different picture. Its growth accelerated, and by the end of fiscal 1979, it had pulled ahead. By the end of fiscal 1987, non-guaranteed debt was two and one-half times as large as guaranteed debt. To appreciate the pervasiveness of this trend, glance at Table 1–5, which compares the increases in non-guaranteed debt by levels of government with those in tax-backed obligations over the ten years ended in 1987.

While lower borrowing costs beginning in 1982 and a resurgence in new construction beginning in 1983 stimulated the issuance of new debt securities generally, two additional reasons contributed significantly to the acceleration in non-guaranteed debt over the period. First, taxpayer resistance to tax increases made governments more eager to resort to user financing of public-purpose facilities. Second, there was an extraordinary increase in the issuance of IDBs and other private-purpose bonds.

Year-to-year net changes in outstanding tax-exempt securities were based on factors such as bond market conditions and the timing of capital program approvals. But perhaps none caused fluctuation more than the expectation, and enactment, of federal tax legislation. To reduce federal revenue lost on tax-exempt securities, presidents and Congress have periodically made interest from certain types of bonds ineligible for exemption.

The most sweeping reforms were in the Tax Reform Act of 1986. It ended the exemption of most types of IDBs (after specified dates) as well as for certain other private-purpose obligations. IDBs and other targeted securities had been rushed to market in prior years, as Reagan Administration and congressional proposals for tax reform were being advanced. Combined net sales of IDBs and tax-exempt obligations of households and non-profit organizations peaked at nearly $53 billion in 1985. Net liquidation of about $12 billion followed in 1986.

While these securities were being offered to investors by the billions, state and local governments also were stepping up sales of general obligation bonds to finance an increase in construction. A new surge in homebuilding required more roads, sewers and other facilities to serve them. An increase in the birth rate in the late 1970s resulted in the need for additional schools in the mid-1980s. All were the quite familiar symbols of growth. Less familiar—and less welcome—was the sight of overcrowding in prisons, necessitating expansion of correctional facilities.

Despite the new vigor, construction outlays accounted for no more than ten percent of total operating and capital expenditures by state and local governments in the mid-1980s. Other expenditures, especially compensation and transfer payments, were rising more rapidly. By 1987, after a few years of surpluses attributable to increased revenues resulting from tax increases and the nation's economic expansion, deficits (excluding social insurance funds) were back.

Given the backlog of long-deferred infrastructure improvements, limits in the ability of state and local governments to pay for capital expenditures out of current tax revenues, and the dim prospects for more help from Washington, it seems a safe bet that there will be an ample supply of new tax-exempt bonds for the foreseeable future.

CORPORATIONS AND DEBT

Compared to the federal, state and local governments, U.S. corporations are relative latecomers as major issuers of bonds; but they have made up for it.

The issuance of bonds by corporations at a significant rate had, of necessity, to await the growth and evolution of corporate business in America as well as the development of a domestic market for these non-government, long-term debt securities. At the time the Constitution was adopted, there probably were no more than a couple of dozen corporations in the 13 states; by 1800 there probably were no more than 300 in 16 states.

Equity First

At first, entrepreneurs forming corporations had to put up their own equity money. Before they were sufficiently established to sell long-term debt securities, they generally sold additional shares of common stock to the public and borrowed from banks or others. It is not surprising, therefore, that equities as well as government bonds were predominant in the holdings of individuals and businesses with money to invest before corporate bonds were widely issued and actively traded on the New York Stock Exchange and elsewhere.

Corporations engaged in transportation, banking, insurance and public utilities were the first to interest investors while those engaged in manufacturing and trade were still growing. In those early days, of course, transportation meant canal, turnpike and toll bridge companies while the utilities were typically water supply firms.

The Railroad Boom

By the 1850s the railroads dominated the corporate securities market, as their rails, laid at $30,000 or more a mile, covered the landscape. Hundreds of railroad companies were formed and promoted, overcoming opposition from competitors and those who believed that riding at 15 miles per hour would be hazardous to one's health. Given the perceived risks involved, few of the early railroad companies could sell their bonds; most of the millions required were raised through the sale of stock to a cross-section of the population—from the wealthy to ordinary folks who were solicited door-to-door.

With the age of invention and industrialization following the Civil War, the time of large industrial corporations also arrived. As steel, oil and other capital-intensive industries developed, they sold large volumes of stocks and bonds. Eventually, they were joined in the markets by new types of utilities: electric light and power and telephone and telegraph companies, which also had great appetites for capital.

The growing mix of incorporated businesses offering securities, the increasing variety in the types of these securities (including preferred stock, first sold by the railroads in the 1840s), and the companies' range of creditworthiness afforded investors a choice of offerings that they had not previously known. The greater selection, of course, was a mixed blessing. It confronted investors with factors they—and their brokers—didn't have to think about earlier, when buying easy-to-understand Treasury bonds.

The most important factor, of course, was safety. Some corporate bonds were secured by assets, such as railroad cars and factories, while others (known as debentures) were not. In either case, investors had to rely on the earning power of the issuing corporations. They had to try to determine whether the companies' profits would be large enough, for long enough, to make interest payments on schedule and redeem the bonds at maturity.

Poor and Moody

To help investors with their dilemma, men appeared, such as John Moody, a statistician, and Henry Varnum Poor, editor of *Railroad Journal,* and his son, Henry William, who began to collect and regularly publish corporate data, thereby planting the seeds for today's Standard & Poor's Corporation and Moody's Investors Service. In 1868, six years after providing operational and financial details on more than 120 railroads in his major history of the industry, Henry V. Poor brought out the first edition of his *Manual of the Railroads of the United States.* By 1900, when railroad bonds still accounted for as much as $5 billion of the $6 billion corporate bonds outstanding, Henry W. Poor and Moody had followed with manuals offering coverage of public utilities and other industries that were increasing their long-term borrowings.

In 1909 Moody went a step further by introducing a system for rating securities according to their investment qualities, applying it first to railroads and subsequently to utilities and industrials. S&P's predecessor company came out with a comparable concept in 1923. Using similar systems of classification, they gave top ratings to the bonds of the most creditworthy corporations (and subsequently to state and local governments) and bottom rankings to the most speculative.

Expanded and modified, the systems are still very much in use and quite relevant, as we shall see in Chapter 4, to anyone buying or holding shares in mutual funds invested in bonds other than those issued by the federal government. The top rating of Aaa (Moody's) or AAA (S&P) is given bonds whose interest payments are well covered by earnings and whose principal is secure.

From "triple-A" through the next three grades—to Baa in Moody's system and BBB in S&P's—bonds are regarded as being investment grade. That is to say, they are deemed to be suitable investments for conservative investors, including fiduciaries.

The remaining ratings are given to bonds regarded as being speculative. They range from securities whose issuers could have trouble meeting debt service during adverse times to those actually in default. To some people, they're all simply "junk bonds." To others, able and willing to differentiate among them, they represent a conglomeration of issues among which some may deserve a look. (While accounting for 23 percent of corporate issues outstanding at the end of 1988, bonds rated below Baa represented 42 percent of the issuers covered by Moody's.)

From the beginning, the rating systems did more than help investors to find bonds with acceptable risk levels—and remind issuers of the importance of sound management. They also helped to determine what investors' returns on their bonds would be. Whenever a new bond issue was brought to market and assigned a rating by each service, the interest rate of its coupon would reflect its rating as well as prevailing credit market conditions. A higher rating would result in a lower coupon rate; the greater risk indicated by a lower rating would be reflected in a higher interest rate. In subsequent trading, the issue would rise or fall—and its current yield would fall or rise—depending on interest rate fluctuations as well as any upgrading or downgrading by the rating services, which continued to monitor the issuing corporations.

Corporate Debt Accelerates

Between 1900 and the U.S. entry into World War I, corporations' bond debt tripled, from $6 billion to over $19 billion (par value), exceeding the federal debt. The railroads continued their expansion and heavy borrowing—the number of railroad companies had exceeded 1,500 in 1907—but public utilities and industrial companies were expanding even faster.

Following the Armistice, the economy picked up momentum again, and the growth of corporate bond debt accelerated. By 1932 the volume of outstanding corporate bonds reached $32 billion—nearly double the federal debt—due largely to a sharp growth in public utility bonds, which had pulled even with the indebtedness of railroads.

With the Depression and World War II, capital expenditure programs were deferred again. While the government had to borrow more to supplement current revenues, corporations had less need to borrow. Able to retire old bonds, they could let their bond debt decline to around $25 billion by the time the war ended.

In the postwar era the economy underwent an enormous expansion, accompanied by especially heavy borrowing by public utilities and manufacturing firms. Rail debt declined in relative importance, as did the railroads, owing to loss of market share to trucking companies, airlines, passenger cars and pipelines.

Trends of the 1980s

Corporate bonds' growth continued at a steady clip, but they really took off in 1984 with the drop in long-term interest rates. Their total outstanding more than doubled in the five years ended in 1988 (Table 1-6).

A striking characteristic of the growth in the volume of corporate bonds during the 1980s, besides the absolute numbers, is their relationship to the total market value of outstanding corporate equities. As the table indicates, the debt-equity ratio has deteriorated significantly.

Table 1-6 Corporate Bonds* (in billions of dollars at year-end)

Types of Issuers	1963	1968	1973	1978	1983	1988
Non-financial corp. business	$ 88.4	$135.0	$206.9	$320.6	$ 423.0	$ 885.0
Financial corporations	10.6	16.4	37.4	73.7	118.6	418.0
Total	$ 99.0	$151.4	$244.3	$394.3	$ 541.6	$1,303.0
Corporate equities at market value	$571.8	$981.4	$901.4	$982.5	$2,021.6	$3,130.0

*Excludes industrial revenue bonds, issued by state and local governments to finance private investment, for which the corporations are liable.

Source: Flow of Funds Section, Board of Governors of the Federal Reserve System.

Anyone who believes that non-financial corporations issue bonds and stocks to obtain capital to expand and modernize their facilities may be surprised when looking at the data.

During most of the ten years ended in 1988, capital expenditures for plant and equipment could be financed entirely—and in the other years, almost entirely—with internally generated funds: earnings retained after payment of dividends and the cash flow generated by depreciation allowances. Proceeds from net sales of bonds, including tax-exempt industrial revenue bonds, seem to have been unneeded, in the aggregate, for capital expenditures after 1982.

Moreover, non-financial corporations *reduced* their outstanding equities in seven of the ten years by buying back significantly more shares than they were issuing. Of the 33 preceding postwar years, outstanding equities had been reduced in only four, and in each of those years only negligible sums were involved.

Debt for Equity

While retiring equity, corporations, in the aggregate, had sold bonds in the 1980s to generate cash—not to expand their production capacities or improve productivity. The consequent substitution of debt for equity in the 1980s has been simply the result of concurrent strategies aimed at a variety of objectives: financing leveraged buyouts, mergers and acquisitions; defending against takeovers; enhancing shareholder returns; reducing income taxes (interest expenses are deductible for corporations, but dividend payments to shareholders are not).

The underlying long-run tendency to greater use of leverage evoked warnings from those who feared that, in the event of a major drop in corporate earnings, too many companies would be unable to service their debt and bonds would, therefore, go into default. It also led many investors to be more alert to the probabilities of "event risk"—the likelihood of an event, such as an attempt to take over a well-established, highly regarded corporation, that would lead to restructuring, including the creation of too much additional debt. That would cause the rating services to downgrade the corporation's existing bonds, resulting in declines in their prices.

Watching the higher debt-equity ratios and other developments, Moody's and Standard & Poor's downgraded a considerable volume of corporate debt in the 1980s. While the resulting increases in yields, relative to those of high-grade bonds, acted as magnets to some investors, they served as red flags to others.

CHAPTER 2

The Lenders

Over the two centuries since the federal government, the original 13 states, and the first U.S. business corporations began to borrow money by selling bonds,[1] there have always been individuals and businesses ready to lend it—at a price called interest. In this chapter we'll look at the various categories of bond investors, review why they buy bonds and what types of bonds they buy, and see how mutual funds fit into the picture.

All U.S. governmental and corporate bond issues that are privately held in this country, as indeed all U.S. private financial assets, are fundamentally owned by individuals. Only a relatively small percentage, however, are bought, held and sold directly by the beneficial owners.

Most bonds are bought, held and sold in our behalf by the entities we have created: non-financial corporations, financial institutions such as commercial banks and insurance companies, unincorporated businesses, foundations, trusts and so on. We are not keenly aware from day to day that most of us have indeterminate interests in bonds held, for example, by an employer's pension fund so that it can send us monthly checks when we're retired or by a life insurance company so that it can pay our survivors.

WHY PURCHASERS BUY BONDS

Individual and institutional investors alike buy bonds for two reasons: expected income in the form of regular interest payments for specific periods of up to 30 years or even more, and expected safety of principal. Unlike individuals, some institutions may not have freedom of choice; owing to their nature or the laws that regulate them, they may have to invest certain shares of their assets in bonds or mortgages—and even a particular kind of bonds (i.e., government bonds). Money—whether in the form of currency or demand deposits at a bank—is essential for our daily transactions and major purchases, but it doesn't earn interest. Institutions *have* to invest to generate income and meet their long-term obligations. And most of us want no more of our financial assets to be non-earning than is necessary for current expenditures.

A portion, enough to accommodate foreseeable and unforeseeable expenditures for the next several months, has to be kept both productive and highly liquid—that is, it should be convertible, without loss, back into cash at any time. It belongs in savings accounts, time deposits, U.S. Treasury bills or money market mutual funds, where the principal will be safe, if not actually guaranteed or insured, and where it will earn interest.

Whatever is left over can be considered for investment in bonds or other financial assets. In the case of bonds, the choice of maturities will depend on several factors, including expected interest rates and the period for which the money can be spared and the income is desired.

In theory, interest rates should be highest for bonds with the longest maturities because they expose their purchasers to risks for longer periods. Much of the time, practice follows theory, but occasionally, as happened for awhile in 1989 when short maturities offered more, it does not.

Interest also is higher for issues that are regarded as involving a greater risk of default and are, therefore, rated lower by Moody's or Standard & Poor's. Thus, corporate bonds pay higher interest than U.S. Treasury issues of comparable maturity, and corporate bonds with low credit ratings must pay significantly more than those of highest quality. Issuers of tax-exempt securities (also known as municipals) offer lower rates than the Treasury, but that reflects the exemption of their interest payments from federal, state and/or local income taxes.

Regular payments of interest for stipulated periods and the return of principal at maturity are not the only attractions offered by bonds. They offer another attractive feature: the ease with which they can be converted into cash prior to maturity when necessary or desirable (even if it's at a loss) in contrast with other debt instruments, such as certificates of deposit (CDs) or mortgages, or with non-financial assets.

Bonds are not the choice, however, when stability of principal is more important than income. For stability, along with reasonable—if not maximum—income and maximum safety, nothing is more suitable than U.S. Treasury bills or government-insured time deposits or savings accounts.

Nor are bonds bought primarily for capital appreciation—except in unusual circumstances. Capital gains can be expected over time from a diversified portfolio of good common stocks, invested in directly or indirectly through mutual funds.

The only time bonds are bought for capital gains is when investors are convinced that interest rates are going to fall, lifting bond prices and providing higher total returns. But interest rate forecasting is a tricky business, even for professionals.

While it is important to consider the rewards of investing in bonds, it is even more important to remember the risks. Varying with the types of issuer and issue, they can be severe. They include the failure to receive interest payments when scheduled and even the loss of part or all of one's principal.

By restricting themselves to U.S. Treasury or government-guaranteed agency issues, investors can avoid the risk of default, as long as the nation continues to maintain its record of creditworthiness that goes back to Hamilton. Even corporations whose bonds enjoy high ratings can have their prospects suddenly—if only temporarily—jeopardized by court awards (Texaco), major accidents (Union Carbide), leveraged buyouts (RJR Nabisco) or other unforeseeable events. Thus, when investing in a corporate, state or local government bond, it is clearly imperative to be mindful of the bond issuer's ability to service its debt—and to seek an interest rate commensurate with the level of risk that's incurred.

Buying Treasuries also can usually avoid the risk of a call associated with corporate and tax-exempt securities—that is, an issuer's contractual right to redeem a bond prior to its maturity. (No Treasury securities issued since 1984 have had a call feature, and no one can predict when, or if, there will be others.) This may be done to gradually retire an issue or to refinance debt when interest rates have fallen—and bond prices have risen—and issuers have an incentive to replace outstanding higher-coupon bonds with new lower-coupon bonds. Whether bonds are called for these or other reasons, their owners are unable to continue enjoying income at the interest rates they had expected. Instead, they are left with cash—that awful non-earning asset—and have to reinvest it at then prevailing lower rates.

Holders of Treasury securities *are* vulnerable to two major risks that are common to all bonds: market volatility and inflation. Anyone who intends to hold a bond until it matures should not care that interest rate fluctuations will cause the price of the bond to rise and fall in the interim. One knows what's due at maturity, regardless of fluctuations, and is prepared to wait for it. If the money is required before maturity, however, the bond's price may be below its original cost, and a seller will have to take a loss.

As for inflation, even if the principal is paid in full at maturity, the dollars won't buy what they would when the bond was purchased. How much less depends on how much the dollar has been inflated since the investment.

The loss of purchasing power resulting from inflation is not just limited to the principal; inflation also affects the stream of interest payments for which the bond was bought. This might not bother institutional investors such as pension funds, which try to match income with expected cash requirements, but it could undermine the hopes of individuals who depend on income from bonds.

WHO BUYS BONDS?

At the end of 1988, households owned directly around $1.2 trillion worth of U.S. government securities, tax-exempt obligations, and corporate and foreign bonds, about 23 percent of the $5.4 trillion outstanding and considerably more than any other category of investors (Table 2–1).[2] This sector's commitment to bonds was even greater, however; it also included an estimated $228 billion of bonds held by mutual funds (i.e., households account for 87 percent of fund holdings). Commercial banks, life insurance companies and foreign investors each accounted for 10 percent or more of the total.

By far the largest share of the nation's financial assets is held by *households*. They held only around ten percent of their total in bonds because of their desire for the liquidity and income afforded by checking and saving accounts, time deposits and money market mutual funds; a high dedication to common stocks; large stakes in pension fund reserves; and large investments in non-corporate businesses.

Commercial banks and *savings institutions* had only about 20 percent of their financial assets in bonds because of their functions in the economy and business objectives. Loans to businesses and consumers constituted 63 percent of their financial assets. The levels of banks' Treasury holdings are influenced partly by demand for loans, which are more profitable for them, and partly by the Federal Reserve System's implementation of monetary policy. The principal purpose of savings institutions is to take in savings and time deposits and use the money to make long-term mortgage loans. These amounted to 53 percent of their total.

Non-financial corporate business assets are primarily fixed, being invested in plant and equipment. Of their financial assets, the largest share was in trade credit (41 percent).

Foreign investors, important to the nation since its founding, continue to hold a large stake here. Of the $1.3 trillion they had invested in U.S. financial assets at the end of 1988, bonds accounted for 44 percent.

Private pension funds and *state and local government employee retirement funds* have similar investment objectives—to make sure they can pay retired employees the pensions they were promised—but pursue them differently. The private funds had only about one-half as much of

---

**Table 2–1   Holdings of U.S. Government Securities, Tax-Exempt
Obligations and Corporate and Foreign Bonds* by Sectors
(amounts outstanding at end of 1988 in billions of dollars)**

Sector	Amount	Share
Households**	$1,251	23.0%
Commercial banks	601	11.1
Life insurance companies	583	10.7
Foreign investors	565	10.4
Savings institutions	393	7.2
State & local govt. employee retirement funds	346	6.4
Private pension funds	320	5.9
Other insurance companies***	281	5.2
Mutual funds	262	4.8
Federal Reserve System	241	4.4
State & local government general funds	217	4.0
Securitized credit obligation (SCO) issuers	136	2.5
Money market mutual funds	96	1.8
Non-financial corporate businesses	76	1.4
Security brokers and dealers	32	0.6
Federally sponsored credit agencies and mortgage pools	23	0.4
Total	$5,429	100.0%

*Includes indeterminate volumes of money market securities. Foreign bonds, combined with corporates, are issues of foreign and international agencies that are held in the U.S.
**Sector includes personal trusts and non-profit organizations, which account for a small percent of the total.
***Primarily fire and casualty companies.

Totals may not add due to rounding.

Source: Flow of Funds Section, Board of Governors of the Federal Reserve System.

their assets in bonds as the governmental funds (28 percent vs. 57 percent) while investing larger portions of their financial assets in common stocks (45 percent vs. 37 percent). Public opposition, manifested in constitutional amendments and laws, commonly prohibited or limited investment in stocks by the public pension funds, but attitudes have softened in recent years and the public funds' investment policies have changed accordingly.

Required to invest their reserves safely, *life insurance companies* invest over 50 percent of their financial assets in bonds and 20 percent in mortgages because of their long-term need for predictable income. Less than 10 percent is in stocks. To the extent they can cope with inflation by raising premiums, employer contributions or other revenue sources, they can boost income to match outgo. While the dollars in interest they receive in the future will have less purchasing power than today's, so will

Table 2–2   Changes in Holdings of U.S. Government Securities, Tax-Exempt Obligations, and Corporate and Foreign Bonds by Sectors 1978–1988 (in billions of dollars)

Sector	1988	1978	Change
Households	$1,251	$ 316	295%
Commercial banks	601	275	119
Life insurance companies	583	176	231
Foreign investors	565	153	270
Savings institutions	393	85	360
State & local govt. employee retirement funds	346	109	216
Private pension funds	320	85	277
Other insurance companies	281	100	181
Mutual funds	262	11	2,349
Federal Reserve System	241	117	105
State & local government general funds	217	83	161
Securitized credit obligation issuers	136	—	NMF
Money market mutual funds	96	2	6,273
Non-financial corporate businesses	76	15	398
Security brokers and dealers	32	3	1,050
Federally sponsored credit agencies and mortgage pools	23	2	1,356
Total	$5,429	$1,535	254%

Percent changes are based on numbers (not shown) to the first decimal place.

Totals may not add due to rounding.

NMF = no meaningful figure

Source: Flow of Funds Section, Board of Governors of the Federal Reserve System.

the dollars paid by the funds and insurance companies to pensioners and survivors.

Other insurance companies—mainly fire and casualty companies—were even more heavily invested in bonds (65 percent) and stocks (17 percent). Because their policies typically have terms of one year (or even less) and because they must always be prepared to pay out large claims, they must invest in securities that can easily be sold. Less regulated than life insurance companies but also eager to earn a high return, they are major buyers of stocks.

The 254 percent increase in outstanding government and corporate bonds in the ten years ended 1988 has been unevenly spread across the sectors (Table 2–2). Given the different rates at which their financial assets have grown and their different requirements, that should not be surprising. What may be surprising is the 2,349 percent increase in bond holdings of mutual funds, reflecting the boom in bond funds, about which there is much to be told.

**Table 2-3 How Sectors Allocate Assets to Bonds
(shares of bond holdings outstanding at end of 1988)**

Sector	U.S. Govt.	Tax-Exempt	Corporate
Households	68.7%	22.1%	9.3%
Commercial banks	61.1	25.2	13.8
Life insurance companies	23.2	1.9	74.9
Foreign investors	68.1	—	31.9
Savings institutions	79.6	0.7	19.6
S & L govt. employee retirement funds	53.4	0.1	46.5
Private pension funds	43.6	—	56.4
Other insurance companies	26.9	51.6	21.5
State & local govt. general funds	95.5	4.5	—
Mutual funds	43.9	30.2	26.0
Federal Reserve System	100.0	—	—
SCO issuers	100.0	—	—
Money market mutual funds	31.3	68.8	—
Non-financial corporate businesses	84.1	15.9	—
Security brokers and dealers	(14.0)	23.3	90.7
Federally sponsored credit agencies and mortgage pools	100.0	—	—
Total	60.4%	14.0%	25.6%

Source: Flow of Funds Section, Board of Governors of the Federal Reserve System.

WHICH BONDS DO PURCHASERS BUY?

Table 2-3 shows clearly how the sectors allocate their investments in bonds. Except for the Federal Reserve System and federally sponsored credit agencies, which can only hold U.S. Treasury and federal agency issues, and the issuers of securitized credit obligations, which primarily hold agency issues, all sectors have a variety of mixes. Patterns are discernible, however.

Directly and through mutual funds, households have allocated the largest portion of their bond dollars to U.S. government securities and the second largest to tax-exempts. Holdings of corporates have increased, however. Whether the reduction of the income tax rates for top brackets provided by the Tax Reform Act of 1986 (TRA '86) will significantly reduce the incentive of high-income individuals to buy municipals remains to be seen.

Other sectors that have a high portion of bond holdings in U.S. government securities, such as state and local government general and pension funds, savings institutions, foreign investors and international agencies, not only share households' concerns with safety but may actually be required to trust only the Treasury or federal agencies. Sectors with high portions of their bond dollars in corporate bonds, such as life insurance companies and private pension funds, are shooting for the higher returns that high-quality corporates provide.

Fire and casualty insurance companies and other institutional investors with large commitments to tax-exempt securities buy them when the income from municipals is more attractive than the after-tax returns from taxable securities. When their investment in tax-exempts drops, it is usually due to drops in operating earnings or to actual losses from operations, which eliminate the incentive to buy municipals. While commercial banks' holdings are still large, they have declined since TRA '86 took away a unique privilege: the right to deduct from taxable income 80 percent of the interest cost of acquiring and maintaining their positions in tax-exempts.

ENDNOTES

1. "Bonds" is this book's collective term for publicly traded debt instruments maturing in more than one year. Those maturing in one year or less are collectively referred to as "money market instruments."
2 The Federal Reserve data used throughout this book for federal, state and local government securities include all maturities. For corporations, however, the data are limited to bonds and, thus, exclude money market instruments. Foreign bonds consist of private, governmental and international agency bonds held in the United States.

CHAPTER 3

The Growth of Bond Funds

The American mutual fund industry—that is, the financial sector consisting of open-end investment companies that, with occasional exceptions, continuously offer shares for sale and that, *without* exception, must always stand ready to redeem them—is by now mature, having turned 65 in 1989. Bond mutual funds—funds that invest primarily or exclusively in debt securities maturing in more than one year—are, for the most part, very young.

From 1924, when Massachusetts Investors Trust (MIT), a stock fund, became the first mutual fund to offer shares to the public, until 1958, when 189 mutual funds were registered with the Securities and Exchange Commission (SEC), no more than a dozen could be called bond funds. Indeed, for the industry's first 50 years not enough bond funds were formed to persuade the Investment Company Institute (ICI) to establish a category for the group for statistical purposes. When at last it did so in 1975, it counted only 35 corporate bond funds,[1] a small fraction of the 390 total funds.

It took another decade before bond funds attained anything like the position they now enjoy in terms of numbers of funds and shareholders, assets and sales. While many factors contributed to their sudden, vigorous growth, a few stand out:

1. The introduction of millions of people to mutual funds—and mutual fund families—through investment in money market funds.

2. Changes in the levels of, and spreads between, money market and long-term interest rates.

3. The apparent satisfaction of many new investors with the performance and services of mutual fund organizations, which led them to try bond funds for longer-term investment when yields became appealing.

4. Growth in the volume and variety of debt securities issued by governments and corporations.

5. Changes in the Internal Revenue Code that resulted in increases in both the supply of bonds available through mutual funds and demand for them.

6. Strong competition among financial institutions for investors' money, exemplified by increases in the number of entities sponsoring mutual funds, in the number of fund types, in the size of fund organizations and in the money spent on promotion.

To appreciate fully the explosion of bond funds in the 1980s, it is helpful to recall why it took such funds so long to develop and attract a large following. In doing so, it is important to bear in mind the basic attributes that bond funds share with stock funds—and those they don't:

- Both offer investors diversification, professional management, the opportunity to invest small sums and easy access to their money when necessary.

- Bond and stock funds differ, however, in investment objectives and in the policies employed to attain them. Bond funds are aimed primarily at generating current income. Stock funds, though differing in objectives from one another, place a greater emphasis on capital appreciation. In fact, some stock funds give income no consideration at all.

THE EARLY PURSUIT OF STOCKS

When the first few open-end investment companies were conceived following MIT's debut in 1924—none apparently called itself a mutual fund until November 1929 when Shaw-Loomis-Sayles Mutual Fund[2] was formed—common stocks were the rage. Those who wanted to share in the nation's growth bought them with unbridled enthusiasm, both directly and indirectly through investment vehicles known collectively as investment trusts, most of them closed-end. As waves of buying drove share prices higher and higher, people became dazzled by their paper profits and bought more shares, commonly borrowing money to do it.

While many were enticed by visions of huge capital gains to be made in stocks, the prospects of income from investment-grade[3] corporate bonds, yielding from 4.5 to 5.5 percent or so, appealed to only a relatively few conservative individuals and to institutions. U.S. government bonds, yielding less than 4 percent, evoked even less interest.

Those who had looked to stocks for current income, of course, had a different view of bond yields. Take, for example, Norfolk Investment Corporation, the predecessor of today's Scudder Income Fund, launched in 1928 (and the first no-load mutual fund). Norfolk wanted to pay its shareholders a dividend of around 4 percent but, as stock prices soared, had increasing difficulty finding desirable stocks with adequate yields.

Reviewing the fund's first half-year in his January 21, 1929, report to shareholders, President F. Haven Clark noted:

> the very high prices at which the majority of common stocks have been selling and the enormous speculation taking place in the stock market.

Then he added:

> At the present time high grade common stocks are yielding less than 4%, and were it not for the high return derived from fixed-income-bearing securities, the present dividend would hardly have been earned.

The problem Clark referred to—of stock yields being below bond yields—is a familiar one for those who wish to invest for current income but prefer to use high–dividend-paying stocks as the primary means toward that objective. Given that stocks are generally riskier than bonds and, therefore, high-grade stocks are riskier than high-grade bonds, it should follow that they would offer higher yields to compensate. In the mid-1920s that had been the case (Table 3–1). But stock market speculation inverted this relationship toward the end of the decade; in 1929 when stocks hit their cyclical peak, average yields of triple-A bonds were more than 1 percent higher.

As the stock-buying frenzy continued, feeding on proclamations such as Irving Fisher's of mid-October 1929, that stock prices "have reached what looks like a permanently higher plateau," other investors and analysts became cautious.

BONDS BEFORE BOND FUNDS

Among the cautious was Walter L. Morgan, a young Philadelphia investment adviser who had founded Wellington Management Company and

**Table 3–1   Comparison of Bond and Stock Yields—
Annual Averages 1924–1969**

Year	Aaa Corporate Bond Yields	Common Stock Yields	Year	Aaa Corporate Bond Yields	Common Stock Yields
1924	5.00%	5.87%	1947	2.61%	4.93%
1925	4.88	5.19	1948	2.82	5.54
1926	4.73	5.32	1949	2.66	6.59
1927	4.57	4.77	1950	2.62	6.57
1928	4.55	3.98	1951	2.86	6.13
1929	4.83	3.48	1952	2.96	5.80
1930	4.55	4.26	1953	3.20	5.80
1931	4.58	5.58	1954	2.90	4.95
1932	5.01	6.69	1955	3.06	4.08
1933	4.49	4.05	1956	3.36	4.09
1934	4.00	3.72	1957	3.89	4.35
1935	3.60	3.82	1958	3.79	3.97
1936	3.24	3.44	1959	4.38	3.23
1937	3.26	4.86	1960	4.41	3.47
1938	3.19	5.18	1961	4.35	2.98
1939	3.01	4.05	1962	4.33	3.37
1940	2.84	5.59	1963	4.26	3.17
1941	2.77	6.82	1964	4.40	3.01
1942	2.83	7.24	1965	4.49	3.00
1943	2.73	4.93	1966	5.13	3.40
1944	2.72	4.86	1967	5.51	3.20
1945	2.62	4.17	1968	6.18	3.07
1946	2.53	3.85	1969	7.03	3.24

Sources: Aaa corporate bond yields, reprinted with permission of Moody's Investors Service; common stock yields, 1924–33, Alfred Cowles, 3rd and Associates, *Common Stock* Indexes, 1871–1937, Bloomington, IN: Principia Press, 1937; 1934–69, Standard & Poor's Corporation.

had recently started a mutual fund, Industrial and Power Securities Company, which in 1935 was to change its name to Wellington Fund (and in 1974 to become an original member of the Vanguard Group).

About 75 percent invested in common stocks when it began operations on July 1, 1929, the fund had slashed its stock holdings before the October crash and by the end of the year had reduced them to 37 percent. By then, most of its assets were in cash and cash equivalents (37 percent), bonds (9 percent) and preferred stocks (16 percent). As a result of its timely switches, Morgan reported to shareholders at the year's end that the fund was off 8 percent from the year's peak in comparison with 60 percent for other investment trusts.

Wrote Morgan years later:

> ...we came to a conservative and common sense conclusion in an era of speculation: that the prices stocks commanded were just 'not in the wood'; hence we should not invest the Fund's resources merely in stocks as the other investment trusts had done. Rather we should have 'an anchor to windward' in the form of a large position in fixed-income securities such as bonds and preferred stocks. By this conservative investment decision, what came to be known as the 'balanced fund' concept was born.[4]

Morgan, still coming into his Vanguard office as he turned 91, looked back in an interview in June, 1989, and reaffirmed the belief he held 60 years earlier in the concept of balance—or of asset allocation, a term that came increasingly into use by funds in the late 1980s. "Not many were buying bonds then," he said, "but balance worked, and it still works.... It just didn't make sense to have everything in stocks. It still doesn't."

As a consequence of Morgan's commitment to conserve shareholders' capital in those exuberant times and to provide steady income, Wellington apparently became the first mutual fund to have long-term bonds in its portfolio—before the inception of the first bond funds. As stocks continued their plunge to the low of 1932, other balanced funds were formed.

But it would be years before the balanced fund concept would be recognized in government forms, if not in statutes or regulations. Given the different ways in which balances among asset types were struck by funds, the SEC eventually developed a "working definition" to guide investors. Any fund referring to itself as a balanced fund should have "the multiple objectives of providing income, stability of capital, and possible increases in capital" and have at least 25 percent of the value of its assets in debt securities and/or preferred stocks.

The bear market following the 1929 crash rewarded the balanced fund managers—and their shareholders—as well as others who had reduced their exposure to stocks and bought bonds; it also provided new opportunities for income investors with a preference for equities. Bond yields held their levels for a period, then fell beginning in mid-1932 as investors, seeking security in a world of shattered dreams, bid up bond prices. At the same time, the plummeting prices of stocks caused their yields to rise—so long as corporations could maintain dividends.

Equity mutual funds, although hard hit, generally survived in better shape than the far larger number of closed-end funds, which had flourished in the booming 1920s and whose share prices had dropped sharply. Many, having been highly leveraged, failed altogether.

THE EARLY BOND FUNDS

In 1931–32, with the Depression approaching its trough, promoters of investment companies formed more funds. With stock and bond yields relatively high, the timing was opportune to benefit from any increases in securities prices that business recovery would bring.

Most of the new funds were of the open-end type, including additional balanced funds such as American Business Shares (now Lord Abbett U.S. Government Securities Fund), Commonwealth Investment Company (now American Balanced Fund), Investors Management Trust (now Dodge & Cox Balanced Fund) and Wamad Associates (now Eaton Vance Investors Fund).

Of special interest, however, was the 1932 introduction of the series of eight by Keystone Custodian Funds, offering investors portfolios that were divided into classes of bonds and stocks: "High-grade Bonds," "Business Men's Bonds," "Convertible Bonds," "Semi-speculative Bonds," "Speculative Bonds," "Liberty Bonds—Common Stocks," "Common Stocks" and "Low-Priced Stocks."

Originated and developed by Theodore A. Rehm of Stetson & Blackman, a Philadelphia brokerage firm, and Sidney L. Sholley of Cambridge Associates, Boston investment counselors, the series provided investors a way to allocate assets to meet individual investment goals by picking two or more from a family of funds. Each fund was fully invested, with money divided equally among the fixed group of bonds or stocks chosen for its portfolio.

The investment vehicles offered by their Keystone organization were ten-year fixed-investment trusts in which investors bought certificates of participation. They were not mutual funds, but, like mutual funds, they did provide for redemption at any time.

In 1935, seven years before the trusts were to terminate, Keystone replaced them with trusts structured as mutual funds, having similar investment objectives. Included were four funds that (as far as can be determined) were the first bond mutual funds: B-1, invested in high-grade bonds; B-2, invested in a broad spectrum of bonds selling at a slight discount; B-3, invested in lower-priced bonds; and B-4, invested in high-yield bonds. B-4, concentrated in bonds of railroads and corporations being reorganized, replaced the original speculative bonds portfolio. It seems to have been the first high-yield bond mutual fund.

As yields of high-grade bonds fell and remained below four percent while stock yields were relatively attractive, the new funds formed during the rest of the 1930s were essentially all balanced or equity funds. For anyone seeking high current income, there was little incentive to invest in bond funds. As things turned out, it was, in fact, the beginning of a 24-

year period in which high-grade bond yields would lag behind high-grade stock yields (as Table 3–1 shows).

A TIME FOR REFORM

For both investors and the financial community, an issue even more important than either bond or stock yields had become paramount: the basic honesty of the fund business. The federal government had begun to play a much stronger role in the regulation of financial markets to end dishonest practices that had cost investors money and undermined their confidence in the system. First, Congress passed the Securities Act of 1933 and the Securities Exchange Act of 1934. Having dealt with the various types of investor abuse associated with the issuance and trading of individual securities, Congress in 1935 directed the SEC, which had been established in the 1934 act, to study investment trusts and investment companies and to make recommendations for reform.

Eventually, the SEC study's recommendations were conveyed to Congress and embodied in a bill sponsored by Senator Robert F. Wagner in the Senate and Representative Clarence F. Lea in the House of Representatives. Hearings were held, bringing out not only the self-enriching practices of some unscrupulous fund promoters but also the public disagreements within the industry as to what to do about them. Following the hearings, representatives of the investment company industry and the SEC met with Congressional encouragement to reconcile differences. The result: substitute legislation introduced in both houses in June, 1940. Called the Investment Company Act of 1940, it was passed and signed by President Roosevelt within two months.

Among other things, the law defined investment companies, dividing them into three principal classes—face-amount certificate companies, unit investment trusts and management companies. It further divided the management companies into open- and closed-end companies. The act did not use the term "mutual fund," but mutual fund subsequently became the popular synonym for open-end management companies, used by the government, investors and the industry alike.

In providing for the registration and regulation of mutual funds, the act gave investors confidence that they would be protected against fraud—but not against market fluctuations. In requiring disclosure of essential information in prospectuses and periodic reports, it gave existing and prospective shareholders what they needed to know about a fund's policies, management and so on. And it gave honest promoters the framework for forming and developing funds that would permit them, as well as their shareholders, to prosper.

OVERSHADOWED BY STOCKS

Through the 1940s, 1950s and 1960s—through World War II and the Korean War, booms and recessions—stocks and stock funds dominated the industry. The Dow Jones Industrial Average, which ended 1940 at 131.13 and 1949 at 200.13, soared to 679.36 by the end of 1959 and ended 1969 at 800.36 after coming close to 1000 on several occasions.

Most of the period from 1940 to 1965 was characterized by low interest rates. As Table 3-2 illustrates, people were usually able—except for the war and early postwar years—to earn real interest above the inflation rate by putting money into ordinary savings accounts at banks or savings institutions. The ceiling on commercial bank savings accounts, set at 2.5 percent since 1935, was even permitted to creep up to 4 percent by 1964. As long as Treasury bill rates were kept artificially low—prior to the Fed–Treasury accord of 1951—individual investors had little or no incentive to buy them.

For long-term investors, U.S. government issues also had limited attraction—whether non-marketable savings bonds bearing a 2.9 percent yield or marketable securities. Triple-A corporate bonds became more attractive as their yields passed those of quality stocks at the end of the 1950s, but the annual volumes of new corporate issues remained low. State and local governments' new debt issues were of interest primarily to those in upper-income tax brackets.

Given the environment in the corporate and U.S. Treasury securities markets, it's not surprising that bond funds—and the total bond holdings of all mutual funds combined—showed slow growth. Nor did municipal bonds offer an opportunity for faster growth for mutual funds organized as corporations or business trusts; unlike shareholders of funds organized as partnerships, their shareholders would have had to pay federal income tax on any interest received. During the Eisenhower administration, fund organizations asked members of Congress to pass legislation permitting the pass-through of the exemption and, as a consequence, the incorporation of tax-exempt municipal bond mutual funds. Bills were introduced two or three times but got nowhere.

THE QUEST FOR INCOME

Under the circumstances, the search for high current income led mostly to the continuing growth of balanced funds and stock funds concentrating in high-yield stocks but less to the expansion of the bond fund sector.

One mutual fund sponsor, Shareholders Management Company, took a different approach in 1963 when it changed the investment policy of its recently acquired Kerr Income Fund to concentrate in securities

---

Table 3-2   Treasury Bill and Savings Account Interest Rates vs. Inflation 1940–1969

Year	Annual Averages of 3-Month Treasury Bill Yields	Changes in Annual Averages of Consumer Price Index	Ceilings on Commercial Bank Savings Deposits
1940	0.014%	0.7%	2.5%*
1941	0.103	5.0	
1942	0.326	10.9	
1943	0.373	6.1	
1944	0.375	1.7	
1945	0.375	2.3	
1946	0.375	8.3	
1947	0.594	14.4	
1948	1.040	8.1	
1949	1.102	(1.2)	
1950	1.218	1.3	
1951	1.552	7.9	
1952	1.766	1.9	
1953	1.931	0.8	
1954	0.953	0.7	
1955	1.753	(0.4)	
1956	2.658	1.5	
1957	3.267	3.3	3.0
1958	1.839	2.8	
1959	3.405	0.7	
1960	2.928	1.7	
1961	2.378	1.0	
1962	2.778	1.0	3.5–4.0**
1963	3.157	1.3	
1964	3.549	1.3	4.0
1965	3.954	1.6	
1966	4.881	2.9	
1967	4.321	3.1	
1968	5.339	4.2	
1969	6.677	5.5	

*In effect since 1935.

**3.5% for deposits under 12 months; 4.0% for 12 months or over.

Sources: Treasury bill yields, *Economic Report of the President,* January 1989; CPI changes, Bureau of Labor Statistics, U.S. Department of Labor; savings deposit ceilings, "Responses to Deregulation: Retail Deposit Pricing from 1983 through 1985," Patrick I. Mahoney, Alice P. White, Paul F. O'Brien and Mary M. McLaughlin, January 1987, staff study, Board of Governors of the Federal Reserve System.

convertible into common stock and changed its name to Convertible Securities Fund. Under other managements since 1975, the fund is now called American Capital Harbor Fund.

Another approach taken by fund sponsors to raise income for shareholders was to invest in bonds of lower quality. According to a major study[5] for the SEC of mutual fund practices during the 1952–58 period, 13 bond and preferred stock funds were in existence as of September 1958. U.S. corporate bonds accounted for 63 percent of their $191 million in assets; state and local bonds, 2 percent; and U.S. government securities, a mere 1 percent. But even more interesting (especially in light of the attention given "junk bond" funds in the late 1980s) was the finding that these funds had more than eight times as much invested in corporates *below* investment grade as in those that were of investment grade. Balanced funds, on the other hand, showed a stronger preference for investment-grade corporate bonds as well as a slightly higher percentage of government bonds.

When inflationary pressures intensified with the escalation of the Vietnam War in 1965 and the Fed pursued a more restrictive monetary policy to offset fiscal easing, interest rates began to climb significantly. Of the few announcements of new bond funds during this period, surely the most portentous came in 1969 from Federated Research Corp., a Pittsburgh investment counseling firm. It intended to start a fund whose objective would be to generate income through investment in, of all things, securities guaranteed by the U.S. government or its agencies. Initially given the clumsy, if descriptive, name of the Mutual Fund for Investing in U.S. Government Securities Yielding at Least 6% to Maturity and U.S. Treasury Bills, Inc., the Fund for U.S. Government Securities (as it was later renamed) started a major trend. It was the first of many funds that would be concentrated in government-guaranteed Ginnie Maes and other federally sponsored pools of mortgage-backed securities that in the 1980s were to become immensely popular because of yields exceeding Treasury securities.

BOND FUNDS COME OF AGE

While the 1970s were marked by events of extraordinary importance whose impact permeated the world of finance as they dominated our lives—two oil price "shocks," soaring inflation, unprecedented interest rates, the resignation of an American President—three developments supplied welcome boosts to mutual funds generally and to bond funds especially.

The high interest rates resulting from the inflationary pressures of the late 1960s, which became almost uncontrolled in the 1970s, gave bond funds their first major stimulus to growth. Investors increasingly perceived bond funds as vehicles permitting them to enjoy high rates for a long term, during which, presumably, inflation and interest rates would recede again—and bond prices would rise. And fund promoters obliged by creating a significant number of new ones.

Stock prices, buffeted by the tight monetary policy used to combat inflation and by the impact of two recessions, were extremely volatile but went nowhere during the 1970s. The decade ended with the Dow Jones Industrial Average at 838.74—essentially where it had been at the beginning. Given that many investors were unwilling or unable to await better times, stock funds suffered net *redemptions* of $10.4 billion during the decade—only about half offset by capital appreciation.

Bond and income funds, on the other hand, enjoyed net *sales* of $5 billion, resulting in a 50 percent increase in their net assets as existing funds grew and a host of new ones were started.

In retrospect, it was modest growth, but it was growth. It laid the foundation for future expansion. Consider, for example: the launching of investment-grade and/or high-yield corporate bond funds by major fund organizations such as Capital Research & Management, Colonial, Dreyfus, Fidelity, First Investors, Kemper, Massachusetts Financial Services (whose MIT had started it all 50 years earlier), T. Rowe Price, Putnam and Vanguard; and the emergence of large brokerage firms such as Merrill Lynch as promoters of their own funds.

Money Market Funds.   Of the three major developments that animated the bond fund sector in the 1970s, the first was the conception of the money market mutual fund, which was introduced in late 1971 by the Reserve Fund. As ceilings on savings accounts were held *below* increases in the consumer price index (Table 3-3), people's savings were losing purchasing power. Even Treasury bills, whose yields by the 1970s had long reflected money market forces, did not keep investors whole at times. When they did, most individuals did not have the minimum of $10,000 to buy them.

The money market fund, therefore, was an investment vehicle whose time had come. The concept was a simple one: the fund would invest in government and high-grade corporate debt instruments of very short maturities and large denominations—money market securities such as T-bills, corporations' commercial paper, certificates of deposit—and the portfolio would be managed to maintain net asset value per share at a constant $1. Thus, principal would be stable while yields—and maturities—would fluctuate.

To attract investors, money market mutual funds offered low minimums for initial and subsequent investments, free check writing and other conveniences. More important, they provided all investors—including those of modest means—access to money market interest rates that would better protect their short-term savings against inflation (as Table 3-3 shows).

Table 3-3 Money Market Rates vs. Inflation 1970–1988

Year	3-Month Treasury Bill Yields*	Changes In Annual Averages of Consumer Price Index	Ceilings on Commercial Bank Savings Deposits	Taxable Money Market Fund Total Returns*
1970	6.458%	5.7%	4.5%	NA
1971	4.348	4.4		NA
1972	4.071	3.2		NA
1973	7.041	6.2	5.0	NA
1974	7.886	11.0		NA
1975	5.838	9.1		6.36%
1976	4.989	5.8		5.29
1977	5.265	6.5		4.98
1978	7.221	7.6		7.22
1979	10.041	11.3	5.25	11.08
1980	11.506	13.5		12.78
1981	14.029	10.3		16.82
1982	10.686	6.2		12.23
1983	8.63	3.2		8.58
1984	9.58	4.3	5.50	10.04
1985	7.48	3.6		7.71
1986	5.98	1.9	**	6.26
1987	5.82	3.6	**	6.12
1988	6.68	4.1	**	7.11

*Annual averages
**Ceilings were removed April 1, 1986, pursuant to decontrol legislation enacted in 1980.

Sources: Treasury Bills, 1970-87, *Economic Report of the President,* January 1989; Treasury bills, 1988, *Federal Reserve Bulletin;* changes in CPI, Bureau of Labor Statistics, U.S. Department of Labor; savings deposits ceilings, Mahoney, op. cit.; money market returns; IBC/*Donoghue's Money Fund Report,* Box 6640, Holliston, MA 01746.

Investors' response was enthusiastic (Table 3-4)—from both those who wished to keep their savings highly liquid and those who preferred to keep their money in short maturities until they felt the time was right to invest long term. By the end of the 1970s, when inflation became much worse, money market mutual funds had become an accepted financial institution. By 1980 money market fund assets even *exceeded* those of stock and bond funds combined.

Money market fund sponsors expected that some of the new billions of dollars brought into their organizations would ultimately be moved into their stock or bond funds. They were right. In a survey for the Investment Company Institute, 30 percent of present mutual fund owners said their first fund shares *were* those of money market funds.

Table 3-4   Money Market Fund Assets 1974-1988 (in billions of dollars)

Year	Total Assets	Taxable	Tax-Exempt
1974	$ 1.7	$ 1.7	—
1975	3.7	3.7	—
1976	3.7	3.7	—
1977	3.9	3.9	—
1978	10.9	10.9	—
1979	45.2	45.2	—
1980	76.4	74.5	$ 1.9
1981	186.2	181.9	4.3
1982	219.8	206.6	13.2
1983	179.4	162.6	16.8
1984	233.5	209.7	23.8
1985	243.8	207.5	36.3
1986	292.1	228.4	63.8
1987	316.1	254.7	61.4
1988	338.0	272.3	65.7

Source: Investment Company Institute.

IRAs. The decade's second major development of importance to mutual funds was the creation of individual retirement arrangements (IRAs). Proposed by President Richard M. Nixon in a pension message to Congress in 1971, they were not embodied in law until passage of the Employee Retirement Income Security Act (ERISA) of 1974, signed by his successor, President Gerald Ford, a few weeks after Nixon had resigned in disgrace.

Nixon's proposal, in essence, was to encourage workers to save more toward their retirement. To induce them to supplement their expected retirement income, he proposed establishment of IRAs, which employees would fund with tax-deductible annual contributions of $1,500. As passed, however, ERISA limited eligibility to those who were not covered by employers' pension plans.

Effective in 1975, IRAs were immediately a success. In the first year, according to the Internal Revenue Service (IRS), 1.2 million of 82.2 million income tax returns reported deductions for IRAs of $1.4 billion. By 1980, 2.6 million of 93.9 million returns reported deductions of $3.4 billion.

But that was only the beginning. In the Economic Recovery Tax Act of 1981 (ERTA), President Reagan and Congress extended eligibility for IRAs to all workers and raised the deductible annual contribution to $2,000, effective 1982. In the first year of liberalization, 12 million tax returns (out of 95.3 million filed) showed contributions to IRAs of $28.3 billion. And a good chunk of the money was going into mutual funds: by the end of 1982, employees had 1.9 million IRA accounts in funds, with assets totaling $5.7 billion, according to ICI. By the end of 1988, 15.7 million IRA accounts had $86 billion in assets, about one-third in bond and income funds.

Municipal Bond Funds.   The third development, also emanating from Washington, was the provision in the Tax Reform Act of 1976 (TRA '76) that at last permitted mutual funds organized as corporations or business trusts to pass through to shareholders the federal tax exemption accorded interest on municipal bonds.

Faster than you could say "tax-free income," a score or more of mutual fund groups were ready to submit registration statements for their entries to the SEC. Having waited for this day for 20 years, they were ready to do business—"coming up like mushrooms after a spring rain," said *The New York Times*—as soon as the act became law.

Unlike mushrooms, which proliferate with apparent ease, the germination of the new section of the Internal Revenue Code took considerable time and effort. Imminent tax reform legislation, which would provide an opportune vehicle, encouraged the fund industry to respond. It was led by Robert Augenblick, president of the Investment Company Institute and a longtime advocate, and Donald A. Petrie, a former Chicago attorney, New York investment banker and 1972 treasurer of the Democratic National Committee, who had registered as a lobbyist for Dreyfus to help spearhead this cause.

Persuading important people in many walks of life—including influential union leaders—that the proposal was in their common interest, they developed support among key Democratic and Republican members of Congress. While gaining allies outside the financial community, fund sponsors had to overcome opposition from within: promoters of unit investment trusts, which had built and dominated the tax-exempt investment company field since the early 1960s.

In anticipation of enactment, Dreyfus had incorporated its Tax Exempt Bond Fund in July, well before Senate and House conferees agreed on the ultimate legislation. Having filed its registration statement with the SEC in advance, the fund could begin operations on October 4, the very day President Ford signed TRA '76 into law.

But Dreyfus' fund was not the first municipal bond mutual fund. Kemper Municipal Bond Fund had begun operations as a limited partnership nearly a half-year earlier—four years after Kemper Financial Services had begun to develop the concept. Most of the time was devoted to satisfying the IRS and SEC's various concerns. Once the SEC was assured that individual investors' rights could be adequately protected in a partnership, Kemper searched for a state with a favorable partnership law. It chose Nebraska.

"Nebraska was a good state for us," Robert J. Butler, Kemper senior vice-president, recalls. "Their law only required a minor amendment, and they had a lot of public power districts and other local municipal bond issuers who certainly weren't offended by the idea that we expanded the market for their securities." About a year after the fund had begun to offer its shares, the Nebraska partnership became history. With pass-through extended to shareholders of corporations and business trusts, Kemper incorporated a successor fund in Maryland. (In 1985, Kemper reorganized the fund again, making it a Massachusetts business trust.)

Municipal bond funds brought within the reach of many the tax-exempt interest that had been available only to those who invested in unit investment trusts or limited partnerships or to those who could afford to buy individual tax-exempt securities. It would be three more years before federally tax-exempt interest also would be available in money market mutual funds.

BOND FUNDS IN THE 1980s

With the dawning of the 1980s, the mutual fund industry had the organization, variety of investment vehicles, favorable federal legislation and growing confidence of its shareholders in its honesty and reliability—and in SEC enforcement of both. All the industry—and the nation as a whole—needed was a more favorable economic environment: healthy growth with stable prices.

That was soon to come—probably sooner than most people imagined. After the nation had gone through the agony of *another* recession and the Fed at last had pushed the inflation rate down from double-digit rates to below six percent, an environment favorable to financial assets was in place. Instead of choosing to spend because saving was rewarded in lost purchasing power, or to borrow because debts could be repaid in cheaper dollars, people could finally invest in stocks and bonds with the expectation of receiving a satisfactory, *real* return over the long run, if not an immediate windfall.

The Explosive 1980s

The realization sank in slowly at first, but then it spread, igniting rallies in securities prices in August 1982, which spawned the great bull market of the 1980s—and the explosive growth of stock and bond funds.

Table 3-5   Where Households Put Money To Work—or Took It Out
Net Increase (Decrease) in Financial Assets 1979–1988 (in
billions of dollars)

Year	Deposits*	U.S. Govt. Securities	Tax-Exempt Oblig.	Corp. & Foreign Bonds	Mutual Funds	Other Corp. Equities	Other Financial Assets**	Total
1979	$132	$ 59	$ 8	$ (3)	$ (1)	$ (25)	$ 67	$237
1980	153	33	1	(18)	1	(11)	75	233
1981	185	22	21	1	6	(41)	75	268
1982	170	41	29	(7)	7	(18)	57	279
1983	182	69	27	(9)	24	(24)	111	381
1984	278	100	26	(4)	24	(77)	80	427
1985	155	83	38	4	69	(103)	190	435
1986	217	21	(25)	39	141	(125)	197	466
1987	126	97	43	24	73	(98)	118	384
1988	161	141	25	17	(2)	(116)	219	446

*Includes checking and savings accounts, time deposits and money market mutual funds.
**Includes pension fund and life insurance reserves, mortgages, open-market paper, net investment in non-corporate businesses, security credit and miscellaneous assets.

Source: Flow of Funds Section, Board of Governors of the Federal Reserve System.

To a large extent, the growth of stock and bond funds was attributable to common factors: the disposable personal income that people had available for investment as the economy grew, their increasing inclination to liquidate holdings of individual corporate equities (Table 3–5), the extension of eligibility for IRA deductions to additional millions of workers—until President Reagan and Congress took it away from most of them in the Tax Reform Act of 1986[6]—and the availability of billions in money market mutual funds that could be switched with a telephone call. And bond funds, moreover, could offer yields from investment in governments and high-quality corporates that investors had never known.

Nor can one ignore the contagion of the bull market, becoming more infectious as prices soared, or the persuasiveness of the industry's marketing efforts. As Tables 3–6a through 3–6c make clear, the growth of fund assets during the 1980s was due more to the edge that sales had over redemptions—especially for bond and income funds—than it was to capital appreciation. (The $737.7 billion of gross sales for 1980–88 included about 60 percent of $120.8 billion in income distributions and an indeterminate percentage of the $69.0 billion in capital gains distributions that shareholders elected to reinvest.)

Given the attractions of the merchandise—for example, bonds backed by the full faith and credit of the Treasury, *guaranteeing* interest

Table 3–6a   How Long-Term Mutual Funds Have Grown Through Share Sales and Capital Appreciation 1970–1988 (in billions of dollars)

Year	Sales*	Redemptions	Net Sales (Redemptions)	Capital Appreciation (Depreciation)	End-of-Year Assets
1970	$ 4.6	$ (3.0)	$ 1.6	$ (2.3)	$ 47.6
1971	5.2	(4.8)	0.4	7.0	55.0
1972	4.9	(6.6)	(1.7)	6.4	59.8
1973	4.4	(5.7)	(1.3)	(12.0)	46.5
1974	3.1	(3.4)	(0.3)	(12.1)	34.1
1975	3.3	(3.7)	(0.4)	8.5	42.2
1976	4.4	(6.8)	(2.4)	7.8	47.6
1977	6.4	(6.0)	0.4	(3.0)	45.0
1978	6.7	(7.2)	(0.5)	0.4	45.0
1979	6.8	(8.0)	(1.2)	5.2	49.0
1980	10.0	(8.2)	1.8	7.6	58.4
1981	9.7	(7.5)	2.2	(5.4)	55.2
1982	15.7	(7.6)	8.2	13.4	76.8
1983	40.3	(14.7)	25.7	11.0	113.6
1984	45.9	(20.0)	25.8	(2.3)	137.1
1985	114.3	(33.8)	80.6	34.0	251.7
1986	215.9	(67.0)	148.8	23.7	424.2
1987	190.6	(116.2)	74.4	(44.8)	453.8
1988	95.3	(92.5)	2.8	15.7	472.3

*Sales include reinvested dividend and capital gains distributions.

Note: Totals may not add due to rounding.

Sources: Sales, redemptions and assets, Investment Company Institute; net sales and net capital appreciation (depreciation), author's calculations.

of 10–13 percent or more for many years into the future—bonds and bond fund shares were not difficult to sell. Given the rising volume of offerings by the federal government and its agencies, state and local governments, and corporations, there was enough merchandise to go around.

Search for Guarantees

As short-term interest rates fell from double-digit levels in autumn 1982 investors became persuaded to seek double-digit income by switching to the new government bond funds and government-backed mortgage securities funds that were spreading like dandelions. The magic phrases, "government guarantee", "safety" and "12 percent yield," blinded many investors to the one risk inherent in all bonds: that prices fall when

Table 3-6b   How Bond and Income Funds Have Grown Through Share Sales and Capital Appreciation 1970-1988 (in billions of dollars)

Year	Sales*	Redemptions	Net Sales (Redemptions)	Capital Appreciation (Depreciation)	End-of-Year Assets
1970	$ 0.7	$ (0.5)	$ 0.2	$ (1.5)	$ 9.1
1971	0.8	(0.7)	0.1	1.3	10.5
1972	0.8	(1.0)	(0.2)	0.9	11.2
1973	0.7	(1.0)	(0.3)	(1.3)	9.6
1974	0.7	(0.7)	0.0	(1.8)	7.8
1975	1.0	(0.7)	0.3	1.7	9.8
1976	1.9	(1.4)	0.5	3.0	13.3
1977	3.8	(1.8)	2.0	(0.5)	14.8
1978	4.0	(2.6)	1.4	(0.6)	15.6
1979	3.8	(2.8)	1.0	(0.5)	16.1
1980	4.4	(2.9)	1.5	(0.8)	16.8
1981	3.8	(2.6)	1.2	(1.8)	16.2
1982	7.3	(2.6)	4.7	4.6	25.5
1983	17.0	(5.6)	11.4	0.9	37.8
1984	25.8	(9.4)	16.4	1.5	55.7
1985	84.7	(15.8)	68.9	11.8	136.4
1986	158.1	(39.8)	118.3	7.9	262.6
1987	118.6	(76.0)	42.6	(32.0)	273.2
1988	64.3	(57.7)	6.6	(2.3)	277.5

*Sales include reinvested dividend and capital gains distributions.

Note: Totals may not add due to rounding.

Sources: Sales, redemptions and assets, Investment Company Institute; net sales and net capital appreciation (depreciation), author's calculations.

interest rates rise. It was a risk that fund organizations, as well as brokers and others who sold funds, did not always stress adequately.

Following a firming of interest rates in mid-1984, the Fed eased in September and rates resumed their decline and sales of bond funds gained momentum. Rates having returned to the highest levels since mid-1982, investors perceived another—possibly last—opportunity to obtain high income from high-quality securities and to realize capital appreciation as prices rose. Moreover, with stock prices sluggish, equity funds provided less competition.

After government bond yields fell to 10 percent and lower in 1985, the search for high income led fund promoters and many investors down the quality ladder. As Table 3-7 shows, when Treasury issues were only yielding around 10 percent in 1985, investment-grade corporates (rated Aaa through Baa) were still yielding 11-12 percent, and, thus, corporate

Table 3–6c How Equity Funds Have Grown Through Share Sales and Capital Appreciation 1970–1988 (in billions of dollars)

Year	Sales*	Redemptions	Net Sales (Redemptions)	Capital Appreciation (Depreciation)	End-of-Year Assets
1970	$ 3.9	$ (2.5)	$ 1.4	$ (0.7)	$ 38.6
1971	4.3	(4.0)	0.3	5.6	44.5
1972	4.1	(5.5)	(1.4)	5.5	48.6
1973	3.6	(4.7)	(0.9)	(10.8)	36.9
1974	2.4	(2.7)	(0.3)	(10.3)	26.3
1975	2.4	(3.0)	(0.6)	6.7	32.4
1976	2.5	(5.4)	(2.9)	4.8	34.3
1977	2.6	(4.3)	(1.7)	(2.3)	30.3
1978	2.7	(4.7)	(2.0)	1.1	29.4
1979	3.0	(5.3)	(2.3)	5.8	32.9
1980	5.6	(5.3)	0.3	8.4	41.6
1981	5.9	(4.9)	1.0	(3.6)	39.0
1982	8.4	(5.0)	3.4	9.0	51.4
1983	23.4	(9.1)	14.3	10.1	75.8
1984	20.0	(10.7)	9.3	(3.6)	81.5
1985	29.6	(18.0)	11.6	22.2	115.3
1986	57.7	(27.2)	30.5	15.7	161.5
1987	72.1	(40.2)	31.9	(12.7)	180.7
1988	31.0	(34.8)	(3.8)	17.9	194.8

*See notes under Table 3–6b.

bond funds could provide higher yields for comparable maturities. Most fund investors, however, were content with Treasury and Ginnie Mae securities' interest; their purchase of government and Ginnie Mae fund shares led bond funds to outsell equity funds by a large margin.

When the yields fell further, a large number of investors dipped into sub-investment-grade bond funds. Known as "high-yield" or "junk bond" funds, they offered significantly higher income, to be sure, but also significantly higher risks against which investors could be best—if unevenly—protected by shrewd selections of fund portfolio managers and broad diversification. It was a time when leveraged buyouts and other corporate developments led the rating services to downgrade many existing issues and to give low grades to a high share of new ones, giving portfolio managers plenty to choose from. Many investors realized that sooner or later interest rates would rise again, as eventually they did in 1987 (when bonds crashed before stocks did), and that it might be wise to shorten the maturities of their bond fund portfolios to minimize volatility. Moreover, many investors wished simply to fine-tune the maturities

Table 3–7   Capital Market Rates, Annual Averages, 1970–1988

Year	Standard & Poor's 500 Stock Price Index	U.S. Treasury 10-Year Constant Maturities	Moody's Aaa Corp. Bonds	Moody's Baa Corp. Bonds
1970	3.83%	7.35%	8.04%	9.11%
1971	3.14	6.16	7.39	8.56
1972	2.84	6.21	7.21	8.16
1973	3.06	6.84	7.44	8.24
1974	4.47	7.56	8.57	9.50
1975	4.31	7.99	8.83	10.61
1976	3.77	7.61	8.43	9.75
1977	4.62	7.42	8.02	8.97
1978	5.28	8.41	8.73	9.49
1979	5.47	9.44	9.63	10.69
1980	5.26	11.46	11.94	13.67
1981	5.20	13.91	14.17	16.04
1982	5.81	13.00	13.79	16.11
1983	4.40	11.10	12.04	13.55
1984	4.64	12.44	12.71	14.19
1985	4.25	10.62	11.37	12.72
1986	3.49	7.68	9.02	10.39
1987	3.08	8.39	9.38	10.58
1988	3.64	8.85	9.71	10.83

Sources: Yield on Standard & Poor's 500 Index, Standard & Poor's Corporation; Treasury yields, *Economic Report of the President,* January 1989; Moody's bond yields reprinted with permission of Moody's Investors Service.

of their bond fund holdings to make them more consistent with their investment objectives.

To accommodate those having these concerns and goals, a growing number of fund organizations formed funds concentrating in U.S. government, state and local government and/or corporate bonds of short and intermediate maturities.

Targeting Maturities

A different approach to enable investors to achieve their objectives was taken by two fund sponsors, Scudder, Stevens & Clark and Benham Management Corporation. In 1981, when interest rates were at or near their peaks, Scudder formed Scudder Target Fund, which offered investors the opportunity to invest in series with specific maturities so they would be sure of their shares' ultimate market values regardless of interim fluctuation. The fund provided a choice of portfolios invested in U.S. government or high-grade corporate securities, with maturities that eventually went out to 1994. In 1983 Scudder added the Tax Free Target Fund, providing a similar choice in municipal bonds.

In 1985 and 1986, both Benham and Scudder introduced funds that also had specific maturities but with a different twist: they were invested in U.S. Treasury zero-coupon obligations. Their creation facilitated by the Treasury, zeros were becoming increasingly popular with individual investors who did not want current income but were eager to lock in specific yields to enable them to accumulate targeted amounts of money by certain years. By mid-1989, Benham Target Maturities Trust had six portfolios and Scudder U.S. Government Zero Coupon Target Fund had three.

The zero-coupon portfolios have been successful, but the taxable Scudder Target Fund was not. Scudder found the concept difficult to sell. "Target Fund's total return was OK," said portfolio manager Samuel Thorne, Jr., "but its current return was low." The Scudder Target Fund was replaced in 1989 with the newly created Scudder Short Term Bond Fund.

Going for the World

Another new concept introduced in the 1980s was a bit easier to understand—and to sell: the fund investing partially or totally in the bonds of foreign governments and corporations. It was initiated in 1981, when Massachusetts Financial Services launched its International Trust— Bond Portfolio. In the year's environment—rising U.S. interest rates and falling bond prices—bond investors were discouraged and frustrated. Many were convinced they should cut losses by selling long bonds and replace them with shorter maturities. MFS hit on the international bond fund idea as an alternative.

The concept is not simple to implement—or risk-free. It requires not only understanding and monitoring credit market conditions in a number of countries but also tracking and projecting trends in foreign currency exchange rates that could enhance—or offset—returns when converted into dollars.

From the beginning, MFS made it clear that the fund was a global— not an international—bond fund. Thus, when necessary or desirable, it could be heavily invested in U.S. bonds. In 1988, when interest rates and prospects for total returns were or tended to become higher abroad, the 75 percent of assets invested in long-term bonds were denominated in foreign currencies: Australian dollars, Canadian dollars, Dutch guilders, English pounds, French francs, Irish pounds, Italian lire, Japanese yen,

New Zealand dollars and Spanish pesetas. (As things turned out, the U.S. dollar put on a surprisingly strong performance during the first half of 1988, and the fund's total return for the year was only 4.4 percent.)

TAKING STOCK OF BOND FUNDS

We can speculate about how credit markets in the U.S. as well as abroad are likely to perform in the 1990s, what new ideas will come from innovative fund managements or how investors will respond; but we can't be sure. Therefore, it may be of greater interest at this point to look back— to review how bonds came to exceed stocks in the portfolios of the mutual fund industry, stimulating the extraordinary growth of bond funds.

Table 3-8 shows vividly how bonds rose from less than ten percent of mutual funds' total net assets to more than 50 percent by 1986, while Table 3-9 fills in the details on how the bonds were allocated among the three broad groups. Corporate bonds, long accounting for nearly all of the bonds held by the industry, remained on top through 1982, when tax-exempts edged them. Municipals have continued to lead corporates but, beginning in 1985, were themselves overtaken by securities issued or backed by the U.S. government.

The increase in funds' bond holdings was sustained by the increase in the number of bond funds. At year-end 1988, ICI counted 1,096 bond and income funds vs. 1,015 equity funds as shown in Table 3-10 on page 54. Even if you exclude the 163 flexible, balanced, income-mixed funds, which hold various proportions of stocks and cash equivalents as well as bonds, that's more than 900 pure bond funds, compared with slightly more than 100 at the end of 1980. Notably, almost one-half were municipal bond funds.

You get a slightly different perspective when you see how the sizes of the fund groups, as measured by their net assets, compare as shown in Table 3-11 on page 55. U.S. government and GNMA bond funds, which together accounted for 12 percent of all funds, held 24 percent of all funds' net assets. With 18 percent and 7 percent, respectively, municipal bond funds and high-yield bond funds, on the other hand, held shares of assets closer to their shares of the number of funds (20 percent and 5 percent).

Since changes in net assets reflect net sales (gross sales including reinvestment of income and capital gains distributions less redemptions) as well as capital appreciation or depreciation, Table 3-11 may not readily indicate how the sales picture changed for the different groups from year to year. A glance at Table 3-12 on page 56 makes it clear that net sales of

Table 3–8   The Growing Importance of Bond Holdings by Mutual Funds*
1970–1988 (in billions of dollars)

Year	Bonds**	Preferred Stocks	Common Stocks	Cash and Equivalents	Other***	Total Net Assets
1970	$ 4.3	$1.1	$ 38.5	$ 3.1	$0.5	$ 47.6
1971	4.9	1.2	45.9	2.6	0.4	55.0
1972	5.1	1.0	50.7	2.6	0.4	59.8
1973	4.2	0.6	37.7	3.4	0.6	46.5
1974	3.6	0.4	26.1	3.4	0.6	34.1
1975	4.8	0.5	33.2	3.2	0.5	42.2
1976	7.0	0.7	37.2	2.4	0.4	47.6
1977	10.0	0.4	30.8	3.3	0.6	45.1
1978	9.2	0.4	30.7	4.5	0.2	45.0
1979	9.0	0.4	34.3	5.0	0.2	49.0
1980	10.9	0.5	41.6	5.3	0.1	58.4
1981	12.7	0.4	36.7	5.3	0.2	55.2
1982	21.4	1.6	47.7	6.0	0.1	76.8
1983	30.3	1.5	72.9	8.3	0.5	113.6
1984	41.6	1.6	81.6	12.0	0.4	137.1
1985	106.8	3.8	119.7	20.6	0.9	251.7
1986	229.7	7.4	153.7	30.7	2.7	424.2
1987	230.1	5.6	176.4	38.0	3.8	453.8
1988	244.3	5.7	173.7	45.1	3.5	472.3

*Long-term funds, excluding taxable and tax-exempt money market mutual funds.
**Corporate bonds only 1970–76; corporate, U.S. government and tax-exempt bonds 1977–88.
***Includes any long-term U.S. government and tax-exempt bonds that funds may have owned 1970–76.

Note: Totals may not add due to rounding.

Source: Investment Company Institute.

U.S. government bond, GNMA and municipal bond fund shares in only two years, 1985 and 1986, accounted for more than one-half of all bond and income fund net sales for the ten years shown. Just as clearly, the uptick of interest rates, beginning in 1987, had a negative impact on the major groups; many investors were led to switch (back) to money market funds.

Which bond groups will lead the next surge? Only time will tell. If support from strong sales organizations would suffice as a clue, U.S. government bond funds should be far ahead. According to ICI data, 96 percent of the assets of government bond funds are accounted for by funds sold by their own management companies' personnel, brokers and other salespeople. This compares with 84 percent for high-yield bond funds, 78 percent for GNMA funds and 77 percent for single-state municipal bond funds. In contrast, only between 60 percent and 70 percent

Table 3-9   The Growth and Changing Mix of Bond Holdings by Mutual Funds 1970-1988 (in billions of dollars)

Year	Corporate Bonds	Tax-Exempt Bonds	U.S. Government Bonds
1970	$ 4.3	NA	NA
1971	4.9	NA	NA
1972	5.1	NA	NA
1973	4.2	NA	NA
1974	3.6	NA	NA
1975	4.8	NA	NA
1976	7.0	NA	NA
1977	6.5	$ 2.3	$ 1.3
1978	5.6	2.6	1.1
1979	5.6	2.7	0.8
1980	6.6	2.9	1.4
1981	7.5	3.1	2.2
1982	10.8	6.8	3.8
1983	13.1	13.4	3.9
1984	15.0	18.5	8.0*
1985	25.0	38.3	43.5*
1986	47.3	70.9	111.5*
1987	41.7	68.6	119.9*
1988	54.4	86.1	103.8*

*For years 1984-88, the Flow of Funds Section of the Federal Reserve Board estimated mutual fund holdings of U.S. agency issues at $0.5, $12.0, $34.9, $34.9 and $33.4 billion, respectively.

Source: Investment Company Institute.

of the assets of income-bond, corporate bond, balanced and national municipal bond funds are held by funds sold through sales organizations. (For all equity funds, it's 58 percent.) In other words, more of these groups' assets are held by no- or low-load funds that deal directly with investors who like to make their own decisions without consulting a salesperson.

But, of course, salesmanship may not—should not—be the only determinant. Investors' assessments of what's right for them, given evolving economic and credit market conditions and fiscal policy, also will influence which fund groups will outsell the others. Whether funds of any of these groups belong in *your* portfolio in the 1990s—and if so, which ones—we'll discuss later. First, we'll look more closely in the next chapter at the different types of bond funds.

Table 3–10   Growth in Bond and Income Funds

Investment Objective	Number of Funds	
	1980	1988
Taxable		
Flexible portfolio	NA	39
Balanced portfolio	21	39
Income-mixed	56	85
Income-bond	NA	86
U.S. government income	NA	184
GNMA	NA	62
Global bond	NA	27
Corporate bond	62	57
High-yield bond	NA	102
Tax Exempt		
National municipal	42	172
State municipal	NA	243
Total bond and income	181	1,096
Equity funds	*277*	*1,015*
Total mutual funds	*458*	*2,111*

Source: Investment Company Institute.

ENDNOTES

1. The 35 were among 104 of what ICI calls bond and income (B&I) funds, a broad grouping that includes funds that also may have been significantly invested in government bonds and preferred and high-dividend common stocks. In the absence of complete historical ICI data for pure bond funds, B&I group figures are used in this book.
2. Known as Loomis-Sayles Mutual Fund since 1931.
3. Aaa through Baa, in terms of Moody's ratings.
4. In *Main Street Comes to Wall Street* (New York: Random House, 1964).
5. A *Study of Mutual Funds,* Wharton School of Finance and Commerce, University of Pennsylvania, 1962.
6. Preliminary IRS data show the number of tax returns claiming deductions for IRAs fell from 15.5 million in 1986 to 7.4 million in 1987 and the dollars deducted, from $37.8 billion to $14.2 billion.

Table 3–11   How Bond and Income Funds Have Grown—Net Assets by Investment Objectives (in billions of dollars)

Type	1979	1980	1981	1982	1983	1984	1985	1986	1987	1988
Balanced	$ 3.4	$ 3.4	$ 2.8	$ 3.1	$ 3.1	$ 2.9	$ 4.1	$ 7.5	$ 9.0	$ 9.5
Flexible portfolio	NA	NA	NA	NA	NA	NA	NA	1.5	4.3	3.5
Income-mixed	NA	NA	NA	NA	NA	NA	NA	10.3	11.4	8.8
Income-bond	NA	NA	NA	NA	NA	NA	NA	11.4	12.6	10.7
Income	4.5	4.8	4.5	5.9	8.8	7.1	11.0	NA	NA	NA
Bond	5.1	5.7	5.9	9.1	11.3	NA	NA	NA	NA	NA
U.S. government	NA	NA	NA	NA	NA	6.4	40.0	82.4	88.9	82.7
GNMA	NA	NA	NA	NA	NA	4.0	17.9	39.6	34.2	28.7
Corporate bond	NA	NA	NA	NA	NA	14.6	24.0	9.1	9.5	10.5
Global bond	NA	NA	NA	NA	NA	NA	NA	0.5	2.1	3.0
High-yield bond	NA	NA	NA	NA	NA	NA	NA	24.6	24.2	33.4
Long-term municipal	3.0	2.9	3.1	7.5	14.6	16.0	27.9	49.9	49.2	54.3
State municipal	NA	NA	NA	NA	NA	4.8	11.5	25.8	27.8	32.4
Total	$16.1	$16.8	$16.2	$25.5	$37.8	$55.7	$136.4	$262.6	$273.2	$277.5
Memo:										
Equity funds	32.9	41.6	39.0	51.3	75.8	81.4	115.3	161.6	180.7	194.8
Total funds	$49.0	$58.4	$55.2	$76.8	$113.6	$137.1	$251.7	$424.2	$453.8	$472.3

Totals may not add due to rounding.

Source: Investment Company Institute.

Table 3-12   Net Sales (Redemptions) of Bond and Income Funds by Investment Objectives 1979-1988 (in billions of dollars)

Investment Objective	1979	1980	1981	1982	1983	1984	1985	1986	1987	1988
Balanced	$(0.4)	$(0.3)	$(0.2)	$(0.2)	$(0.1)	$(0.1)	$ 0.6	$ 2.8	$ 2.2	$(0.4)
Flexible	NA	NA	NA	NA	NA	NA	NA	0.3	2.5	*
Income	*	0.2	*	0.4	2.6	0.8	2.8	NA	NA	NA
Income-mixed	NA	NA	NA	NA	NA	NA	NA	3.4	1.1	(0.7)
Income-bond	NA	NA	NA	NA	NA	NA	NA	3.8	2.2	0.9
Bond	0.6	0.8	0.7	1.7	2.1	NA	NA	NA	NA	NA
Corporate bond	NA	NA	NA	NA	NA	2.5	7.2	3.6	1.5	0.4
High-yield bond	NA	NA	NA	NA	NA	NA	NA	10.9	4.1	4.3
Government	NA	NA	NA	NA	NA	5.1	31.8	40.4	16.6	(4.3)
GNMA	NA	NA	NA	NA	NA	2.4	11.6	21.9	0.3	(2.6)
Global bond	NA	NA	NA	NA	NA	NA	NA	0.4	0.6	0.8
Long-term municipal	0.8	0.8	0.8	2.8	6.8	3.7	9.3	18.3	6.3	4.3
State municipal	NA	NA	NA	NA	NA	2.0	5.8	12.5	5.2	3.8
Total	$ 1.0	$ 1.5	$ 1.2	$ 4.7	$11.4	$16.4	$68.9	$118.3	$42.6	$ 6.6
Memo:										
Equity funds	(2.3)	0.3	1.0	3.4	14.3	9.3	11.6	30.5	31.9	(3.8)
Total funds	$(1.2)	$1.8	$2.2	$8.2	$25.7	$25.8	$80.6	$148.8	$74.4	$2.8

* Less than $0.1.

Totals may not add due to rounding.

Source: Investment Company Institute. Calculated from ICI data.

CHAPTER 4

The Many Types of Bond Funds

You may have the impression by now that there is an infinite variety of bond funds. You may want to bet that even the most creative mutual fund marketers cannot come up with one more type. While you could err in selling short the imaginations of fund marketers who almost overnight have built a financial sector with over 15 million shareholder accounts holding over $300 billion in net assets, you might be right.

How many types of bond funds are there, really, for you to consider? It depends on who does the counting and how they're counted. To the SEC, which regulates them (in addition to state authorities), they're all simply bond or income funds. It's satisfied if each bond fund merely identifies itself as that on the cover page of its prospectus, states its investment objective—for bond funds, that's principally or exclusively income—and spells out the types of debt securities in which it will invest. Although twice a year it asks bond funds to report what percentage of assets are in various types of debt securities, divided into two broad maturity classes, it doesn't subdivide the funds into groups accordingly.

THREE MAJOR CRITERIA

In the absence of an official system for classifying bond funds, we have to rely on others who gather fund statistics and disseminate them. ICI, the industry trade association, has divided the universe of bond and income funds into 11 groups since 1986; for these it calculates monthly and annual totals[1] of assets, share sales and redemptions, exchanges, security purchases and sales, and liquidity ratios.

Lipper Analytical Services, Inc., the company whose comprehensive data on the performance of individual funds and fund classes are the most widely used, has divided the universe into 21 groups (including balanced funds and counting single-state municipal bond funds as a group). Because of the firm's concern for completeness and accuracy, its performance data have become the industry standard.

Since the spectrum of Lipper categories and Lipper performance data should be useful to you in choosing the fund(s) that might enable you to achieve your individual investment objectives, the Lipper categories will be used throughout this book.

Table 4–1 shows how Lipper's analysis of fund policies and practices resulted in its classification of the 1,027 bond and balanced funds that had been in existence at least one year at the end of September 1989—excluding the nearly 100 more formed during the year—as well as how the 21 groups grew in number over the previous decade. Looking at the table, you can see how Lipper's classification can help you to identify those of greatest potential interest to you on the basis of the three most important criteria.

Taxability of Income

Income is either subject to or exempt from federal income tax. It is exempt when distributed in dividends by funds that receive interest from investment in tax-exempt securities. All other distributions of investment income, whether taken in cash or reinvested in additional shares, are federally taxable. (Of course, income distributed by bond funds held in IRAs is not taxable until money is taken out of the IRAs.)

Income from federally tax-exempt funds may be taxable by state and/or local governments that impose income taxes. Patterns vary. Some states exempt income from state and local government obligations issued within those states but tax income from those issued in other states. This has stimulated the growth of single-state municipal bond funds, promising to be "triple tax-free."

The reverse of the federally tax-exempt but state-taxable funds occurs in the case of some U.S. government securities funds. Income distributions from these funds is taxable at the federal level but may be partially or totally exempt from state and local income taxes, depending on state laws.

Credit Risk

Debt securities in which bond funds invest range in credit risk from those backed by the full faith and credit of the U.S. government, and corporate and municipal bonds accorded the highest credit ratings, to corporate

Table 4-1   Bond Fund Groups: How Long They've Been in Existence As of September 1989

Classification	Number of Funds in Existence			
	1 Year	3 Years	5 Years	10 Years
		Taxable		
A-rated corporate	36	31	28	19
BBB-rated corporate	41	23	17	11
Balanced	48	34	28	22
Convertible securities	30	17	5	5
Flexible income	20	17	10	10
GNMA	42	33	14	4
General bond	17	13	8	7
High-yield	82	58	39	25
Intermediate U.S. government	21	10	5	1
Intermediate investment-grade	24	10	8	4
Short U.S. government	23	8	4	0
Short investment-grade	27	12	7	0
U.S. government	121	59	15	5
U.S. mortgage	21	13	6	1
World income	35	5	1	0
Total	588	343	195	114
		Tax-Exempt: National		
General	99	70	51	28
High-yield	26	18	8	3
Insured	22	17	4	1
Intermediate	27	14	8	2
Short	17	13	11	1
Total	191	132	82	35
		Tax-Exempt: Single-State		
Arizona	5	2	0	0
California	47	32	13	1
Colorado	6	1	0	0
Georgia	6	3	0	0
Maryland	6	4	0	0
Massachusetts	18	8	3	0
Michigan	12	6	1	0
Minnesota	17	10	2	0
New Jersey	9	0	0	0
New York	42	25	13	0
North Carolina	4	3	0	0
Ohio	17	9	1	0
Oregon	7	4	1	0
Pennsylvania	12	4	1	1
Virginia	5	3	0	0
All other states	35	9	1	1
Total	248	123	36	3
Total bond funds	1,027	598	313	152

Source: Lipper Analytical Services.

and municipal issues whose prospects for timely interest payment or principal repayment are in doubt.

If a fund's name doesn't indicate the level of risk inherent in its investment policy, its statements of investment objectives and policies

must. Nothing is given more emphasis in the wording and enforcement
of the Investment Company Act of 1940 than that funds express clearly
the degree and types of risk incurred in their operations. If a fund is primarily invested in U.S. government or other high-grade securities, it will
be glad to say so; perhaps its name will reflect its concentration. But if a
fund is invested lower on the rating scale, it must make this equally clear.

The SEC doesn't care what a fund's management wants to call it or
what its investment objectives and policies are. It does care, however, that
neither name, objectives nor policies mislead prospective shareholders—
and it watches to ensure that a fund's practices are consistent with its
stated objectives and policies. Little has given the SEC's Division of Investment Management as much concern in recent years as implications
that the full faith and credit of the U.S. government stand behind a
fund's shares instead of behind the government securities that the fund
holds. The SEC also has been careful to keep an eye out for fund literature that could be interpreted to suggest that the government guarantee
of Treasury securities prevents fund share prices from falling when interest rates rise.

To help investors understand the levels of credit risk inherent in their
holdings of corporate and tax-exempt securities, funds make use of
Moody's and Standard & Poor's simple ratings in their prospectuses, just
as they use ratings in managing their portfolios. (The better-managed
funds supplement ratings with their own credit research.) If a fund states
that its policy is to hold only triple-A securities, or triple-A and double-A
securities, no one can wonder about the relative degree of credit risk of
its portfolio. If, on the other hand, it aims at higher income by investing
in bonds receiving Baa/BBB or lower ratings, just stating the minimum
ratings of the bonds it will buy isn't enough. The fund has to disclose
clearly the risks involved in such investments. In fact, the decline in junk
bonds led the SEC in October 1989 to ask funds to elaborate on such
risks as the sensitivity of high-yield bond prices to adverse economic
changes or corporate developments, as well as the thinness of the high-
yield bond market.

Maturity

Taxable or tax-exempt, the debt securities held by the funds with which
we're concerned have maturities running essentially from 1 to 30 years.
Prices of securities with short maturities tend to fluctuate less in response to changes in interest rates than those of long maturities, and,
thus, net asset values (NAV) per share of short-term funds tend to be
more stable than those of long-term funds involving comparable credit
risks.

Under normal circumstances, short-term bond funds pay lower interest because short-maturity bonds pay lower interest. Lenders (investors) normally insist on higher interest for longer maturities because their money is subject to risks—such as inflation and default—over a longer period.

Conditions are not always normal, however. There are times when long and short rates are very close, as they were most recently in 1989. There are other times when financial market supply/demand balances result in short maturities having higher yields. When interest rates for the range of maturities are plotted in a chart at such times, with the rates on the vertical axis and maturities on the horizontal axis, the curve slopes down as it goes from left to right—that is, out into the future. This is called "an inverted yield curve," and it was also seen in 1989.

When buying individual bonds, one can choose maturities based on prevailing interest rates as well as on the time when one wishes to have the principal repaid. One knows that no matter what happens to rates—and, therefore, to bond prices—one will get back a specific amount at a specific time (unless the issue is called earlier or the issuer defaults, of course).

When buying shares of bond funds—other than target funds (page 49)—one cannot specify a maturity with the assurance of getting back a principal amount on a certain day in the future. A bond fund does not mature. Its policy may require adherence to a narrow range of short, intermediate or long maturities, except under circumstances necessitating changes; it may permit its portfolio manager wide discretion to achieve a desired goal under changing market conditions; or it may be vague on the point. Whatever the case, as maturities of a portfolio's securities become shorter, the managers may sell them and reinvest the proceeds in new issues that will permit them to maintain the portfolio's weighted average maturity at a level the management deems appropriate. (Fewer sales may be necessary if sufficient cash is available from net sales of fund shares and from reinvestment of dividends in behalf of shareholders.)

So much for the three major bond fund criteria. Let's now focus on the classes of funds. Brief descriptions of each follow, beginning with the specific criteria that Lipper employs to classify them.

TAXABLE BOND FUNDS

A-Rated Corporate Bond Funds

At least 65 percent[2] of assets are invested in corporate bonds rated A or better or in government securities.

These are the funds most concentrated (as high as 85 percent for Pioneer Bond Fund, 80 percent for D.L. Babson Bond Trust's Portfolio L and Dreyfus A Bonds Plus) in corporate bonds that at the time of purchase carried the three highest ratings—Aaa, Aa or A (Moody's); AAA, AA or A (Standard & Poor's)—and, perhaps, in securities issued or guaranteed by the U.S. or Canadian government or their agencies. Collectively known as "high grade," these corporates are the taxable bonds whose yields are lowest of all, except for governments. Thus, these funds undertake perhaps the greatest challenge in attaining the investment objective of providing shareholders "high" current income consistent with "prudent" risk and/or "conservation of principal."

How do you produce *high* income from *low* yields? Managers employ various strategies. They may mix their core holdings in different proportions, such as by leaning more to the relatively higher-yielding A-rated bonds than to those rated Aaa/AAA or to government securities. Or they invest their remaining assets in higher-yielding securities. Most commonly, they buy bonds rated Baa/BBB. Several also invest in bonds below investment grade (i.e., Ba/BB or lower), convertible securities, foreign bonds denominated in U.S. dollars, preferred stocks, dividend-paying stocks, collateralized mortgage obligations and even limited partnership interests.

As market conditions change, managers adjust the mixes. When, for example, yield spreads widen, some may buy Ba/BBs in the expectation that the higher income will offset the slightly higher risk.

Fund managers may decide to sell bonds when the rating services downgrade them. "If, after purchase...the rating of a portfolio security is lost or reduced," says the prospectus for SteinRoe Income Trust's Managed Bonds portfolio, "the Fund would not be required to sell the security, but the Adviser (Stein Roe & Farnham) would consider such a change in deciding whether the Fund should retain the security in its portfolio."

Another, concurrent strategy may involve maturities. A fund's fundamental policy may require it, under normal circumstances, to be invested in long maturities to obtain their higher yields. It may express its policy in terms of a range, as in the cases of Twentieth Century's Long-term Bond or Vanguard's Investment Grade Portfolio, whose weighted average portfolio maturities are expected to run from 15 to 25 years. Alternatively, a fund's management may prefer the greater price stability—if normally lower yields—expected of intermediate-term maturities, as in the case of Babson, which expects a weighted average beyond five years. Or a fund may say its policy is not to aim at specific maturities. In any case, fund managers commonly change maturities as market conditions and expectations change, shortening portfolio maturities when rates are expected to rise and lengthening them when they are expected to fall.

To accommodate redemption needs and to help reduce volatility, all have some money invested in high-grade money market instruments; percentages vary.

Given the adjustments that managers make, high rates of portfolio turnover (i.e., 100 percent or higher), with correspondingly increased transaction costs, are not unusual. Most fund prospectuses disavow the practice of short-term trading, however.

BBB-Rated Corporate Bond Funds

At least 65 percent of assets are invested in corporate bonds rated in the top four grades—so-called "investment-grade" corporates—and in governments.

Funds that Lipper assigns to this group have investment objectives and policies similar to those of the previous category. By dropping one level below A to include (more) Baa/BBB-rated issues, thereby raising income, they incur a shade more risk than A-rated funds but remain relatively conservative nonetheless. As the prospectus for SteinRoe High-Yield Bonds points out, the issuers of both A- and Baa/BBB-rated bonds, in which the fund is principally invested, "possess adequate, but not outstanding, capacities to service their debt securities."

These funds' stated policies on portfolio composition call for minimums as high as 90 percent of assets (in the case of IDS Selective Fund) in the top four bond grades, governments, money market instruments and certain other high-quality securities. To maximize income, some fund managers have large shares in Baa/BBB issues as long as yield spreads provide the incentive. When their assessment of market prospects indicates the desirability of even radical change, however, managers will change their mixes.

In addition to bonds of the top four grades, governments and money market instruments, funds in this group also are likely to invest in speculative securities. American Capital Corporate Bond Fund, for example, is permitted to invest as much as 40 percent in securities below investment grade.

Most of this group's funds tend not to specify portfolio maturity targets in their prospectuses. Those that do range from T. Rowe Price

New Income Fund's average maturity of 4-9 years to New England Bond Income Fund's 5-15 years.

Balanced Funds

The primary objective of these funds is to conserve principal by maintaining at all times balanced portfolios of both stocks and bonds. Typically, their stock/bond ratios range around 60/40 percent.

Whether defined by Lipper or by the SEC, which requires any fund saying it's balanced to have at least 25 percent of its assets in bonds and/or preferred stocks, balanced funds are not strictly bond funds. But, given the large proportion of bonds they hold, they are not strictly equity funds either.

Some managements, such as those of American Balanced Fund, Dodge & Cox Balanced Fund and Wellington Fund, consider their funds to be complete investment programs for long-term investors while others, such as Eaton Vance Investors Fund and Fidelity Balanced Fund, say theirs are not intended to be complete programs.

In summarizing their investment objectives, funds commonly cite capital preservation, as expected, but most also add current income, capital appreciation or total return (i.e., both). A few, such as American, Composite Bond and Stock Fund, Dodge & Cox, Federated Stock and Bond and Massachusetts Financial Total Return Trust, also mention long-term growth of income.

While a large number state in their prospectuses that their policies don't call for the allocation of specific percentages to each asset type, several specify the *minimum* of 25 percent of assets in bonds or bonds plus preferred stocks to satisfy the SEC requirement. Twentieth Century Balanced Investors goes as high as 40 percent.

Other balanced funds express targets in terms of a *maximum* level of equities, stating they will allocate no more than 75 percent to common stocks (65 percent, in the cases of IDS Mutual and Strong Investment Fund, 60-70 percent, in the case of Wellington). Thus, they reassure cautious investors that they're not full-fledged equity funds—and retain the flexibility to buy enough senior securities to achieve their objectives.

Vanguard STAR Fund, which invests in other Vanguard funds, states its allocation policy in terms of ranges—60-70 percent in equity funds, 20-30 percent in bond funds and 10-20 percent in a money market fund—but has maintained fixed targets since its inception in 1985: 62.5 percent, 25 percent and 12.5 percent, respectively.

"This policy," the prospectus says, "reflects the Board of Trustees' belief that holding relatively steady proportions of stocks, bonds and money market instruments is more likely to provide favorable long-term investment returns, with moderate risk, than frequently rebalancing [STAR's investment holdings] based on short-term events."

Convertible Securities Funds

These funds are primarily invested in convertible bonds and/or convertible preferred stocks.

Convertible bonds and preferreds are hybrid securities that may be converted into a specific number of shares of the common stock of the company that issued them, at a specific price, within a specific period. In a corporation's capital structure, convertibles are junior to non-convertible bonds but senior to common stocks. Until their conversion, holders of convertible bonds or preferreds receive regular interest or dividends.

Like the prices of non-convertible fixed-income securities, the prices of convertibles tend to rise when interest rates fall and to fall when interest rates rise. When the prices of the underlying shares rise, the prices of convertibles rise and may exceed the market values that their interest/dividend income would indicate. When prices of the stocks fall, the prices of the convertibles fall, too, but eventually find support at levels consistent with their yields.

While interest and dividend payments make convertibles suitable investments for those who want stable current income, their issuers offer lower yields than they would for non-convertible securities of similar quality. That's because of the opportunities for capital appreciation arising from the conversion possibility. Yet, the yields tend to be higher than those of the dividends paid on the underlying stocks.

Given the nature of convertibles—combining the risks and rewards of both common stocks and fixed-income securities—they don't fully belong in either camp. Convertible securities funds sometimes are grouped with bond funds, sometimes with growth and income equity funds.

More like equity or balanced funds than like bond funds, convertible funds state that their investment objectives are capital appreciation as well as current income, or, simply, total return. Some add that they seek high current income or high total return.

While a large majority say they aim to have at least 65 percent of their assets in convertible securities, a few shoot for more: RNC Convertible Securities Fund and Vanguard Convertible Securities Fund seek a minimum of 80 percent; Alliance Convertible Fund, 75 percent; and Value Line Convertible Fund, 70 percent. On the other hand, American Capital Harbor Fund, the oldest, has a fundamental policy of merely investing "over 50 percent" of assets excluding cash and governments in convertibles and, in fact, has been running at below 55 percent of total assets in them.

A fund's selection of convertibles typically involves consideration of how much of the portfolio should consist of high-grade issues versus those with lower credit ratings and, therefore, higher yields. At least one, Noddings Convertible Strategies Fund, focuses on convertibles of small- to medium-size companies in the expectation that the long-term appreciation of their stocks will be greater.

The portions of portfolios invested in non-convertible assets are used to enhance income, prospects for appreciation or to reduce risk. American Capital Harbor appears to be the most enthusiastic for common stocks, having a policy that permits it to devote as much as 45 percent of total assets to them.

Flexible Income Funds

These funds emphasize generation of income by investing in bonds, preferreds, convertibles and/or common stocks and warrants.

As indicated, the funds in this group emphasize current income—some say maximum current income—by investing primarily in whatever types of securities will provide it consistent with prudent risk. Maximum total return, with emphasis on income, is given as the objective by Janus Flexible Income Fund and IDEX Total Income Trust (whose investment adviser, IDEX Management, Inc., is 50 percent owned by Janus Capital Corporation, which is investment adviser to the Janus fund). Among funds with explicit secondary objectives, long-term growth of income or capital is given most frequently.

The group's designation suggests that the funds' policies give their managers the flexibility to make portfolio switches, when deemed advantageous, between fixed-income securities and equities; among short, intermediate and long maturities; among high, medium and lower grades; between corporates and governments; and between U.S. and foreign issues. Some are very actively managed indeed, resulting in a high rate of portfolio turnover—as high as 400 percent for Strong Income Fund in 1988; Others, such as Nicholas Income Fund, have a turnover as low as 12 percent.

Inasmuch as bonds have provided higher yields than common stocks for quite a few years, it's not surprising that bonds tend to account for the largest percentages of portfolios. Northeast Investors Trust, for example, notes that since 1970 more than 90 percent of its assets have been in bonds, preferreds and cash. Fixed-income securities also account for 90 percent or more of the portfolios of IDEX, Janus and Nicholas Income Fund (whose policy requires that 10–50 percent of its net assets be in electric utility securities) and 75–80 percent of the assets of Mutual of Omaha Income Fund and Seligman Income Fund.

To help provide long-term growth of income and/or capital, some of the funds add a greater dose of dividend-paying equities. Vanguard's Wellesley Income Fund, for example, devotes around 35 percent to such stocks, while Unified Income Fund goes as high as 45 percent.

GNMA Funds

A minimum 65 percent of the assets of the funds in this group are in mortgage-backed securities guaranteed by the Government National Mortgage Association.

These funds were organized and flourished in the 1980s, investing in the government-guaranteed securities that were conceived after Congress created GNMA in 1968 to encourage home construction and ownership by attracting mortgage capital from new sources.

All have essentially the same investment objective: high current income consistent with safety of principal. To achieve that objective, nearly all state that they maintain at least 65 percent of their assets in GNMA securities, which provide higher yields than Treasury issues but are also backed by the full faith and credit of the U.S. government. A few—such as Federated GNMA Trust, Lexington GNMA Income Fund and Vanguard's GNMA Portfolio—aim at an 80 percent minimum.

That the funds have been successful in attracting investors to the GNMA program is attested by the size of several of these. They include the largest bond fund, Franklin U.S. Government Securities Series, with assets of over $11 billion, and such other giants as Dean Witter U.S. Government Securities Trust ($10 billion), Kemper U.S. Government Securities Fund ($4 billion), Merrill Lynch Federal Securities Trust, AARP GNMA & U.S. Treasury Fund and Vanguard GNMA (over $2 billion).

To understand the appeal of Ginnie Maes, you have to remember just what they are.

GNMA was established as a government corporation (within the U.S. Department of Housing and Urban Development) to expand the secondary market for Federal Housing Administration and Veterans Administration mortgages by making it attractive for all types of investors to invest in them indirectly. The investment vehicles that were developed, and which evolved into magnets for mutual fund sponsors and investors alike, were GNMA certificates—securities backed by the mortgages.

The program works like this: A private, GNMA- and FHA-approved lender—say, a commercial bank—makes a number of mortgage loans that are insured by the FHA or guaranteed by VA (now the Department of Veterans Affairs). Instead of holding them as income-producing assets for 30 years, the bank bunches $1 million worth of the same type, with common interest rates and maturities, in a "pool" and applies to GNMA for a guaranty of securities, to be backed by the mortgages that it proposes to issue. Having received GNMA's—that is, the government's—additional guaranty of timely payment of interest and repayment of principal, the bank creates 40 $25,000 GNMA certificates—Ginnie Maes—each of which represents partial ownership in the pool's mortgages. It agrees to sell the certificates to securities dealers, GNMA authorizes its transfer agent to make delivery and, with the proceeds, the bank can make new mortgage loans, starting the cycle all over again. Although it turned over the $1 million in mortgages to a custodian, it can't forget them. Each month it receives principal and interest from the homeowners who borrowed the money and sees that both are paid to the investors who bought its GNMA-guaranteed certificates.

In theory, investors in the certificates will receive the monthly "pass-through" of principal and interest on the pooled mortgages for, say, 30 years from the issuer or GNMA's agent, even if the borrowers do not make their payments on time. In practice, mortgages are liquidated earlier because people prepay them as they move or refinance when interest rates fall or because they are foreclosed by lenders when borrowers fail to pay and GNMA has to step in. Experience has shown the average life of a pool is no more than 12 years.

Owing to the government guaranty, Ginnie Maes are as safe as U.S. Treasury securities. But the shares of funds investing in them are not guaranteed. When interest rates fluctuate, the prices of Ginnie Maes fluctuate, as do the share prices of the funds that hold them.

Yields on Ginnie Maes tend to run one percent or so higher than those for Treasury issues of comparable maturity (Figure 4–1) to compensate investors for prepayment risk. With a Ginnie Mae, an investor receives the scheduled interest and principal every month as well as unpredictable payments of principal that have to be reinvested at interest rates that may be lower than that of the Ginnie Mae. Prepayments rise when interest rates fall and homeowners refinance the pool's mortgages.

When interest rates rise, Ginnie Maes fall, but when interest rates are falling and investors want to lock in relatively high yields and benefit from capital appreciation, Ginnie Maes do not rise as much as comparable Treasuries because of the prepayments. As James M. Benham,

---

Figure 4–1   GNMA vs. 10-Year Treasury Note

Yields

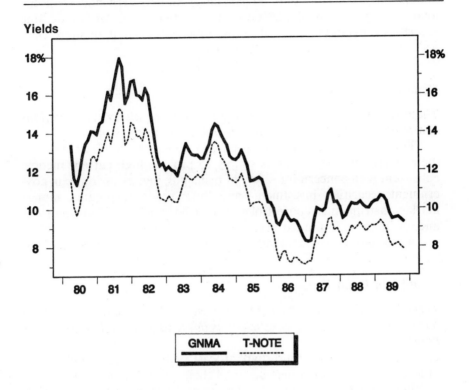

Source: Benham Capital Management Group

---

chairman of the Benham GNMA Income Fund, said in his 1988 annual report to shareholders: "...relative stability is the ideal market environment for an investment in GNMAs."

To achieve their long-term objective of high current income, fund managers must choose pools on the basis of whether they judge a coupon rate to be enough to maximize income for their shareholders but not so high that the risk of prepayment is too great. They also have to decide whether to adjust the maturities of their portfolios, to raise or lower the portions of their assets not allocated to Ginnie Maes and how to invest those portions (typically, in other government or government-related securities). It's in the formulation of such strategies that differences in performance emerge.

As long as managers calculate that it's advantageous to be in Ginnie Maes, they should have little trouble finding them for sale, even if the volume of new issues may ebb with residential construction. For a number of years, more than 90 percent of all new FHA and VA home loans have gone into GNMA pools, raising the volume of Ginnie Mae securities outstanding to well above $300 billion—out of more than $500 billion issued—as the 1980s ended.

General Bond Funds

These funds have no particular credit quality or maturity restrictions and tend to invest in both corporate and government bonds.

This rather heterogeneous group of funds, most of which state their investment objectives as simply to provide high current income consistent with concern for safety of principal, invests variously in government securities, investment- and lower-grade corporates, money market instruments, convertibles, preferred stock, foreign securities and/or interests in limited partnerships.

A few also engage in a variety of trading and hedging techniques.

High-Yield Bond Funds

These funds aim at high current yield from fixed-income securities. They have no quality or maturity restrictions but tend to invest in lower-grade bonds.

The funds in this group share at least two things: their investment objective—to seek high income—and their characterization by others as "junk bond" funds. A large number also share a secondary objective, capital appreciation, which they pursue so long as it is consistent with the primary one.

High-yield funds aim to provide their shareholders a higher rate of current income per dollar invested than any other group of funds. The securities they choose tend to be corporate bonds rated below investment grade, with coupon rates as high as 16 percent or higher—several percent above long-term Treasury bonds. The issuers' ability to pay interest and repay principal on these bonds—rated Ba or lower by Moody's, BB or lower by Standard & Poor's or unrated—may be questionable; the bonds already may be in default. Purchasers also expose themselves to the risk that junk bond prices can fall when economic conditions deteriorate or that the limited market for these securities may make sales difficult. Including some of the best-known corporate names in the nation, these bonds fall essentially into two categories:

1. New bond issues, including not only bonds issued by emerging companies that seek debt capital or by existing companies wanting

to expand but also bonds issued to finance mergers, acquisitions and leveraged buyouts of established companies; and

2. Existing issues whose ratings are lowered when their issuers have, or are expected to have, financial problems that have resulted—or could result—in default.

An ample—not to say excessive—supply of such bonds exists owing to the increased leveraging of corporate America and downgrading of existing issues in the 1980s. At the end of 1989, some $210 billion in bonds rated Ba or lower by Moody's were outstanding; this followed the issuance of over $180 billion of such bonds in the previous five years. Net assets of high-yield bond funds at the same time, according to Lipper, exceeded $30 billion. (Not all of their assets, as we will see, consisted of lower-rated bonds.)

The premise on which high-yield bond funds operate, as Kemper High Yield Fund says in its prospectus, is "that over the long term a broadly diversified portfolio of high-yield, fixed-income securities should, even taking into account possible losses, provide a higher net return than that achievable on a portfolio of higher-rated securities."

The margin of high-yield bonds' yields over those of high-quality bonds is not constant. During most of the 1980s it ran from three to five percent. "Market prices of high-yield, fixed-income securities may fluctuate more than market prices of higher-rated securities," Kemper adds. They "tend to reflect short-term corporate and market developments to a greater extent than higher-rated securities, which, assuming no change in their fundamental quality, react primarily to fluctuations in the general level of interest rates."

Investment in high-yield bonds clearly necessitates that portfolio managers and other investors address the risks of loss of income and even principal that are inherent in them.

They can do so in at least four ways, each of them beyond the capabilities of an average individual investor, thus making a case for investing in high-yield bonds via mutual funds, if one is to invest in them at all.

1. Thorough research into and monitoring of the financial condition and prospects of issuers. Most funds say that they treat ratings only as one piece of evidence. Some funds deliberately include bonds of corporations in bankruptcy when their research leads them to expect the companies to come out of bankruptcy and eventually pay bondholders.

2. Diversification. Given that inevitably some bonds will go into default, it is critical that an investor have a portfolio sufficiently di-

versified among both companies and industries to absorb the losses without materially hurting a portfolio's total return. Some funds hold as many as 200 issues or more.

3. Credit market analysis. Changes in interest rate levels and in the spread between rates for high- and low-quality issues create opportunities to adjust portfolios. Spotting the opportunities requires understanding market conditions.

4. Economic analysis. Because investments in high-yield bonds depend on their issuers' ability to service their debt, it is important to be aware of the likelihood of any downturns in the economy that could significantly reduce the issuers' profits, or even cause them to suffer losses and lead to defaults. Managers may reduce investment in cyclical industries when a recession seems probable and turn instead to companies less vulnerable to contractions.

Differences in performance among high-yield funds arise not only from the differences in their managers' abilities to assimilate, analyze and act on pertinent information but also from the clear differences in the policies on which they base their investment decisions. Although most say they primarily invest in high-yield fixed-income securities, they vary in how they define "primarily"—for some it's 80 percent; for others, 65 percent—and in the universes from which they choose the securities. Some express their target universes in terms of bonds rated at a certain level—such as Baa/BBB—or lower; some express them in terms of bonds rated at a certain level—such as B—or higher; and others use both maximum and minimum ratings. Still other funds include high-yield equities. High-yield funds also vary in their policies regarding investment of the remaining 20–35 percent of their assets.

Intermediate U.S. Government Funds and Intermediate Investment-Grade Debt Funds

These funds invest in bonds with maturities averaging five to ten years. At least 65 percent of their assets are invested, respectively, in securities issued or guaranteed by the U.S. government or its agencies and in investment-grade debt issues.

Funds in these groups invest for high current income in a way that's consistent with capital preservation and is likely, under normal circumstances, to result in less share price volatility than is expected of funds investing in similar quality bonds of longer maturities.

While the government funds are concentrated in government securities, most of the investment-grade funds also are invested in varying degrees in securities of the U.S. government and its agencies. (Shareholders of those invested in government securities may find their income partly or totally exempt from state and local income taxes.) Mixes of the government securities in which both groups invest vary from fund to fund. There are also slight quality differences in the core corporate holdings of the investment-grade group.

The funds' targets of weighted average maturities vary, too; some are expressed as broad ranges: Benham Treasury Note Fund (U.S.), 13 months to 10 years; and Fidelity Intermediate (I.G.), American Funds' Intermediate Bond Fund (I.G.), and Prudential-Bache Government Securities Trust's Intermediate Term Series (U.S.), three to ten years. Others are more limited.

Two investment-grade group funds, the SEI Bond Index Portfolio (available to institutional investors) and the Vanguard Bond Market Fund are, in a sense, managed by the market. They are index funds, designed to duplicate the performance of the Salomon Brothers Broad Investment Grade Bond Index, nearly 55 percent of whose $2.7 trillion market value is accounted for by U.S. Treasury and agency issues; the balance is divided between mortgage-backed securities (over 26 percent) and corporates (over 18 percent). The average maturity of the 4,900 issues represented in the index is around 9.5 years.

Short U.S. Government Bond Funds and Short Investment-Grade Debt Funds

These funds invest in bonds with maturities averaging less than five years. At least 65 percent of their assets, too, are invested respectively, in securities issued or guaranteed by the U.S. government and its agencies and in investment-grade corporates.

Both groups of funds have essentially one investment objective: to provide high current income consistent with minimum fluctuation in principal. They try to provide returns that are higher than those of money market funds but, unlike money market funds, their share prices fluctuate.

In brief periods, such as occurred in 1989, when money market yields were rising and even higher than those of longer-term securities, short-term bond fund returns have lagged behind those of money market funds. Inasmuch as such a situation may have come as a surprise to some, Edward A. Taber III, president of the T. Rowe Price Short-Term Bond Fund, reminded his shareholders of some basics:

> In seeking the highest possible income consistent with minimum principal fluctuation, the Fund can earn an incremental return

over money funds when rates are stable or falling. In such an environment, the Fund's high income is augmented by a steady or rising net asset value. When rates are moving higher—and particularly when money market rates are greater than intermediate yields—money funds have an advantage because their principal remains stable. Over the long term, however, the total return from a fund such as [ours] should outpace a money fund's.

As in the case of the intermediate groups, both of these categories invest in U.S. government securities. The investment-grade funds also have various proportions of investment-grade corporates. A few fund families, such as Fidelity and Vanguard, offer both pure government securities funds (Fidelity Short-Term Government Portfolio and Vanguard Short Term Government Bond Portfolio) and funds that combine corporates and governments (Fidelity Short-Term Bond Portfolio and Vanguard Short Term Bond Portfolio).

Investment policies generally stipulate a maximum for average weighted maturities of around three years, but some will buy securities maturing in as many as seven years (T. Rowe Price) or even ten (Strong Short-Term Bond Fund) so long as the weighted average does not exceed three. During periods of rising interest rates, fund managers tend to reduce average maturities to two years or less.

U.S. Government Funds

These funds invest at least 65 percent of their assets in U.S. Treasury and U.S. agency issues.

Funds in this group should be the safest of all long-term bond funds because their assets are concentrated in securities that are backed by the full faith and credit of the U.S. Treasury or by agencies or instrumentalities of the government. Thus, they really should expose investors to only one major risk: market risk. A given increase in interest rates, which may reflect an increase in the actual or anticipated inflation rate, causes prices of longer maturity bonds to fall more than prices of shorter maturity bonds. It's an axiom to which government securities are not immune.

Changes in interest rates present problems that astute portfolio managers of government bond funds can mitigate through changes in portfolio maturities and composition and through hedging strategies. Since they don't have to worry about the credit or industry risk inherent in the bonds of hundreds of corporations, they're able to focus on a relatively short list of government securities types—and perhaps some corporate money market instruments, if policies permit. To the extent that they're invested in Treasury securities, they usually don't have to worry about calls prior to maturity—the Treasury has not issued callable bonds since 1984—as they would with corporates. But to the extent that they're also invested in Ginnie Maes or other mortgage-backed securities, they must be concerned with the likelihood of early, unscheduled prepayment of principal and make adjustments accordingly.

While running government securities portfolios to consistently provide shareholders reasonable returns with minimum loss of sleep should be sufficiently challenging for anyone, some fund managements have offered to enhance income by engaging in practices, such as option strategies, that incur additional risks. The policies describing the practices and the risks are spelled out in their prospectuses in passages that usually are neither prominent nor lucid and that seem to be incompatible with the solidity implied in the photos of the Capitol, flag and/or other national symbols that dominate the funds' colorful promotional literature. When these speculative practices are successful, they do enable the funds to distribute more money. But when they fail, shareholders feel the results, which they probably had not expected and which are not felt by shareholders of more prudently designed "plain vanilla" government securities funds.

The common investment objective of U.S. government securities funds is "a high level of current income." Some qualify this by adding: "...consistent with safety of principal." Others go on to say: "...by investing primarily in obligations issued or guaranteed by the U.S. government, its agencies or instrumentalities." Those engaged in risky practices add right up front that they will "seek to enhance (their) current return" by whatever means they've adopted. Moreover, part or all of the distributions of interest income may be exempt from state and local income taxes.

As if these points aren't sufficient to sell shares easily, making the category the largest of all fund groups, many of these funds also offer to distribute their income monthly. This is a compelling attraction to those who want cash distributions, instead of reinvesting dividends in more shares, and who prefer monthly checks to the semiannual payments of interest they would receive if they owned individual government securities directly.

Important as the quality of the merchandise, promotion and salesmanship have been to the growth of U.S. government securities funds, they would not have been enough if the government had not provided such an ample inventory in the 1980s.

You are well aware by now of the volume of securities that the Treasury has been selling each year, but you may not be aware of the frequency with which it offers them, as is shown here, by maturities:

Treasury bills ($10,000 minimum):
   13- and 26-week bills, auctioned each week
   52-week bills, every four weeks
Treasury notes (ten years or less) and bonds (over ten years):[3]
   2-year notes ($5,000 minimum), once a month
   3-year notes ($5,000 minimum), once a quarter (February, May, August and November)
   4-year notes ($1,000 minimum), once a quarter (March, June, September and December)
   5-year, 2-month notes ($1,000 minimum), once a quarter (February, May, August and November)
   7-year notes ($1,000 minimum), once a quarter (January, April, July and October)
   10-year notes ($1,000 minimum), once a quarter (February, May, August and November)
   30-year bonds ($1,000 minimum), once a quarter (February, May, August and November)

Obviously, fund portfolio managers have a large range from which they can select[4] and plenty of opportunities to buy. Not that they're limited to buying Treasury securities when they're issued or that they're limited to these maturities. By going to dealers in the secondary market, they also can buy Treasuries with an infinite variety of periods remaining until maturity, ranging from a few days to 30 years.

Of course, the 200 or so issues of Treasury notes and bonds outstanding at any time, plus bills, are *not* the only government securities to be considered by managers of government bond funds whose investment policies also permit investment in other instruments:

1. Obligations issued or guaranteed by agencies or other instrumentalities of the government and also backed by the full faith and credit of the Treasury. These include Ginnie Maes (see above) and obligations of the Export-Import Bank, Farmers Home Administration, Federal Housing Administration, General Services Administration, Small Business Administration and the Maritime Administration.

2. Obligations not explicitly backed by the full faith and credit but endowed with the government's implicit moral support and backed by the issuing agency or instrumentality (some of which have the right to borrow from the Treasury). These include the securities of the Federal Home Loan Mortgage Corporation (FHLMC, or "Freddie Mac") and Federal National Mortgage Association (FNMA, or "Fannie Mae") as well as securities of the Banks for Cooperatives, Federal Farm Credit Banks, Federal Home Loan Banks, Federal Intermediate Credit Banks,

Federal Land Banks, Student Loan Marketing Association, Tennessee Valley Authority and Postal Service.

No securities are as abundant or as widely held among U.S. government securities funds as those of the Treasury. They have accounted for 90 percent or more of the assets of such funds as American Capital Government Securities, Colonial Government Securities Plus Trust, Dean Witter Government Securities Plus, Massachusetts Financial Services (MFS) Government Income Plus Trust and Vanguard U.S. Treasury Bond Portfolio. And Benham Target Maturities Trust and Scudder U.S. Government Zero Coupon Target Fund portfolios are totally or almost totally invested in Treasury zeros. Most funds in the group, however, also have invested substantially in agency securities to earn higher yields for comparable maturities.

Ginnie Maes have predominated in such funds as Freedom Government Plus, (Federated) Government Income Securities, IDS Federal Income Fund, Lord Abbett U.S. Government Securities Fund, SteinRoe Governments Plus and Value Line U.S. Government Securities Fund.

Funds going beyond these full faith and credit securities tend to invest significantly in Freddie Macs and Fannie Maes. They include AMEV U.S. Government Securities Fund, Eaton Vance Government Obligations Trust, Equitec Siebel U.S. Government Securities Fund and Federated Income Trust.

Many portfolio managers try to do more than fulfill the objective of "a high level of current income." They also try, with varying intensity and success, to see that flows of income to shareholders and/or share prices remain stable. Although funds point out (often in fine print) that income and share prices—even of U.S. government securities funds—can fluctuate with interest rates, managers know that changes in either can be unsettling to many shareholders. So they act to mitigate the effects.

Many funds have policies permitting managers to change the average maturities of their portfolios—in some cases over a very wide range—as they believe is warranted by expected interest rate levels for various maturities. Their shareholders, therefore, have to trust them to make the right moves. If the yield curve is normal—that is, if interest rates rise with the length of maturities—and if higher rates are expected, the managers may significantly shorten maturities to minimize fluctuation in share prices. If rates are expected to drop, those wishing to maximize income may go for longer maturities to "lock in" higher rates.

Some, such as Vanguard U.S. Treasury Bond, which is concentrated in Treasury issues, favor long maturities as a matter of policy to maximize long-run return. Its average weighted maturity is expected to range from 15 to 25 years, and it has been running close to 30. "We're trying to offer investors a tightly defined policy of potential risk and reward," says Ian A. MacKinnon, senior vice-president of the Vanguard Group. Others favor average maturities closer to ten years in the hope that this will reduce fluctuation.

Managers able to invest across the broad range of Treasury and agency securities have to weigh the higher yields offered by Ginnie Maes, Freddie Macs, Fannie Maes and the rest against the likelihood of prepayment of the mortgage-backed securities. Capital appreciation, which is not a primary objective of any government bond fund but which can be realized with Treasury securities when interest rates fall—especially with longer bonds—is less attainable with mortgage-backed securities because of prepayments.

In managing their portfolios, many managers do more than buy and sell government and money market securities. They also engage in supplemental, somewhat risky strategies, using options and futures contracts to a limited extent. They may hedge against an increase in interest rates and a drop in bond prices. Or they may act to remain fully invested or to expand their positions when they expect bond prices to rise but don't want to use up their cash reserves.

A number of funds, several of which use the word "plus" in their names, employ options and futures more aggressively to generate more cash for distribution to shareholders than could be expected from investment in government securities alone (and, presumably, from competitors' funds). (Since "plus" has not been defined in law or SEC regulation, funds appear to be able to employ it at their discretion.) Most commonly, they sell calls against securities in their portfolios to generate premium income.

Until the SEC issued, in mid-1988, its rules standardizing the computation of what funds could call yield—and prescribing its use in ads and sales literature—the "income-plus"-type funds vigorously promoted the rates of their payments. They stressed the margins by which their distributions exceeded interest income from government securities alone—income on which less daring fund managements and their shareholders were relying. The additional income attributable to options, which did not fall within the definition of investment income, could not be included with income dividends; when paid out, it was combined with any other short-term capital gains. But that did not keep funds such as MFS Government Securities High Yield Trust (now MFS Government Income Plus Trust) from proclaiming in a promotional leaflet: "Higher yield through options—In addition to high current income, the Fund's goal is to provide an 'extra' level of income by writing covered-call and secured-put options against its holdings...."

After the SEC blew the whistle, however, the only yield funds could cite in ads or pamphlets was the figure based on investment income (defined by SEC to reflect interest income plus or minus the net amortization of bonds' premiums and discounts), and it could only be used in combination with specific total return data. The total of actual cash distributions, including whatever may have been derived from options, could no longer be featured in ads. It could only be used in prospectuses and sales literature in combination with SEC-defined yield and total return.

To the extent that funds had earned a lot of premium income and/ or interest income from high coupon bonds whose premiums had to be amortized, their yields fell below their distribution rates. Explanations had to be provided to puzzled shareholders.

Nor has the government's action on yield advertising been the "income-plus" funds' only challenge. As luck would have it, some managers made some wrong calls on interest rates, subjecting shareholders to the downside of "income enhancement" strategies. When interest rates rose, they didn't only absorb declines in the values of their portfolios' securities—and thus their share prices—as they suffered realized and unrealized losses on bonds; they also had losses on options and futures. When interest rates fell, the enjoyment of increasing portfolio values was marred by the relinquishment of bonds against which they had sold calls, depriving their shareholders of appreciation from which they could have benefited.

A decline in interest rates has predictable, and understandable, consequences for all bond funds: lower investment income and, therefore, lower dividends. It has had additional consequences for those "government income-plus" funds whose ads and leaflets had emphasized the stability of their monthly distributions, implicitly to be achieved by adroit portfolio management. "Regular monthly distributions derived primarily from interest on government securities in the Fund's portfolio," proclaimed a flier of the $8 billion Putnam High Income Government Trust, the group's largest fund, for example. Distributing a constant amount is feasible as long as it can be supported by investment income, option premium and other short-term capital gains, and long-term capital gains. But when income is down and there are losses instead of gains, funds have only two choices: cut the distribution rate or return investors' capital. Managements such as Putnam have decided to keep distributions relatively constant by including certain amounts per share as a non-taxable return of shareholders' capital. Of Putnam's $1.20 per share distribution for fiscal 1989, for example, 33 cents was a return of capital. In fiscal 1988, it had been 36 cents of $1.28.

The practice raises at least two questions: whether shareholders are adequately advised that the funds have such a policy and whether it makes sense from the shareholders' point of view. The 1940 act and SEC regulations are silent on distribution-smoothing but emphatic on disclosure: funds have to describe their distribution policies in their prospectuses and to report at the time of distribution where the money came from.

Some prospectuses say that managements may engage in the practice. Others may give a different impression. For example, the March 9, 1988, prospectus of Prudential-Bache Government Plus Fund II said that it may "reserve (and not distribute) a portion of any net short-term capital gains in order to preclude the distribution of a return of capital." It said nothing about the circumstances under which a distribution would *include* a return of capital. Yet the annual report for the year ended October 31, 1988, announced: "In periods when the Fund does not generate sufficient income from option sales to maintain the targeted distribution level, the Fund's Board of Trustees has voted to return capital to shareholders in order to help keep the dollar amount of quarterly distributions relatively constant over time."

Does return of capital to keep distributions stable make sense for shareholders? Can it optimize their return, or does it just make them feel comfortable? Since, as Prudential-Bache noted, it results in a reduction of shareholders' cost bases, how long could it take until the capital working for them has been significantly reduced?

Presumably, shareholders decide how much to invest in a fund and then want that money working for them. Do they want to get the money back after paying a fund to manage it for them and, as is more than likely with a government securities fund, after paying a broker a front-end load to handle the investment?

One can understand that a fund's management might want to maintain a monthly flow of constant distributions because investors expect them and may be unsettled by unexpected fluctuation in the amounts of their monthly checks. But, if they're advised ahead of time of the possibility that distributions can vary, depending on interest rates or other factors that can be cited, and if the reports issued at the times of distribution are sufficiently informative, perhaps return of capital would not be necessary. This seems to work for "plain vanilla" government securities funds.

Ironically for the many investors in "income-plus" funds who reinvest their distributions, the return *of* capital is immediately returned *to* capital.

U.S. Mortgage Funds

These funds invest a minimum of 65 percent of their assets in mortgages/securities issued or guaranteed as to principal and interest by the U.S. government or its agencies.

This group of funds seeks to provide shareholders with a high level of current income by investing primarily in three types of government or government-related securities representing interests in pools of (mostly) residential mortgages with similar characteristics: Ginnie Maes, Freddie Macs and Fannie Maes. Thus, their investment policies are more narrowly focused than those of the U.S. government securities funds yet not as narrowly defined as those of pure Ginnie Mae funds.

Of the mortgage-backed securities (MBSs) in the funds' portfolios only Ginnie Maes have the full faith and credit of the U.S. Treasury behind them. The credit quality of those issued and guaranteed by the Federal Home Loan Mortgage Corporation (Freddie Mac) and the Federal National Mortgage Association (Fannie Mae), being securities of agencies or instrumentalities of the government but without its full faith and credit support, is also high but not as high as that of Ginnie Maes.

The three types of MBSs have more in common than government links and the collateral of mortgage pools. They all provide for passing through to bond funds (and other holders) the monthly payments of both interest and principal made by mortgagors—a key feature that distinguishes them from conventional long-term debt securities whose issuers don't repay principal until maturity, when they do so in one lump sum.

Even with their high credit quality, Ginnie Maes, Freddie Macs and Fannie Maes are not riskless. Inherent in all three types of securities is prepayment risk: the likelihood that mortgagors will pay off their mortgages before they mature and investors have to reinvest the unscheduled prepayments of principal at lower rates. Whatever the reason for prepayments, they can deprive investors of income flows they had expected to continue for years and necessitate reinvestment. That's why these MBSs have to offer higher yields than Treasury issues of comparable maturities.

Prepayment risk is highest when interest rates are falling and greatest for the MBSs with the highest coupon rates. Under the circumstances, a fund doesn't only face reinvesting the prepayments at lower rates. If a fund had bought high-coupon MBSs at prices above par, it could suffer losses of as much as the premiums because prepayment is guaranteed at par.

Because of the risk of prepayment, the average lives of MBSs are considerably shorter than their stated terms. On the average, MBSs backed by 30-year mortgages are assumed to have lives of 12 years. Those backed by 15-year mortgages are assumed to have correspondingly shorter average lives.

For the funds that invest in them, the characteristics that distinguish MBSs from each other and from conventional long-term debt securities provide challenges. Their market prices fall when interest rates rise, but there is no commensurate benefit to balance interest rate risk when things go the other way. Because of the prepayment risk, funds cannot effectively lock in high yields by investing in MBSs, as they can by investing in Treasuries.

Taking all such factors into consideration, funds have adopted different policies. Some, reflecting a greater concern for credit quality, have limited themselves to investing in government and government-related securities. They include Federated Investors' Fund for U.S. Government Securities (the oldest), Merrill Lynch Retirement/Income Fund, SLH Managed Governments and Van Kampen Merritt U.S. Government Fund (the largest). Others, such as Seligman Secured Mortgage Income Series and Alliance Mortgage Securities Income Fund, also invest in private mortgage-backed securities, which may be supported by insurance or guarantees and other high-quality corporate debt, much of it collateralized by mortgages, to earn higher yields.

Portfolios of U.S. mortgage funds contain different proportions of Ginnie Maes, Freddie Macs and Fannie Maes, as well as Treasury securities, based on the different strategies and market assessments of their portfolio managers. Most change proportions frequently. If, for example, interest rates are likely to fall, they may want to pick up more Treasuries to reduce their exposure to prepayment risk and benefit from the expected appreciation. They also consider whether changes in yield spreads or other factors indicate the desirability of changing the relative weights given each of the agencies or of adjusting the coupon or maturity mixes. An active manager, such as Fidelity Mortgage Securities Portfolio's James R. Wolfson, for example, could switch within a single year from 38 percent Ginnie Maes on July 31, 1988, to 29 percent on January 31, 1989, to 50 percent on July 31, 1989. When cutting back on Ginnie Maes, he piled on more Fannie Maes. When adding Ginnie Maes, he slashed his positions in the other two.

World Income Funds

These funds invest primarily in U.S.-dollar and non-U.S.-dollar debt instruments. They also may invest in common and preferred stocks.

Although funds in this group have invested in U.S. dollar bonds and foreign stocks, their policies call primarily for investment in debt securities of foreign governments and corporations that are denominated in foreign currencies.

Started in 1981 when Massachusetts Financial Services (MFS) launched its International Trust—Bond Portfolio to provide investors an alternative to plummeting U.S. bonds, the group has grown in number as other fund families perceived a potential—albeit, still relatively modest—demand among U.S. investors.

The years since the inception of these funds have not been easy ones for their managers. They've not only had to bear all of the major risks (and, of course, rewards) that foreign bonds have in common with U.S. bonds but they've also had to stay on top of exchange rate volatility and the political risks associated with investments in other currencies, to say nothing of such risks as exchange controls, expropriation of corporate property, confiscatory taxation or even renunciation of governmental debt.

To get an idea of how leadership of world bond markets rotates—and how this could pay off for world income funds that buy and sell bonds at the right time—you can glance at Salomon Brothers' World Government Bond Market Performance Indexes. They measure the returns of government bonds denominated in U.S. dollars and eight other currencies.

They show that in the ten years, 1980–89, government bonds denominated in the U.S. dollar outperformed all the others in U.S. dollar terms only once (in 1984). Those denominated in the Japanese yen led in three years and those in the British pound and Canadian dollar, in two. Those denominated in the Australian dollar and the French franc led the pack once each. (Australian securities were included only for half of the decade.) Of the nine, only those denominated in the West German Deutschemark, Swiss franc and Dutch guilder failed to make the leadership list during that period.

Given that U.S. government securities are outperformed with such regularity—sometimes by wide margins—it's noteworthy that foreign bonds are available in abundance. Non-U.S.-dollar bonds account for nearly 55 percent of the $10 trillion total of outstanding publicly issued bonds in the world's 13 major bond markets (i.e. also including Belgium, Denmark, Italy and Sweden).

Of the funds formed to seek investment opportunities abroad, about half have high current income as an investment objective, with capital appreciation accorded a secondary priority; the other half aim at total return. One, G.T. Global Bond, aims for capital appreciation first and "moderate" income second.

Unlike most U.S. bond funds, which have current income as their objective, world income funds also hold out the potential of capital appreciation because of the gains they expect from changes in currency exchange rates, interest rates, or—ideally—both. Several of them say that, while they look for securities offering high yields with the expectation that they'll benefit from appreciation as interest rates decline, they also will invest in bonds of lower yields if currency trends indicate a possibility of appreciation.

To achieve their objectives, most of these funds state they will normally be at least 65 percent invested (a couple say 80 percent) in U.S. and foreign government and corporate bonds. A few, such as T. Rowe Price International Bond Fund and Scudder International Bond Fund, put the emphasis on non-U.S. bonds. Some, such as G.T. Global Government, New England Global Government Fund and Putnam Global Governmental Income Trust, put the emphasis on government securities. And Merrill Lynch Global Convertible Fund, formed in 1988, expects to be 65 percent invested in convertible securities.

With respect to corporate bonds, nearly all stress that, at least for their primary holdings, they will only invest in high-grade securities. Some limit themselves to bonds rated Aa/AA or higher, or of comparable quality. Others, such as American Funds' Capital World Bond Fund, will invest in bonds rated Baa/BBB.

To obtain adequate diversification, virtually all funds say they must be invested in at least three currencies, including European Currency Units (ECUs). In actuality, most have invested in quite a few more, including currencies of countries beyond the 13 major bond markets: those of Finland, Ireland, New Zealand, Norway and Spain.

TAX-EXEMPT BOND FUNDS

More than 400 bond funds, with net assets exceeding $100 billion, are eligible in the SEC's eyes to call themselves tax-exempt: their fundamental policies require them to be invested so that at least 80 percent of their income is federally tax-exempt or to have at least 80 percent of their assets in tax-exempt securities. Also known as municipal bond funds, they are concentrated in the debt securities of states, counties, townships, school districts, special districts and authorities created by state governments as well as municipalities.

The state and local government bond market is large. Each year $100 billion or more of such securities are issued to raise new capital or to refund old bonds—and tax-exempt bond funds are among the leading purchasers (along with individuals, unit investment trusts, and property and casualty insurance companies).

Lipper has divided municipal bond funds into six classifications. To minimize redundancy, some general comments, applicable to all six, are offered first. Descriptions of the categories follow.

Interest payments that investors receive from issuers of municipal bonds are almost always exempt from federal income tax; when funds, in turn, distribute their net investment income to their shareholders, the exemption is passed through.

Exemption from federal income tax isn't the only benefit of owning municipal bonds, directly or indirectly. Investors subject to state and local income taxes also are likely to be exempt from such taxes on the interest income attributable to securities issued in the states where they live. They may be liable, however, for state and local taxes on income attributable to other states' securities—hence, the development and expansion of single-state municipal bond funds and the promotion of double tax-exempt and even "triple tax-free" income.

No exemption is accorded capital gains, however—whether distributions of capital gains that funds have realized when selling securities or those that individuals have realized when selling fund shares. They can be taxable at all three levels of government.

The Tax Reform Act of 1986 (TRA '86) changed and complicated the tax-exempt bond picture in several ways. It reduced the supply of new issues by narrowing the definition of public purpose obligations and by ending the tax exemption for the interest received from certain types of private-activity bonds. It designated the interest from others as tax preference items, thereby exposing investors to the possibility of paying the alternative minimum tax (AMT).

TRA '86 also has had an impact on individuals' demand for traditional, fully tax-exempt securities. By cutting individual income tax rates, it reduced the incentive for many to seek tax-exempt income. On the other hand, in eliminating tax shelters, TRA '86 may have expanded the demand for tax-exempts among those who find them a convenient alternative way to earn non-taxable income.

Owing to the tax-exempt feature, issuers of municipal bonds are able, under normal market conditions, to offer lower interest rates than are offered for taxable bonds of comparable quality and maturity. How much lower is a function of supply-demand balances in the bond market. As Figure 4-2 shows, at times their yields may be only slightly lower. Because of the lower yields, municipals normally make no sense for individuals' tax-sheltered portfolios, such as IRAs for tax-exempt institutional investors, or for anyone else not required to pay U.S. income tax. (You'll find thoughts on whether they may make sense for you in Chapter 7.)

Except for the differences arising from their tax-exempt income, municipals have much in common with U.S. government and corporate bonds. Like other bonds, municipals involve market risk: the risk that prices will fall as interest rates rise. Unlike Treasuries but like corporates, municipals expose investors to credit risk: the risk that a governmental unit will default on its obligations. And, as is the case with corporates,

Figure 4–2   Yield Comparisons

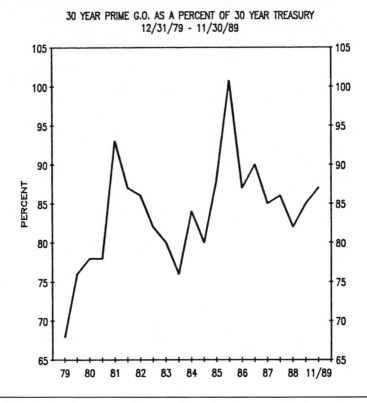

Source: T. Rowe Price Associates, Inc.

municipals may involve unpredictable call risk. Investors cannot count on earning fixed-interest payments until maturity because call provisions permit issuers to call the bonds under certain circumstances. Money managers always have to keep these in mind.

Given all of these risk considerations and the commitment to earn a desired level of tax-exempt income for shareholders, a portfolio manager must make choices:

General Obligation vs. Revenue Bonds.   General obligation bonds are serviced out of appropriations and backed by the credit and tax base of the issuing unit of government. Interest and principal on revenue bonds are paid from the revenues of the facilities (turnpike, airport, hospital, etc.) that were built with the money received from their sale.

General obligation bonds account for around 30 percent of all new municipal issues, but typically they account for a smaller percentage of long-term bond funds' assets. For one thing, the supply of revenue bonds is normally greater in longer maturities while the supply of general obligation bonds is greater in intermediate maturities. Thus, managers looking for longer maturities are more likely to invest in revenue bonds, all other things being equal. Moreover, general obligation bonds offer a slightly lower yield, even when maturities and other key factors are comparable, because, with taxing authority behind them, they are regarded as a better credit risk.

Credit Quality.   Both general obligation and revenue bonds are rated for credit quality by Moody's and Standard & Poor's. As with corporates, municipals rated Aaa/AAA through Baa/BBB are regarded as investment grade. And as with corporates, the higher-grade securities offer a lower yield; the lower grades, a higher yield. Even given the underlying power to tax, the general obligation bonds of some state and local governments are judged not to be as good a risk as others and are avoided by cautious managers. Diversification by region and sector (in the case of revenue bonds) is critical to help reduce funds' vulnerability to any decline in issuers' abilities to service their debts. Some funds have policies that permit investment only in municipals of the highest grades because these tend to be more liquid—an important consideration because they may be easier to sell when it becomes necessary or desirable.

Maturities.   Municipal bonds frequently are issued for terms of 30 years—as long as the longest Treasury issues—but maturities of 40 years and even longer are offered from time to time.

State vs. Local Governments.   All other things being equal, state securities may be more desirable than local obligations because the markets for state securities tend to be larger and more liquid.

In dealing with these and other variables, managers run their portfolios to achieve similar investment objectives in ways that reflect a variety of management policies, managerial styles and assessments of the commonly available data. While they generally are actively managing their portfolios, they vary in activity, the emphasis they give alternative strategies and, of course, their effectiveness.

General Municipal Bond Funds

These funds invest 65 percent or more of their assets in municipal debt issues in the top four credit ratings.

This is by far the largest category, accounting for about half of the number and net assets of national municipal bond funds. Within the group, there are differences in quality requirements, policies on maturities and other aspects of management emphasis, all pursued to generate current income for shareholders at reasonable risks.

Scudder Managed Municipal Bonds may have the highest stated quality standards of all, saying that, under normal market conditions, 100 percent of its investments in municipal securities will be rated A or higher and at least 50 percent will be rated Aa/AA or higher. Benham National Tax-Free Trust is almost as selective for its Long-Term Portfolio, restricting its municipals to those rated A or better. Vanguard Municipal Bond Fund's Long-Term Portfolio and D.L. Babson Tax-Free Income Fund's Portfolio L are right behind; 95 percent and 90 percent, respectively, of their municipal securities must be rated a minimum of A. Shearson Lehman Tax-Exempt Income Portfolio is at the other extreme, targeting bonds rated A through Ba/BB and willing to invest up to 35 percent of its assets in bonds rated B or lower.

Whatever the ratings, bonds held by the funds in this group are primarily long-term bonds. Of the funds commenting on maturity policies in their prospectuses, the largest number tend to aim at weighted averages of 10 or 15 to 25 years or more. They differ in their apparent inclination to adjust average maturities up and down in response to, or anticipation of, changes in interest rates. Some tend to stay at the upper end of the range to benefit from higher yields.

Within the context of their quality and maturity policies, fund managements employ several different techniques with varying degrees of aggressiveness.

The portfolios of few, if any, general municipal bond funds have been as actively managed as that of MFS Managed Municipal Bond Trust, whose portfolio turnover rate ranged between 164 percent and 642 percent in the ten years ended 1989.

"Instead of just buying for high yields and hanging on, we're looking for the highest total return," says John B. Jamieson, senior vice-president of Massachusetts Financial Services Company and manager of its municipal bond department. "We believe in the theory that the market is inefficient and that we can add value to our portfolio by playing the spreads regardless of whether the market is moving up or down—spreads between discount and premium bonds, between Aaa and Baa bonds, between bonds of different sectors, between high-tax states and low- or no-tax states. Spreads are constantly moving targets."

What he and others who "play" the spreads are doing is maintaining a continual watch for issues whose prices in the "inefficient" bond market are higher, or lower, than they believe warranted on the basis of their analysis of pertinent data. Their objective is twofold: to spot undervalued securities for purchase before others do and to identify bonds in their own portfolios that have become overvalued so that they can unload them before the market marks them down.

Stephen C. Bauer of the SAFECO Municipal Bond Fund is another portfolio manager who tries to "play" the spreads but not with such intensity. He's not willing to trade for small increments, he says, and opportunities for larger ones are becoming harder to find. "There are fewer disparities than there were a few years ago," Bauer explains, "and dozens of firms are tracking the spreads to find them. We're all trying to increase value."

Sometimes those who monitor spreads between high-grade and lower-grade municipal bond yields make switches to enhance the quality of their portfolios. When these spreads become narrow enough, they replace lower- or medium-grade holdings with higher-grade securities in the conviction that they're not being sufficiently rewarded for taking higher credit risks. When spreads widen, they switch to lower-grade bonds if they believe that their total return goals are not in jeopardy.

Other managers, such as Peter J.D. Gordon, portfolio manager of the T. Rowe Price Tax-Free Income Fund (and chairman of Price's Tax-Free Funds Investment Advisory Committee), take a different approach. When they expect rates to rise, they shorten maturities to reduce volatility and place themselves in position to pick up bonds offering high yields—if their expectations turn out to be correct. On the other hand, when it looks as if interest rates are falling, they lengthen maturities to gain capital appreciation.

"We try to catch the major trends rather than actively trading for a few basis points," Gordon says. "We would rather move the weighted average maturity significantly to protect our portfolio against inflation or to take advantage of a rise in bond prices.

"Our policy permits us to manage the portfolio so that the average maturity can range from 15 to 30 years. If we have a strong conviction about long-term interest rate trends and think that prices are going up, we go long. If we want to be defensive, we shorten the average to 15 years. And we won't want to be fully invested. We'll want cash reserves of five percent so that we won't be forced to sell bonds."

Of the funds whose prospectuses mention the private-activity bonds that subject investors to the possibility of paying alternative minimum tax, a few state that that they want to avoid them altogether. A larger number say they will invest in them only to a limited degree to obtain higher income; most of these cite a maximum of 20 percent of their assets.

Alliance Municipal Income Fund takes the opposite position with respect to its National Portfolio. It was organized in 1986 for the purpose of investing in AMT-subject bonds and was 92 percent invested in them at the end of its 1989 fiscal year. Says Susan G. Peabody, portfolio manager: "Only 0.2 percent of taxpayers are subject to the AMT. For the benefit of all the others who don't pay the tax, we see this as an opportunity to offer a higher yield—some 50 to 75 basis points—without additional risk."

High-Yield Municipal Bond Funds

These funds may invest 50 percent or more of their assets in lower-rated municipal debt issues.

These are the municipal bond funds that try to provide the highest current return by investing in long-term bonds that combine two kinds of risk: interest rate and credit.

On the question of maturities, there seems to be a consensus. Prospectuses indicate the funds are aiming at weighted average maturities of 15 or 20 years. They properly point out the degree of share price volatility that investment in high-yield municipals for such periods may involve.

On the question of credit quality, the funds span a wide spectrum. At one extreme, Scudder High Yield Tax Free Fund states it will only invest in securities rated investment grade—but concentrate in medium-quality (A–Baa/BBB) issues. Then there are several that concentrate in medium-quality bonds for the 65–80 percent of assets that constitute their principal holdings but will invest the rest of their assets in below investment-grade securities. These include funds such as Fidelity High Yield Municipals, Merrill Lynch Municipal Bond Fund High Yield Portfolio, T. Rowe Price Tax-Free High Yield Fund and Vanguard Municipal Bond Fund High-Yield Portfolio. At the other extreme funds such as Fidelity Aggressive Tax-Free Portfolio, Fidelity's second entry in the group, and Franklin High Yield Tax-Free Income Fund usually can invest in securities rated below investment grade (i.e., Ba/BB or lower).

These funds generally reserve the flexibility to invest in high-grade bonds when yield spreads are narrow and managers feel they'd be poorly compensated for added risk or when enough attractive medium- or lower-quality bonds are not available; they advise shareholders that current income might be reduced as a result. Most also say they may buy lower grades than the quality range from which they normally choose when it's justified.

More than anywhere else in the municipal bond sector, these fund managements credit their research staffs for helping them to identify the high-yield securities to be bought—and those to be avoided—by supplementing the work of the rating agencies. There are lags between the time an issuer's financial situation changes—for better or worse—and the time the agencies change their ratings, some managers say.

"We try to identify credits before they deteriorate and sell them; we also try to pick up ones that have already deteriorated but have stabilized," Guy Wickwire, portfolio manager of Fidelity High Yield, wrote shareholders in his 1988 annual report. "About 15 percent of our holdings had their ratings upgraded during the course of the year, so that shows how good credit analysis can help in the selection process."

If diversification is essential to the prudent management of any mutual fund group, it's crucial to this one, given the credit risks inherent in low-grade bonds. Fortunately for the funds and their investors, they have a diverse list of revenue bond issues to choose from. Some may be favorites one year, candidates for sale the next.

Insured Tax-Free Bond Funds

These funds invest at least 65 percent of their assets in municipal debt issues whose timely payment is insured.

This is the small group of funds that are primarily (65–80 percent) invested in long-term municipal bonds whose timely interest and principal payments are covered by insurance. Given that the insurance is to protect the funds against loss in the event of a state or local government's default, the securities in the funds' portfolios would appear to remain exposed only to market risk.

The funds point out, sometimes in bold print, that insurance does *not* protect investors against fluctuations in the market prices of the bonds held by the funds, the share prices of the funds themselves or their yields. They also note, if not always prominently, that the insurance is no more reliable than the credit of the companies that write the policies.

Three types of insurance are involved:

1. New-issue insurance is what state and local governments (or their underwriters) obtain if the issuers qualify, if it would help them to sell new bond issues and if it would reduce borrowing costs. If the premium would cost less than the government would save in interest owing to the higher rating resulting from the coverage, insurance would be economically advantageous. If the cost would exceed the savings, it would not. Once the premium is paid, coverage remains in force as long as the bonds are outstanding (with their resale value enhanced) and the insurance companies are in business.

2. Secondary market insurance is purchased by investors—such as mutual funds—to cover eligible bonds already outstanding.

3. Portfolio insurance is bought by funds to cover bonds in their portfolios that are not already insured by policies of the first two types.

First Investors Insured Tax Exempt Fund and Merrill Lynch Municipal Bond Fund's Insured Portfolio were the first mutual funds to concentrate in insured tax-exempts. They commenced operations in August, 1977, and October, 1977, respectively—a year after general municipal bond funds were launched, three years after the first policy was written for a unit investment trust, and six years after AMBAC Indemnity Corporation introduced new-issue insurance for municipal bonds.

Because investor demand for the new type of fund took time to build, as did the insurance companies' ability and willingness to undertake this new type of business, First Investors and Merrill Lynch had the field to themselves for several years. Criterion's Insured Quality Tax Free Bond Portfolio (now called Transamerica Tax Free Income Fund) came along in 1983, and others followed in ensuing years. No doubt they were encouraged by the expectation that investors would want the protection of insurance after the Washington State Public Power Supply System defaulted on two of its bond issues in 1983.

In building their core portfolios, funds follow three patterns. Some buy insured municipals of investment grade (a few will only buy Aaa/AAAs), others buy uninsured investment-grade bonds for which they obtain insurance, and the rest do both. (They may round out their portfolios with uninsured, high-grade short-term securities.)

It's not enough that the insured bonds bought by funds have ratings that meet their standards. It's also important that no one doubts the claims-paying abilities of the insurance companies providing the coverage. (Besides AMBAC, which has been 97 percent owned by Citibank since 1988, companies that write such insurance include Capital Guaranty Insurance Company, Financial Guaranty Insurance Company and Municipal Bond Investors Assurance Corporation.) Most funds make certain the insurance companies are rated triple-A, and several say they check periodically to ensure that they remain triple-A.

Funds are able to raise their yields without raising their portfolios' credit risk by buying uninsured bonds that are rated Baa/BBB—and, therefore, offer higher yields than Aaa/AAAs—and having triple-A-rated insurance companies cover them. They're also able to take advantage of the fact that outstanding insured triple-A bonds are available in the market at lower prices in relation to their coupon rates than uninsured triple-As, enabling them to earn an additional 20–30 basis points for every dollar invested.

Why would uninsured triple-As provide a lower yield, implying lower risk, than insured triple-As?

Portfolio managers offer a couple of explanations.

"It's a paradox," says Ian A. MacKinnon, senior vice-president of the Vanguard Fixed Income Group. "Maybe the market doesn't wholeheartedly believe in the insurers."

"It's the uninsured triple-As' scarcity value," says Jerry R. Eubank, portfolio manager of First Investors' Insured Tax Exempt Fund. "There are states, such as Minnesota, where there is a chronic shortage of triple-A bonds. When Minneapolis comes to market—Minneapolis doesn't need insurance to have its bonds rated triple-A—investors bid up the prices."

The cost of insurance is felt by tax-exempt funds—and, in turn, by their shareholders—in one of two ways. For bonds that are insured when funds buy them, premiums are reflected in the prices paid. For uninsured bonds, funds pay the premiums directly.

Portfolio insurance costs run from 0.2–0.4 percent of the value of the bonds insured, according to fund prospectuses. How much they can add to a fund's expenses depends not only on the premium rate but also on the portfolio's composition—i.e., on how much of the portfolio consists of bonds for which the fund obtained coverage. Funds reports show that yearly premiums can run from around 0.1 percent to around 0.75 percent of average net assets.

Intermediate Municipal Bond Funds

These funds invest in municipal debt issues with maturities averaging five to ten years.

These are funds that, under normal circumstances, provide a lower yield and more stability than long-term tax-exempt funds but a higher yield than funds invested in municipals of shorter maturities.

Except for Scudder Tax Free Target Fund's portfolios, the funds in this group tend to have flexible targets for weighted average maturities, which they adjust with interest rates.

The targeted maturities are expressed in terms of caps (such as 12 years or less for Fidelity Limited Term Municipals) or ranges (from 8–12 years for Prudential-Bache Municipal Bond Fund Modified Term Series and 7–12 years for Vanguard Municipal Bond Fund's Intermediate-Term Portfolio to 2–10 years for Benham National Tax-Free Trust Intermediate-Term Portfolio and 3–10 years for Dreyfus Intermediate Tax Exempt Bond Fund).

Differences among funds in credit risks incurred appear to be slight. They generally want primary holdings to be rated at least A but differ in whether, and how much, remaining holdings may include bonds rated Baa/BBB (from 40 percent for Pru-Bache and 25 percent for SteinRoe Intermediate Municipals to five percent for the Scudder and Vanguard funds and none for Benham) to raise yields.

Short Municipal Bond Funds

These funds invest in municipal debt issues with maturities averaging less than five years.

The few funds constituting this group try to offer investors yields that normally are slightly higher than those offered by tax-exempt money market funds but that involve the risk of fluctuations in interest rates and, therefore, the risk of slight fluctuations in share prices. Fluctuations in rates are produced not only by market factors but also by changes in the Federal Reserve Board's monetary policy, which usually have their greatest immediate impact on short-term yields.

To minimize share volatility when rates are rising or to benefit from higher short-term rates when they may have hit a cyclical peak, fund managers adjust their weighted average maturities (with the exception of Scudder Tax Free Target Fund portfolio). Some have more maneuvering room than others. Vanguard Municipal Bond Fund's Short-Term Portfolio, the oldest (started in 1977) and the largest, aims at an average of between one and two years. So does Merrill Lynch's Municipal Bond Fund Limited Maturity portfolio. Others permit averages to run up to three (Federated Short-Intermediate Municipal Trust, Dreyfus Short-Intermediate Tax Exempt Bond Fund and USAA Tax Exempt Short-Term Fund) and four years (Fidelity Short-Term Tax-Free Portfolio.)

All managements insist on high credit quality. Most require that investment be primarily in issues rated A or better. As its name implies, the AARP Insured Tax Free Short-Term Fund primarily buys securities that are insured and, therefore, rated triple-A.

Single-State Municipal Bond Funds

These funds limit their assets to securities that are exempt from taxation of a specific state or city.

The large number of federally tax-exempt funds in this group are structured for investors who are subject to state (and perhaps local) income taxes, who may be exempt from such taxes on interest income from securities issued by their own state or local governments, and who want to maximize the benefits offered by such securities. (To benefit from double or triple exemption, those investing in national municipal bond funds usually can only deduct income attributable to their own state and/or local governments' securities when preparing their state and local income tax returns.)

The first single-state municipal bond funds, DMC Tax-Free Income Trust-PA and Franklin California Tax-Free Income, were started shortly after the first incorporated municipal bond funds were launched in late 1976. By now they exist in a large majority of the more than 30 states that impose income taxes on other states' securities but not on their own. Most are fairly small, but several exceed $1 billion in assets. Understandably, California and New York have many more funds than other states.

Single-state municipal bond funds may involve greater credit risk than national funds because, by definition, they lack geographic diversification. The risk of default may be associated with cyclical economic problems or secular decline in a state's major industry, but it also can be raised by other events, such as a court ruling or the threat of a taxpayer rebellion, which could jeopardize appropriations required to service general obligation bonds.

In recognition of the risk, most fund managements tend to invest primarily in bonds rated Baa/BBB or higher. Some try to go no lower than A. Others offer insured bond portfolios. On the other hand, some offer high-yield funds that may invest in lower-grade bonds.

Portfolios of single-state funds tend to have weighted average maturities of 15–25 years. Some fund sponsors also offer intermediate-term single-state funds.

ENDNOTES

1. ICI aggregates data reported by its members, which represent about 90 percent of the industry's assets, and certain non-members.
2. Sixty-five percent is required by the SEC as the minimum level of assets that a fund—other than a tax-exempt or money market fund—must invest, under normal circumstances, in the particular type of security that its name implies it's concentrated in. For tax-exempt and money market funds it's 80 percent.
3. Regular sales of 15-year, 1-month and 20-year, 1-month issues were discontinued in 1986.
4. Treasury officials in late 1989 were studying the pros and cons of resuming the issuance of 40-year bonds, last sold—with three percent coupons—in 1955.

CHAPTER 5

How Bond Funds Have Performed—and Why

Now that we have seen how the various types of taxable and tax-exempt bond funds compare in investment objectives, policies and practices, we'll look at how they have performed for their shareholders and try to understand why they performed as they did.

Of all the words of caution that the SEC requires mutual funds to use in their pamphlets, none are truer than those declaring that past performance may not indicate future results. Yet the record of past performance is important. It tells us how well or how poorly a fund was managed, in its effort to achieve its stated investment objective, during good *and* bad markets. Ideally, the record should be long enough to reflect both. Without this information, we know too little to make rational investment decisions. Even with this information, we cannot be sure how a fund, under the same policies and portfolio manager, may perform in the future.

Before looking at data for the top performers among bond funds, let's recall the investment environment in which they were managed.

THE PERFORMANCE OF DEBT SECURITIES

As Table 5-1 shows so vividly, the ten years from 1979 through 1988 provided quite a roller coaster ride for debt securities—and for those who managed and invested in them. Total returns—that is, interest plus (or minus) capital appreciation (or depreciation)—ranged from over 40 percent to a *negative* 3 percent for both long-term high-grade corporate and long-term government securities. Intermediate-term governments had only positive total returns but did drop below 3 percent after ranging as high as 28 percent. In as many as four of the years, Treasury bills outper-

96

Table 5–1   Annual Rates of Total Return of Debt Securities Compared with Cost of Living 1979–1988

Year	L/T Corp.	L/T Trea.	Int. Trea.	T-bills	CPI	SB/BIG	FI Funds
1979	NA	NA	NA	10.0%	13.3%	NA	2.8%
1980	(2.6)%	(3.2)%	4.5%	11.4	12.5	2.8%	3.3
1981	0.2	1.3	9.3	14.2	8.9	6.5	5.9
1982	41.2	40.6	27.9	10.9	3.8	31.8	30.2
1983	8.3	1.5	7.1	8.9	3.8	8.2	10.0
1984	16.9	14.9	14.5	9.8	3.9	15.0	10.9
1985	29.2	31.5	20.7	7.3	3.8	22.3	19.8
1986	19.3	24.1	14.7	5.8	1.1	15.5	12.7
1987	0.5	(2.8)	2.7	5.2	4.4	2.6	1.3
1988	10.9	9.3	6.1	6.1	4.4	8.0	7.9

Notes: L/T Corp. = Corporate bonds with maturities of over ten years; L/T Trea. = Treasury securities with maturities of over ten years; Int. Trea. = Treasury securities with maturities of three to seven years; T-bills = U.S. Treasury bills; CPI = Percent changes in consumer price index (December to December); SB/BIG = Salomon Brothers Broad Investment-Grade Bond Index; FI Funds = fixed-income mutual funds.

Sources: Corporate and Treasury securities and BIG index, Salomon Brothers, Inc.; T-bills, CDA Investment Technologies, Inc.; CPI, Bureau of Labor Statistics, U.S. Department of Labor; FI funds, Lipper Mutual Fund Performance Analysis, published by Lipper Analytical Services, Inc.

formed both long-term and intermediate-term securities, but in two of the ten years—years of double-digit inflation—even they failed to keep pace with the cost of living.

To ascertain how taxable investment-grade debt securities behaved in the aggregate, you can look at an index such as Salomon Brothers' Broad Investment-Grade Bond Index (BIG). It captures all generally available Treasury, federal agency, mortgage and investment-grade corporate (i.e., Baa/BBB or higher) securities with a maturity of at least one year—securities with a total market value of $2.7 trillion at the end of 1989.

As you can see, this index has shown only positive total returns since 1980, the first year for which it was calculated. It soared, if not quite as high as long-term corporates and governments, in 1982 and 1985, the best years for bonds.

If BIG appears to have a close correlation with intermediate-term Treasuries, it's no coincidence. The investment-grade bond market as a whole has been characterized by a weighted average maturity in the intermediate range: eight to ten years. (At the end of 1989, it was 9.5 years; the effective duration, 4.6.) The weighted average maturities of Treasury, federal agency and mortgage securities, which account for around 80 percent of the index, have tended to be close to that range (seven to eight years for Treasuries and agencies, five to eight years for mortgage securities). Corporates, on the other hand, have exceeded 13 years, but their combined market value accounts for only 20 percent of BIG's weight.

BOND FUNDS: SIMILARITIES AND DIFFERENCES

If you get the impression that the performance of taxable bond funds has followed a pattern closer to that of the BIG index, you're right. In the aggregate, they're also primarily invested in government and investment-grade corporate securities and have an intermediate-weighted average maturity.

Compared to the index, bond funds didn't do badly on the average, even exceeding BIG in two years. In fact, you could have expected their average annual returns to slightly lag those of the index for at least two major reasons:

1. Bond funds keep portions of their assets in cash equivalents to meet redemption requirements. (Portfolio managers may invest significantly in T-bills to implement defensive strategies. In some years, as you can infer from the table, T-bills can lift a fund's total return.)

2. Bond funds are encumbered by investment advisory fees and other expenses—some, as we'll shortly see, a lot more than others.

Because of the importance of focusing on longer-run tendencies instead of year-to-year fluctuations when considering investments in mutual funds or individual securities, the performance of debt securities during 1979–88 is presented in Table 5–2 in terms of average annual returns for the entire ten-year period and for the two five-year periods that constituted it. It shows that bond funds, on the average, performed more

Table 5–2   Total Returns for Investment Alternatives: Comparison of Recent 5- and 10-Year Periods (compound annual rates)

	1979–1983	1984–1988	1979–1988
Fixed-Income Mutual Funds	10.2%	10.8%	10.7%
Long-Term Corporate Bonds	6.8	15.1	10.9
Long-Term Government Bonds	6.4	15.0	10.6
Intermediate-Term Governments	10.4	11.5	11.0
U.S. Treasury Bills	11.1	7.1	9.1
Consumer Price Index	8.4	3.5	5.9
All Equity Mutual Funds	21.0	11.0	15.8
S&P 500 Index	17.3	15.4	16.3

Sources: Mutual fund data, Lipper—Mutual Fund Performance Analysis, published by Lipper Analytical Services, Inc. Bond, bill, CPI and S&P 500 data, Roger G. Ibbotson and Rex A. Sinquefield, *Stocks, Bonds, Bills and Inflation* (SBBI), 1982, updated in *Stocks, Bonds, Bills and Inflation 1989 Yearbook,* Ibbotson Associates, Inc., Chicago. All rights reserved.

consistently, in line with intermediate-term governments, than long-term bonds, whose average results were lower during the period of high interest rates (1979–83) and higher during the period of falling rates (1984–1988).

The apparently even average performance of bond funds, calculated by annualizing cumulative data for both periods, is misleading, however. We know from Table 5-1 (if not from our personal experience) that their actual rates of return fluctuated significantly from year to year. Did all categories of bond funds behave similarly? If not, how did they differ?

DIFFERENCES AMONG FUND GROUPS

Even if you exclude the world income group (a special case because it consisted of only one fund for all of 1984–88), you'll find a mixed pattern among taxable bond fund groups, as depicted in Table 5-3a, but generally predictable performance.

For the entire ten-year stretch, funds having some linkage to common stocks—the convertible securities and flexible income funds as well as balanced funds—led the pure bond funds. Among bond funds, those involving the greatest risk, high-yield funds, provided slightly higher rewards. Those invested in investment-grade corporate and government bonds did better than those concentrated in GNMA and other

---

Table 5–3a   Taxable Bond Fund Rates of Return for 5-Year and 10-Year Periods by Category

Category	1984–1988	1979–1988
	(Compound Annual Rates)	
World Income	17.6%	—
Flexible Income	12.5	11.9%
Corporate BBB-Rated	11.6	10.3
General Bond	11.4	10.4
Corporate A-Rated	11.3	10.4
High-Yield	10.6	11.5
GNMA	10.4	8.5
Intermediate	10.4	10.4
Convertible Securities	10.1	14.9
U.S. Mortgage	10.1	9.4
U.S. Government	10.0	10.5
Short-Intermediate	9.7	—
Balanced	13.1	14.5

Source: Lipper—Fixed Income Fund Performance Analysis; Lipper—Mutual Fund Performance Analysis, published by Lipper Analytical Services, Inc. (rates of return annualized by author).

mortgage-backed securities. Intermediate bond funds performed as well as those invested in longer maturities.

From 1984 through 1988, the flexible-income group benefited from higher bond prices. Investment-grade corporate bond funds edged government and mortgage securities funds. High-yield funds, on the average, did not score returns high enough to reward investors for the risks they incurred. Short-intermediate funds, which were developed during this time, scored about as expected, given lower short-term interest rates.

Allowing for the fact that their yields are lower to reflect the lower interest rates available from the tax-exempt securities in which they're invested, municipal bond funds (Table 5–3b) gave a reasonably good account of themselves for 1984–88 when compared with taxable funds.

COMPARING THE FUNDS

So much for the fund group averages. Since we can only invest in individual funds—not a group as a whole—let's see which bond funds have been the leading performers in the various groups, exceeding group averages. Whether these funds will remain leaders or be replaced by others, no one can say. Regardless, scanning historic data should help us to get an idea of what to look for when checking such rankings in the future.

Most of the tables from 5–4a through 5–4t show the average annual compounded rates of total return for the five- and ten-year periods ended in September 1989 for the top ten funds in each group that are generally available to individual investors. If there weren't ten, fewer funds are listed. For groups having only two or three funds in existence for as many as ten years, data are provided for three- and five-year periods.

Consistent, genuinely superior long-term performance is what we want to look for when considering mutual funds in which to invest. For bond funds, it is best demonstrated in results for periods long enough to

---

Table 5–3b   Tax-Exempt Bond Fund Rates of Return for 5-Year and 10-Year Periods by Category

Category	1984–1988	1979–1988
	(Compound Annual Rates)	
General Municipal	11.6%	7.9%
Insured	10.8	8.0
High-Yield Municipal	10.7	9.0
Intermediate	8.5	7.1
Short-Intermediate	6.6	6.4

Source: Lipper—Fixed Income Fund Performance Analysis published by Lipper Analytical Services, Inc.

include higher and lower interest rates. Periods of five and ten years generally have been accepted as meeting this objective. Beginning in 1988, all income funds have been required by the SEC to use total return data for these periods, on a uniformly calculated basis, whenever making performance claims.

Some general comments are in order before we look at the tables.

Emphasis on Total Return.   Since many people invest in bond funds for income, you may wonder why funds are ranked here by total return for five (or three) years instead of by yield, or why yield isn't even shown. Three reasons may suffice:

1. Total return—the rate of change in the value of an investment, assuming reinvestment of income dividends and capital gains distributions—is the most meaningful measure of fund performance for a given period because it reflects realized and unrealized capital gains and losses as well as income. Ranking bond funds by their annual rates of income distributions would not indicate whether they were performing poorly or losing value because of the risks their managers incurred to achieve them.

2. Bond funds are now required to calculate annualized yields on the basis of SEC-defined investment income earned during the most recent 30-day period. No purpose would be served in printing here yield figures that are susceptible to such frequent change. (Since yields reflect the amortization of bond premiums and discounts, as well as interest income, they differ—sometimes considerably—from distribution rates with which investors are more familiar.)

3. One-half or more of bond fund dividends are reinvested. Whether income is a few cents higher or lower shouldn't matter to anyone reinvesting, except for the tax liabilities resulting from the crediting of taxable interest income.

Changes in Objectives or Managers.   Funds may have significantly changed investment objectives or policies during the period(s) for which total return figures are provided. Thus, returns may reflect results achieved when a fund belonged in another category. Funds also may have changed investment advisers or portfolio managers during the period(s), causing changes in performance.

Front-End Sales Charges.   Although some funds impose maximum front-end loads as high as the 8.5 percent permitted by the National Association of Securities Dealers, no-load funds regularly appear among leaders. If fewer no-loads make the lists of the top ten, it's because there are fewer of them—especially among bond funds—not because load funds provide superior management. The loads, which usually decrease as transaction sizes increase, do not go to the portfolio managers as incentives or rewards for performance. They go primarily to sales forces as compensation for selling shares. When data services' fund performance data are not adjusted for loads, they overstate the total returns that people have actually earned on the money they invested in load funds. In promoting their yields and total returns, funds *are* required to reflect any sales charges.

Deferred Sales Loads.   A number of funds impose deferred sales loads instead of front-end loads, reducing capital gains and increasing capital losses. Fees usually are levied according to a sliding scale, falling each year the shares are held until they're eliminated after around five years. If a fund performs poorly during the time the load is in effect, its shareholders have to weigh the cost of redeeming shares vs. the cost of holding them.

Sales Loads on Reinvested Dividends.   Some funds—fewer than five percent, according to the SEC—charge a sales load for the purchase of shares through the reinvestment of dividends, year after year after year. This load also—if slightly—reduces return on shareholders' investments. Since most funds encourage reinvestment—for one thing, it's cheaper than attracting new shareholders—imposition of this load is hard to understand. So is its apparent acceptance by shareholders.

Operating Expenses.   Unlike one-time sales charges, which are not reflected in Lipper total return data, annual operating expenses *are* reflected. As you run down the lists, you may see how low expenses help to lift performance and how high expenses serve to weigh it down.

Since 1988, the SEC has required every fund to divide operating expenses into three categories—management/advisory, 12b-1 distribution expenses, and all other—and to report them prominently in the prospectus. This makes it easy for shareholders to see why a fund's expense ratio is high or low.

Among the top A and BBB corporate bond funds, for example, management/advisory fees range from 0.18 percent for Vanguard Investment Grade Bond Portfolio to 0.70 percent for Calvert Income Fund. (No fund family's expense ratios are as consistently low as Vanguard's.) About one-half do not impose 12b-1 fees. Among those that do, they run as high as 0.75 percent for Shearson Lehman Hutton's SLH Investment Grade Bond Portfolio. "Other" expenses range from 0.10 percent for IDS Selective Fund to 0.88 percent for Alliance Bond Fund's Monthly Income Portfolio.

In several cases, you'll see a correlation of high expense ratios with deferred sales charges. This usually reflects policies of compensating sales people out of 12b-1 plan distribution money when there's no front-end sales load from which they can be paid.

Waived and Reimbursed Expenses. In a considerable number of cases, funds' expense ratios would have been higher, and returns would have been lower, if investment advisers had not waived or reimbursed portions of the funds' scheduled expenses.

LOOKING AT THE LEADERS

Looking at Tables 5–4a and 5–4b, you can see how difficult it was for most funds concentrated in investment-grade corporates to achieve an average annual total return of 13 percent in the five years ended in September 1989, and how impossible it was for all but two of them to achieve a 12 percent rate in the ten-year period. Strategies varied.

Table 5–4a   Corporate Bond Funds A-Rated (Performance for Periods Ended September 1989)

	1984–1989 (Compound Annual Rate)	1979–1989 (Compound Annual Rate)	Maximum Sales Charge*	Operating Expense Ratio**
United Bond Fund	13.8%	11.3%	8.50%	0.65%
(American Funds)				
Bond Fund of America	13.5	12.1	4.75	0.75
SLH Investment Grade Bond	13.4	—	5.00 D	1.63
John Hancock Bond Trust	12.9	10.4	8.50	0.82
Vanguard Investment Grade	12.8	11.4	None	0.38
Dreyfus A Bonds Plus	12.6	11.6	None	0.94
Merrill Lynch High Quality A	12.5	—	4.00	0.60
Scudder Income	12.4	10.7	None	0.94
Kemper Income &				
Capital Preservation	12.4	10.8	4.50	0.69
SteinRoe Managed Bonds	12.3	10.6	None	0.73
GROUP (number of funds)	12.2 (28)	10.7 (19)		

Notes: Performance data for Tables 5–4a through 5–4t are for periods ended September 1989. Asterisked reference data and sources below apply to Tables 5–4a through 5–4t. Group averages may reflect Lipper data for funds not shown because they are not generally available to individual investors or have ceased operations.

*Front-end sales charge unless deferred sales charge (D) indicated.
**Operating expenses as percent of average net assets for most recent calendar or fiscal year.
***Front-end sales charge also imposed on reinvested dividends.
****Excluding charges waived or reimbursed by investment adviser.

Sources: Performance data, Lipper—Fixed Income Fund Performance Analysis (rates of return annualized by author); sales charges and expense ratios, fund prospectuses and reports.

Table 5–4b   Performance: Corporate Bond Funds BBB-Rated

	1984–1989 (Compound Annual Rate)	1979–1989	Maximum Sales Charge*	Operating Expense Ratio**
Axe-Houghton Income Fund	13.7%	12.0%	None	1.35%
Calvert Income Fund	13.5	—	4.50%	0.94****
IDS Selective Fund	12.9	11.7	5.00	0.78
Alliance Bond Monthly Income	12.9	10.4	5.50	1.81
Mass. Financial Bond Fund	12.7	11.1	7.25***	0.83
American Capital Corp. Bond	12.6	10.2	4.75	0.74
IDS Strategy Income	12.6	—	5.00 D	1.74
Financial Bond Select Income	12.4	10.3	None	1.00
Fidelity Flexible Bond	11.6	10.0	None	0.66
Columbia Fixed Income	11.6	—	None	0.77
GROUP (number of funds)	12.1 (17)	10.6 (11)		

Note: See Table 5–4a for asterisked references.

Robert G. Alley, portfolio manager of United Bond Fund, credits his fund's strategy of diversification: investing wherever he found values, including non-dollar securities, electric utilities, mortgage-backed securities and certain high-yield bonds. He reduced holdings of U.S. industrials that could expose the fund to event risk. He also tried aggressively to adjust the portfolio's duration[1] to maximize the benefit of falling interest rates and minimize the impact of rising rates.

Robert E. Manning, portfolio manager of the Axe-Houghton Income Fund, attributes his fund's performance to staying with long maturities, even though they may cause under-performance when interest rates are rising, and to investing selectively in some lower-quality issues. "Our record does not owe much to market timing," he says.

Table 5–4c   Performance: General Bond Funds

	1984–1989 (Compound Annual Rate)	1979–1989	Maximum Sales Charge*	Operating Expense Ratio**
FPA New Income	13.2%	10.9%#	4.50%	1.52%****
CIGNA Income Fund	13.2	11.2	5.00	0.97
IDS Bond Fund	13.0	11.8	5.00	0.75
Colonial Income Trust	12.0	10.5	4.75	1.13
Composite Income Fund	11.2	9.4	4.00	1.01
Keystone Series B-2	11.1	11.3	4.00 D	1.68
GROUP (number of funds)	12.4 (8)	10.8 (7)		

Note: See Table 5–4a for asterisked references.

Investment objective or policy was changed to the present one during the period.

Tables 5-4d through 5-4f also can be looked at together, given their common denominator of U.S. Treasury and other government-backed and -related securities. You can quickly see that even though the funds invested in very similar, if not identical, securities, they produced different results. In addition to operating expenses, the differences were largely a function of portfolio managers' assessment of interest rate prospects, the degree to which they were actively managing their portfolios and the nature of their portfolio strategies. Alternatives included choice of targeted maturities or durations, choice of coupon rates, analysis of prepayment risks of Ginnie Maes and other mortgage-backed securities, the mix of such securities, the blend of non-callable Treasury notes and bonds, short-term trading and the use of options and futures.

Of the more than 135 U.S. government funds and more than 40 GNMA funds, only 15 and 14 had been in business for as many as five years as of September 1989. The records of the great majority are really too short to judge. Because the top performers for 1979–89, listed in Tables 5-4d and 5-4e, were not concentrated in U.S. government or GNMA securities for all of the ten years, the total return data should not be taken as an indication of results that could have been produced by such investments—with two exceptions: Fidelity Government Securities Fund, which commenced operations in April 1979, and Mutual of

Table 5-4d   Performance: U.S. Government Funds

	1984–1989 (Compound Annual Rate)	1979–1989	Maximum Sales Charge*	Operating Expense Ratio**
Lord Abbett U.S. Govt. Securities	12.4%#	11.7%#	4.75%	0.88%
Value Line U.S. Govt. Securities	12.0#	—	None	0.66
AMEV U.S. Govt. Securities Fund	11.7#	11.0#	4.50	0.87
Colonial Govt. Securities Plus	11.4	—	6.75	1.13
Carnegie High Yield Govt.	11.1	—	4.50	1.27
United Govt. Securities	11.1	—	4.25	0.77
Fidelity Govt. Securities	10.9	10.9	None	0.79
Federated Income Trust	10.8	—	None	0.52
Composite U.S. Govt. Securities	10.4	—	4.00	1.03
Mutual of Omaha America Fund	10.2	9.7	None	1.03
GROUP (number of funds)	10.9 (15)	10.4 (5)		

Note: See Table 5-4a for asterisked references.

Investment objective or policy was changed to the present one during the period.

Table 5–4e   Performance: GNMA Funds

	1984–1989 (Compound Annual Rate)	1979–1989	Maximum Sales Charge*	Operating Expense Ratio**
Kemper U.S. Govt. Securities	12.5%	10.2%#	4.50%	0.50%
Vanguard GNMA	12.3	—	None	0.35
Federated GNMA Trust	12.1	—	None	0.53
Franklin U.S. Govt. Securities	11.7	9.2#	4.00***	0.53
Merrill Lynch Federal Securities	11.4	—	4.00	0.69
Putnam U.S. Govt. Guaranteed	11.2	—	4.75	0.61
Lexington GNMA Income Fund	11.1	8.9#	None	1.07
PaineWebber GNMA Portfolio	10.5	—	4.25	0.67
(Integrated) Home Investors Govt. Guar.	10.3	—	5.00 D	1.78
Prudential-Bache GNMA Fund	9.9	—	5.00 D	1.52
GROUP (number of funds)	10.7 (14)	9.0 (4)		

Note: See Table 5–4a for asterisked references.

Investment objective or policy was changed to the present one during the period.

Table 5–4f   Performance: U.S. Mortgage Funds

	1986–1989 (Compound Annual Rate)	1984–1989	Maximum Sales Charge*	Operating Expense Ratio**
(Federated) Fund for U.S. Govt. Securities	8.3%	10.8%	4.50%	0.96%****
MIMLIC Mortgage Securities	7.8	—	5.00	1.05****
Alliance Mortgage Securities Inc.	7.5	11.2	5.50	1.11
Van Kampen Merritt U.S. Govt.	7.4	11.9	4.90	0.71
Fidelity Mortgage Securities	7.4	—	None	0.81
Kidder, Peabody Govt. Income Fund	7.1	—	4.00	1.68
Seligman Secured Mortgage	6.8	—	4.75	1.05****
Financial Indep. U.S. Govt. Securities	6.6	10.3	4.00	1.37
Merrill Lynch Retirement/ Income	6.6	—	4.00 D	1.37
First Investors Govt. Fund	6.3	10.1	7.25	0.99****
GROUP (number of funds)	6.9 (13)	10.7 (6)		

Note: See Table 5–4a for asterisked references.

Omaha America Fund, which has invested exclusively in governments since 1973.

In the U.S. mortgage fund group, six funds had been in operation for as many as five years. Only one has a long history: Federated Investors' Fund for U.S. Government Securities, whose operation goes back to 1969.

Leading high-yield funds, shown in Table 5–4g, rewarded their investors with the superior long-run returns that they had expected for taking greater risk in lower-quality portfolios—despite periods such as 1989, when high-yield bond prices slumped and many investors redeemed their shares. For those invested in the better funds who reinvested their dividends, the compounding of high income was an important offset to the impact of actual and expected defaults on share prices.

None performed better through the years, on average, than Kemper High Yield Fund. William R. Buecking, head of Kemper Financial Services' fixed-income group and one of the two Kemper High Yield Fund portfolio managers, credits the achievement primarily to the firm's methodology for selecting both attractive sectors and low-quality issues within those sectors. "Careful credit research was very important," he says. "So was choosing companies with stable or improving creditworthiness—companies not susceptible to economic downturns."

Selection wasn't everything, however. Management also changed average quality and average maturity from time to time. On two occasions in the early 1980s, for example, Buecking says, the fund performed well

Table 5–4g Performance: High-Yield Funds

	1984–1989	1979–1989	Maximum	Operating
	(Compound Annual Rate)		Sales Charge*	Expense Ratio**
Kemper High Yield Fund	14.5%	13.3%	4.50%	0.72%
Eaton Vance Income of Boston	14.2	12.6	4.75	1.31
Financial Bond HY Portfolio	13.8	—	None	0.82
Delaware High Yield Delchester I	13.7	11.7	6.75	0.87
CIGNA High Yield Fund	13.5	12.1	5.00	0.96****
(Kemper) Investment Portfolios HY	12.7	—	5.00 D	2.10
Vanguard High Yield Bond	12.7	11.7	None	0.41
Fidelity High Income Fund	12.4	12.6	None	0.77
Colonial High Yield Securities	12.4	11.3	4.75	1.17
Merrill Lynch High Income A	12.4	11.1	4.00	0.64
GROUP (number of funds)	10.7 (39)	10.9 (25)		

Note: See Table 5–4a for asterisked references.

because management shifted most of its assets out of "junk bonds" and into investment-grade securities: "When the yield spread between BBs and GNMAs narrowed to 100 basis points, we reduced risk even if it meant reducing yield. We manage for total return." The Kemper managers are permitted to vary the portfolio's weighted average maturity between five and twelve years. During the 1980s, they found it necessary to adjust the average periodically.

Despite the performance of Kemper, and other leading funds, the group's average was pulled down by funds that did poorly. During 1984–89, when the leaders' returns attained a higher average annual rate than they had in the previous five-year period—as did bonds generally—the high-yield fund average was encumbered by the weight of laggards. First Investors Bond Appreciation and Bull & Bear High Yield Funds managed average annual total returns *below* the 6.5 percent that their investors could have obtained from Treasury bills. American Investors Income and National Bond Funds' returns were only slightly higher.

Data for the five years ended in September 1989, of course, do not fully reflect the drop in high-yield funds' net asset values resulting from 1989's plunge in junk bond prices. It affected the portfolios of all of the group's funds, albeit unevenly. Many investors, fearing the worst, were persuaded to switch to money market funds and/or other investment alternatives. Many others hung on, presumably eager to preserve—and, if possible, reinvest—the flow of dividends, confident that their portfolio managers could pilot their funds through the choppiness caused by increased fear of defaults and high-yield market illiquidity, and hopeful that the low-quality bond market would eventually recover.

Funds that concentrate in U.S. government and investment-grade corporate bonds of short or intermediate maturities are mostly of recent origin, and there aren't many of them (Tables 5–4h through 5–4k). Only nine short and 12 intermediate funds were in operation for all of the five years ended in September 1989.

Differences in the performance of short and intermediate funds were due largely to whether they were concentrated in government or corporate issues, to how they weighted the maturities, and, in the case of corporates, credit qualities.[2] The Boston Company's Managed Income Fund earned the return that enabled it to lead the pack in 1984–89 by selectively investing 25–30 percent of its net assets in high-yield bonds, according to J. David Mills, senior vice-president. "We've looked for value while trying to avoid the original-issue junk and the companies that have to sell assets to make interest payments," he said. "When we didn't find merchandise that met our criteria, we didn't buy."

Bonds and preferred stocks convertible into common stocks offer opportunities for both long-term capital appreciation and income, albeit

Table 5–4h   Performance: Intermediate U.S. Government Funds

	1986–1989 (Compound Annual Rate)	1984–1989 (Compound Annual Rate)	Maximum Sales Charge*	Operating Expense Ratio**
Eaton Vance Govt. Obligations	8.0%	10.4%	4.75%	1.19%
Benham Target Maturities 1995 Portfolio	6.7	—	None	0.70****
Scudder U.S. Govt. Zero Coupon 1995 Port.	6.6	—	None	1.00****
Rushmore U.S. Govt. Interm.	6.5	—	None	0.81
Voyageur Granit Govt. Securities	6.5	—	4.00	1.25****
Prudential-Bache Govt. Interm. Term	6.3	10.7	None	0.83
John Hancock U.S. Govt. Securities	5.6	10.9#	8.50	1.02
SLH Intermediate Term Govt.	5.3	—	5.00 D	1.61
Benham Treasury Note Fund	5.2	10.3	None	0.75****
GROUP (number of funds)	6.4 (10)	10.7 (5)		

Note: See Table 5–4a for asterisked references.

Investment objective or policy was changed to the present one during the period.

less appreciation than common stocks and less income than bonds. The funds that invest in convertible securities, however, have performed unevenly, as Table 5–4l indicates. Virtually all funds in the group experienced negative total returns in 1987—for some, it was the second time in four years—as they were buffeted by breaks in prices of both fixed-income securities and equities to which their convertibles were linked. Better performances over the 1986–89 period were achieved by funds whose portfolios had dropped less in 1987, then bounced back more vigorously in 1988. Those recovering more sluggishly tended to be invested in securities of smaller firms at a time when common stocks of such companies, as a group, lagged behind those of large corporations.

The better performers among flexible income funds (Table 5–4m), which may invest in stocks as well as bonds and cash equivalents, turned in respectable scorecards. Their strategies in pursuing income and, secondarily, capital appreciation have varied but have had one inescapable common denominator: acceptance of more risks than those associated with fixed-income securities alone.

National Total Income Fund, the leading performer, has an asset allocation policy that permits it to go heavily into cash, as it did in the autumn of 1987, but it has been about 50–60 percent invested in common stocks during the 1980s. "We have looked for dividend-paying stocks

Table 5–4i   Performance: Intermediate Investment-Grade Funds

	1986–1989 (Compound Annual Rate)	1984–1989	Maximum Sales Charge*	Operating Expense Ratio**
Boston Co. Managed Income	8.3%	12.8%#	None	1.14%
MassMutual Investment Grade	8.0#	11.3#	4.50%	1.09
Merrill Lynch Corp. Interm.	7.0	11.8	2.00	0.62
Fidelity Intermediate Bond	6.9	11.6	None	0.63
UMB Bond	6.6	10.4	None	0.87
Connecticut Mutual Income	6.2	—	4.50	1.24
GROUP (number of funds)	7.2 (10)	11.5 (8)		

Investment objective or policy was changed to the present one during the period.

Note: See Table 5–4a for asterisked references.

that are undervalued," says Mark L. Lipson, president. "Once a stock has reached what we believe is its maximum potential, we have not hesitated to liquidate our position even though the stock may have done well for us." For the bond portion of the portfolio, Lipson said, the fund has focused on governments and investment-grade corporates, looking at each for its capital appreciation possibilities, not yield, and trying to stay in intermediate maturities.

Vanguard's Wellesley Income Fund has tended to have a lower proportion in common: around 35 percent. Its investment policy, which stresses current income, calls for the preponderance of its assets to be invested in long-term fixed-income securities, primarily investment-grade bonds, so long as the general level of interest rates remains in excess of dividend yields available on common stocks. At the end of September 1989, it held about 35 percent corporates and 25 percent government and agency securities. Seligman Income Fund, which has tended toward a similar 70–30 bond-common split, has devoted 20 percent or more of its assets to convertibles. Northeast Investors Trust has invested over 90 percent—essentially even 100 percent—of its total assets in bonds through the limited use of leverage.

Only one world income fund, Massachusetts Financial International Trust—Bond Portfolio, had been around for as many as seven years by September 1989, and for the five years ended then it had an average total return of 17.9 percent. Only three other world income bond funds had been in operation for three years: Merrill Lynch Retirement Global Bond Fund, T. Rowe Price International Bond Fund, and Templeton Income Fund. The largest, $1.1 billion PaineWebber Master Global Income Fund, had been in operation for two and one-half years.

Table 5–4j   Performance: Short U.S. Government Funds

	1986–1989 (Compound Annual Rate)	1984–1989	Maximum Sales Charge*	Operating Expense Ratio**
Federated Short-Interm. Govt.	6.7%	9.2%	None	0.47%****
Federated Intermediate Govt.	6.6	10.3	None	0.50
Delaware Treasury Reserves Investors	6.5	—	None	0.90
Benham Target Mat. 1990 Port.	6.2	—	None	0.70****
20th Century U.S. Governments	6.1	9.0	None	1.00
Baker U.S. Government	5.9	—	None	1.00****
Scudder U.S. Govt. Zero Coupon 1990 Port.	5.8	—	None	1.00****
Midwest Income Trust Intermed.	5.7	9.2	2.00%	1.04
GROUP (number of funds)	6.2 (8)	9.5 (4)		

Note: See Table 5–4a for asterisked references.

Table 5–4k   Performance: Short Investment-Grade Funds

	1986–1989 (Compound Annual Rate)	1984–1989	Maximum Sales Charge*	Operating Expense Ratio**
DFA 1-Year Fixed Income Port.	7.4%	8.7%	None	0.22%
Vanguard Short Term Bond	7.4	10.6	None	0.34
Sit "New Beginning" Investment Reserve	7.0	—	None	1.00****
IAI Reserve Fund	6.8	—	None	0.85****
Neuberger & Berman Ltd. Mat.	6.8	—	None	0.63****
Scudder Short Term Bond†	6.8#	11.7#	None	0.50****
T. Rowe Price Short-Term Bond	6.5	8.8	None	0.94
IDS Strategy Short-Term	6.4#	6.3#	5.00% D	1.74
Fidelity Short-Term Bond	6.3	—	None	0.89
GROUP (number of funds)	6.9 (12)	9.2 (7)		

Note: See Table 5–4a for asterisked references.

† Successor to Scudder 1994 Target Fund.

Investment objective or policy was changed to the present one during the period.

Table 5–4I   Performance: Convertible Securities Funds

	1986–1989 (Compound Annual Rate)	1984–1989 (Compound Annual Rate)	Maximum Sales Charge*	Operating Expense Ratio**
Dreyfus Convertible Securities	11.7%	16.6%#	None	1.09%
Phoenix Convertible Fund	11.2	14.2	6.90%	0.83
American Capital Harbor Fund	11.2	14.1	5.75	0.87
Dolphin FRIC Convertible	10.2	—	4.50	2.34****
Alliance Convertible	9.8	—	5.50	1.54****
SLH Convertible	9.3	—	5.00 D	1.75
Putnam Convertible Income	9.0	13.6	8.50	0.97
Value Line Convertible	8.7	—	None	1.03
Vanguard Convertible	8.3	—	None	0.88
Calamos Convertible Income	7.1	—	None	1.10
GROUP (number of funds)	7.8 (17)	13.4 (5)		

Note: See Table 5–4a for asterisked references.

Investment objective or policy changed to the present one during the period.

No meaningful comparison of long-term performance is feasible for the entire group, but Table 5–4n gives you an idea of the rates of annual performance of which such funds are capable. With total returns ranging from Templeton's 10.2 percent to Price's 1.3 percent for the one year ended September 1989, you can see that there can be substantial differences among the funds and, for individual funds, from one year to the next. The total group, grown to 35, averaged 6.0 percent for the year.

Perhaps George Putnam, chairman of the even younger Putnam Global Governmental Income Trust, put it as vividly as anyone when he wrote in an annual report that a world income fund portfolio manager has to display the "uncanny sense of timing" of Fred Astaire and Ginger Rogers—that is, to exhibit "a similar, though less theatrical, knack of being in the right place at the right time." Managing such a fund requires not only making the types of judgments necessary to run a domestic bond fund—interest rate projections, choices of credit qualities, maturities and so on—but making such judgments for government and corporate securities of a dozen or more countries and, in addition, forecasting currency exchange rate trends. Only after doing all of these things can he or she decide where to invest the fund's assets. Those that have done well in all of these respects have turned in impressive performances, providing shareholders with generous income as well as double-digit total returns. Those that have gotten everything right but the currencies—failing to anticipate strength in the U.S. dollar against the Deutschemark or yen, for example—won no applause.

Table 5–4m   Performance: Flexible-Income Funds

	1984–1989	1979–1989	Maximum	Operating
	(Compound Annual Rate)		Sales Charge*	Expense Ratio**
National Total Income Fund	18.5%	16.8%	7.25%***	1.07%
(Vanguard) Wellesley Income Fund	15.8	14.5	None	0.51
JP Income Fund	13.9	10.8	6.75	0.85
Northeast Investors Trust	13.8	11.8	None	0.72
Seligman Income Fund	13.8	13.0	4.75	0.80
Mutual of Omaha Income	13.8	11.6	8.00	0.80
USAA Income Fund	12.8	12.0	None	0.61
(Capstone) Investors Income Fund	12.7	10.4	4.75	1.29
Nicholas Income Fund	11.4	10.0	None	0.83
Unified Income Fund	7.9	10.2	None	1.35
GROUP (number of funds)	13.6 (10)	12.3 (10)		

Note: See Table 5–4a for asterisked references.

Although they're not really bond funds, balanced funds are normally at least 25 percent invested in bonds. Table 5–4o shows the long-term leaders, each reporting consistently respectable average total returns, ahead of those for average bond funds largely because of the boosts provided by their equity holdings.

For municipal bond funds and their investors, the two five-year periods constituting the decade that ended in September 1989, were as different as night and day. The period of 1979–84 was appalling. Prices of outstanding tax-exempt bonds—and of municipal bond fund shares—slumped as interest rates soared, then recovered as rates receded.

The years 1984–89 brought lower rates and less volatility. Moreover, conditions in the municipal bond market further improved as supply and

Table 5–4n   Performance: World Income Funds

	1986–1989	1984–1989	Maximum	Operating
	(Compound Annual Rate)		Sales Charge*	Expense Ratio**
Mass. Financial Intl. Bond	11.1%	17.9%	7.25%	1.13%
Merrill Lynch Ret. Global B	10.7	—	4.00 D	1.78
Templeton Income Fund	8.7	—	8.50	1.10
T. Rowe Price Intl. Bond Fund	7.2	—	None	1.20
GROUP (number of funds)	9.3† (5)	17.9 (1)		

Note: See Table 5–4a for asterisked references.

† Reflects inclusion of 8.8% average return for one fund that is not a bond fund: International Cash Portfolios—Global Cash Portfolio, which invests in U.S. and foreign money market instruments.

Table 5–4o   Performance: Balanced Funds

	1984–1989	1979–1989	Maximum	Operating
	(Compound Annual Rate)		Sales Charge*	Expense Ratio**
Loomis-Sayles Mutual Fund	21.5%	16.7%	None	1.01%
Mass. Financial Total Return	19.0	16.4	7.25%	0.71
Dodge & Cox Balanced Fund	18.6	15.2	None	0.77
Alliance Balanced Shares	18.4	15.2	5.50	1.42
IDS Mutual	18.1	15.6	5.00	0.67
(Vanguard) Wellington Fund	17.8	16.3	None	0.47
Phoenix Balanced Fund	17.7	17.5	8.50	0.80
George Putnam Fund of Boston	17.4	15.1	8.50	0.80
American Balanced Fund	17.1	14.9	5.75	0.76
Delaware Fund	16.7#	17.0#	6.75	0.77
GROUP (number of funds)	15.9 (28)	14.9 (22)		

Note: See Table 5–4a for asterisked references.

Investment objective or policy was changed to the present one during the period.

demand were brought into better balance, owing primarily to a reduction in supply.

This combination of factors was made to order for long-term municipals, so it's no wonder that the general municipal bond fund group led other tax-exempt categories in total return for 1984–89. In fact, as Table 5-4p shows, the group's leaders had average annual returns matching those of taxable bond funds despite the lower coupons of their portfolio securities.

Interestingly, the leaders followed slightly different strategies to achieve their results.

John M. Holliday, manager of United Municipal Bond Fund, managed his portfolio "actively," he says. His turnover rate during the period averaged well above 200 percent.

"The market is so imperfect that there are constantly opportunities to improve your holdings," Holliday adds. "We're constantly restructuring the fund, buying the best values nationwide. If California issues a lot of bonds and they become cheap, we'll buy more California. Then, when they become scarce, we'll sell them and buy, say, Missouri. We'll buy whatever is cheap. You can't be a top performer unless you're willing to take advantage of opportunities and also to take gains."

David A. Snowbeck, president of SteinRoe Tax-Exempt Income Trust, says he was "moderately active" in managing SteinRoe Managed Municipals: shortening the duration of his normally long portfolio when

Table 5-4p   Performance: General Municipal Bonds

	1984–1989 (Compound Annual Rate)	1979–1989	Maximum Sales Charge*	Operating Expense Ratio**
United Municipal Bond Fund	14.2%	7.4%	4.25%	0.58%
Delaware Group Tax-Free USA	13.8	—	4.75	0.77
Mutual of Omaha Tax-Free Income	13.4	7.4	8.00	0.64
SteinRoe Managed Municipals	13.4	9.3	None	0.65
Financial Tax-Free Income	13.3	—	None	0.77
Putnam Tax-Exempt Income	13.2	10.8	4.75	0.52
Seligman National Tax-Exempt	13.1	—	4.75	0.83
Kemper Municipal Bond Fund	12.9	8.6	4.50	0.51
Safeco Municipal Bond Fund	12.8	—	None	0.60
Lord Abbett Tax-Free National Portfolio	12.7	—	4.75	0.66
GROUP (number of funds)	11.9 (51)	8.1 (28)		

Note: See Table 5–4a for asterisked references.

interest rates turned up during the period and "modestly" switching from bonds selling at premium prices to those selling at discounts.

"We took advantage of unique supply-demand distortions, whether on an issue or sector basis or in the entire market," he recalls. "With the help of our own research, we were able to buy securities that were undervalued and to extricate ourselves before overvaluations were spotted in the marketplace. We didn't automatically buy securities just because they were cheap. Some that we looked at might have been cheap, but they had call provisions that were too onerous."

Total returns of leading insured municipal bond funds for 1984–89 and 1986–89 (Table 5-4q) slightly lagged behind those of leading general municipal bond funds with comparable weighted average maturities, primarily because of the insurance premiums that they have to pay (directly or indirectly), thereby reducing their yields. The funds benefited increasingly, however, from the greater competition among bond insurance companies, which resulted in a drop in premiums that began in 1986 and accelerated in 1988.

Assurance of timely payment of interest and principal on the insured bonds in their portfolios, of course, did not protect fund investors against large declines in bond prices in 1987, when several insured bond funds reported negative returns, as reflected in the 1986–89 average

Table 5–4q   Performance: Insured Municipal Bond Funds

	1986–1989 (Compound Annual Rate)	1984–1989	Maximum Sales Charge*	Operating Expense Ratio**
Vanguard Municipal Insured Long-Term	7.8%	11.7%	None	0.29%
First Investors Insured Tax Exempt	7.7	11.3	7.25%	1.04
AARP Insured Tax Free General Bond	7.1	—	None	0.92
Merrill Lynch Municipal Bond Insured A	7.1	11.6	4.00	0.49
Van Kampen Merritt Insured Tax Free	7.0	—	4.90	0.86
Principal Preservation Insured Tax-Exempt	7.0	—	4.50	1.35****
Delaware Group Tax-Free USA Insured	6.9	—	4.75	0.82
Franklin Insured Tax-Free Income	6.7	—	4.00***	0.58
Integrated Tax Free STRIPES	6.5	—	4.75	1.30
IDS Insured Tax-Exempt	6.4	—	5.00	0.72
GROUP (number of funds)	6.4 (17)	11.3 (4)		

Note: See Table 5–4a for asterisked references.

results. Those who led the group during the three-year period had to take advantage of every opportunity to excel.

Jerry R. Eubank, portfolio manager of the $1 billion First Investors Insured Tax Exempt Fund, attributes his fund's performance partly to having fresh money available from sales of shares and dividend reinvestment so that he could invest in additional bonds as their interest rates were falling (and prices were rising). He also shopped for the best values, buying uninsured bonds and purchasing insurance for them when the yield spreads between them and insured bonds of comparable maturities were wide, but buying bonds that were already insured when the spreads narrowed enough to make that more attractive.

Kenneth A. Jacob, vice president and senior portfolio manager of Merrill Lynch Municipal Bond Fund, credits the performance of its $2 billion Insured Portfolio in part to the stream of income from its higher coupon bonds, half or more of which it could reinvest in behalf of its shareholders. Dating back to 1977, it is one of the three oldest insured bond funds, and, therefore, higher coupon bonds have accounted for a significant portion of its assets. But, Jacob noted, Merrill Lynch, of course, has not hesitated to dispose of high-coupon bonds whose call dates were approaching.

The high-yield municipal bond fund average total return (Table 5–4r) did not quite match that of general municipal bond funds in the five years ended September 1987, partly because high-yield bond prices may not have been as sensitive to falling interest rates as those of higher-rated issues. Nor did the leaders quite match the performance of the leading general municipal funds. But, at 12 percent or higher annually, the leaders' total returns are not to be minimized. (Ironically, the Vanguard and IDS funds' average annual total returns were slightly ahead of those of the taxable Vanguard and IDS high-yield bond funds.)

Thomas J. Conlin, portfolio manager of SteinRoe High-Yield Municipals, says his fund's performance was "more a function of avoiding bonds of issuers with deteriorating credit than of selecting big winners." Looking at the creditworthiness of governments and certain nonprofit organizations while seeking bonds offering high tax-exempt yields, he spotted issues whose ratings were on the verge of being raised to investment grade, resulting in higher prices.

In his bond selection strategy, Conlin also pursued certain themes: the resurgence of industrial America ("rust belt" pollution control revenue bonds linked to the credit of major steel companies, Cleveland general obligation bonds); the aging of America (housing for the elderly, well-managed hospitals in the "sun belt"), and special situations featuring new business opportunities (New Jersey solid waste transfer projects, Texas prisons) and regional economic development and housing authorities (revenue bonds to fund mortgage loans for single-family homes).

Table 5–4r   Performance: High-Yield Municipal Bond Funds

	1984–1989 (Compound Annual Rate)	1979–1989	Maximum Sales Charge*	Operating Expense Ratio**
SteinRoe High-Yield Municipals	13.1%	—	None	0.73%
Vanguard Municipal High-Yield	12.9	8.1%	None	0.29
IDS High Yield Tax-Exempt	12.7	8.8	5.00%	0.61
Fidelity High Yield Municipals	12.2	8.3	None	0.60
Merrill Lynch Municipal Bond High Yield A	12.0	—	4.00	0.55
GIT Tax-Free High Yield Portfolio	10.6	—	None	1.16
MFS High Yield Municipal Bond	10.2	—	4.75	0.65****
Venture Muni (+) Plus	7.3	—	5.00 D	2.46
GROUP (number of funds)	11.4 (8)	8.4 (3)		

Note: See Table 5–4a for asterisked references.

Having done the credit research and bought, Conlin has not necessarily held on. As soon as bonds became fully valued, he replaced them, raising his portfolio turnover rate to over 200 percent in the year ended June 1989, and, as yield spreads narrowed, raising the portfolio's quality as well.

The Vanguard Municipal Bond Fund High Yield Portfolio's results during the five years are largely attributable to Vanguard's early emphasis on maximizing call protection by buying bonds selling at significant discounts or those with the longest periods prior to call dates, according to Ian A. MacKinnon, Vanguard senior vice president. "During much of 1987 and 1988, call protection could be purchased at very low relative 'cost' (that is, reduced yield)," he said. MacKinnon added that the fund also was aided by the "very successful" use of bond futures contracts during the latter part of the period. They reduced the fund's need to sell desirable bonds to raise cash when shareholders responded to 1987's second bond market break by inundating Vanguard (and other fund families) with requests for redemption. Thus it was able to participate more fully in the subsequent recovery of bond prices than would have been possible otherwise.

Another Vanguard fund, the Intermediate-Term Portfolio, led the small group of intermediate municipal bond funds in total return for both 1984–89 and 1986–89 (Table 5-4s). Factors contributing to his fund's performance, MacKinnon says, were the same as those that produced results for the High Yield Portfolio: maximum call protection, use of futures contracts and lower operating expenses. The fund also maintained its weighted average maturity at around nine to ten years, thereby earning higher income than other funds in the group with shorter maturities until the yield curve flattened in 1989.

Short municipal bond funds—those investing in securities maturing in from one to five years—filled the bill for investors who wanted tax-exempt income that would be slightly higher than that of tax-exempt money market funds and who agreed to accept slight risk to earn it. The 7.0 percent average total return of the eleven funds that were in operation for the five years ended in September 1989 (Table 5-4t) exceeded the 4.9 percent annual average of tax-exempt money market funds by nearly 220 basis points, or 2.2 percent, and that of the period's best-performing tax-exempt money market fund (Calvert Tax-Free Reserves Money Market Portfolio) by about 170 basis points, or 1.7 percent. Although the average for the latest three years was considerably lower, the 5.4 percent rate still exceeded the tax-exempt money market fund average by about 60 basis points.

The leader among short municipal funds for the three years ended September 1989—and, save for a Scudder Target portfolio, also for five

Table 5–4s   Performance: Intermediate Municipal Bond Funds

	1986–1989	1984–1989	Maximum	Operating
	(Compound Annual Rate)		Sales Charge*	Expense Ratio**
Vanguard Municipal Intermediate	7.1%	11.0%	None	0.29%
UST Master Tax-Exempt Intermediate	7.0	—	4.50%	0.68
Dreyfus Intermediate Tax Exempt	6.4	9.9	None	0.73
USAA Tax Exempt Intermediate-Term	6.1	9.6	None	0.49
Fidelity Limited Term Municipals	5.7	9.9	None	0.67
Scudder Tax Free Target 1996 Portfolio	5.7	—	None	0.98
Zweig Tax-Free Limited Term	5.5	—	1.50	0.73****
Benham National Tax-Free Intermediate	5.5	7.9	None	0.50****
SteinRoe Intermediate Municipals	5.4	—	None	0.80****
(Rushmore) Fund for Tax-Free Investors Intermediate	5.0	7.8	None	0.93
GROUP (number of funds)	5.7 (14)	8.8 (8)		

Note: See Table 5–4a for asterisked references.

years—was Limited Term Municipal Fund's National Portfolio. To provide income above tax-exempt money market fund rates, Brian J. McMahon, president, says he has maintained its weighted average maturity at between four and five years. That's longer than the averages of other funds in the group, some of whose managers try to stay under two years to hold down share price volatility—even if at a sacrifice in yield.

McMahon buys securities with maturities staggered from one to ten years; the proportions, he says, depend in part on which maturities offer the best values. He also seeks to lift income by going outside the universe of municipal bonds to invest in municipal leases,[3] which, according to the fund's prospectus, "frequently have special risks not normally associated with general obligation or revenue bonds."

While Scudder Tax Free Target Fund's 1990 and 1993 portfolios were among the ten leading performers in this classification, one cannot jump to the conclusion that such funds, with few and declining numbers of years remaining until their targeted maturities, always will outperform conventional short-term funds. Much depends on the level and shape of the yield curve over time.

Table 5–4t   Performance: Short Municipal Bond Funds

	1986–1989	1984–1989	Maximum	Operating
	(Compound Annual Rate)		Sales Charge*	Expense Ratio**
Limited Term Municipal Fund				
National Portfolio	6.5%	8.7%	2.75%	1.15%
Calvert Tax-Free Reserves				
Limited-Term	6.0	7.0	2.00	0.81
USAA Tax Exempt Short-Term	5.5	6.9	None	0.51
Vanguard Municipal				
Short-Term	5.4	6.2	None	0.29
Scudder Tax Free Target 1993				
Portfolio	5.4	8.8	None	0.80
Babson Tax-Free Income				
Portfolio S	5.3	7.6	None	1.00
Merrill Lynch Municipal Bond				
Limited Maturity Portfolio	5.2	6.1	0.75	0.41
Scudder Tax Free Target 1990				
Portfolio	5.0	7.6	None	0.79
Federated Short-Intermediate				
Municipal	4.8	5.7	None	0.46****
Midwest Group Tax Free				
Limited Term Portfolio	4.8	6.1	2.00	1.19****
GROUP (number of funds)	5.4 (13)	7.0 (11)		

Note: See Table 5–4a for asterisked references.

THE TOP PERFORMERS

When the top 1984–89 performers of all taxable and tax-exempt bond fund groups are ranked according to total return, as Table 5–5 does, it's interesting to see which groups are represented and which are not.

As many as ten of the twenty-five—the six flexible income funds and four convertible securities funds—are not straight bond funds. Their performance was linked to the stock market as well as to the bond market. (If the list had been consolidated with that of the best-performing balanced funds (Table 5–4o), which also invest in stocks, ten of the top twenty-five funds would have been balanced funds.)

Of the fifteen conventional bond funds, five are high-yield bond funds. One, the only world income fund in operation for the entire period, benefited from investment in high-yielding non-U.S.-dollar bonds. Of the remaining nine that invested in domestic investment-grade bonds, only five come from the ranks of A- and BBB-rated corporate bond funds. As many as four funds, perhaps surprisingly, are general municipal bond funds.

Funds characterized by lower credit or interest rate risks are not on the list. None of the funds is concentrated in U.S. government or

Table 5–5   The Top 25 Performers: Bond Funds that Led the Group in the Five Years Ended September 1989

Assets (Millions)	Fund	Fund Type	Average Annual Total Return	Latest 12-Month Yield	Maximum Sales Charge*	Operating Expense Ratio**
$ 187	National Total Income	Flx	18.5%	5.8%	7.25%***	1.07%
135	Mass. Financial Intl. Bond	WI	17.9	10.2	7.25	1.13
267	Dreyfus Convertible Securities	CV	16.6#	4.2	None	1.09
723	Wellesley Income Fund	Flx	15.8	6.1	None	0.51
1,552	Kemper High-Yield Fund	HY	14.5	13.4	4.50	0.72
157	Phoenix Convertible Fund	CV	14.2	5.6	6.90	0.83
594	United Municipal Bond	GM	14.2	6.8 TE	4.25	0.58
86	Eaton Vance Income of Boston	HY	14.2	12.1	4.75	1.31
385	American Capital Harbor	CV	14.1	5.9	5.75	0.87
18	JP Income Fund	Flx	13.9	8.9	6.75	0.85
526	Delaware Group Tax-Free USA	GM	13.8	7.3 TE	4.75	0.77
62	Financial Bond High-Yield Portfolio	HY	13.8	12.4	None	0.82
385	Northeast Investors Trust	Flx	13.8	13.8	None	0.72
384	United Bond Fund	A	13.8	9.1	8.50	0.65
160	Seligman Income Fund	Flx	13.8	8.2	4.75	0.80
165	Mutual of Omaha Income	Flx	13.8	8.4	8.00	0.80
669	Delaware High-Yield Delchester I	HY	13.7	12.9	6.75	0.87
63	Axe-Houghton Income	BBB	13.7	9.5	None	1.35
869	Putnam Convertible Income	CV	13.6	6.0	8.50	0.97
23	Calvert Income	BBB	13.5	8.6	4.50	0.94****
1,355	(American Funds) Bond Fund of America	A	13.5	9.5	4.75	0.75
289	CIGNA High-Yield Fund	HY	13.5	12.5	5.00	0.96****
346	Mutual of Omaha Tax-Free Income	GM	13.4	7.1 TE	8.00	0.64
472	SLH Investment Grade	A	13.4	8.1	5.00 D	1.63
515	SteinRoe Managed Municipals	GM	13.4	6.6 TE	None	0.65

\# Investment objective/policy changed to present one during the period.

A	= A-rated corporate	GM	= General municipal
BBB	= BBB-rated corporate	HY	= High yield
CV	= Convertible securities	TE	= Tax-exempt
Flx	= Flexible income	WI	= World income

Note: See Table 5–4a for asterisked references. Yields reflect income distributions divided by September 30, 1989, net asset values per share (adjusted for any capital gains distributions) and may differ from 30-day annualized yields calculated in compliance with SEC definition.

Source: Assets, returns (annualized by author), and yields, Lipper—Fixed Income Fund Performance Analysis; sales charges and expense ratios, fund prospectuses and reports.

government-related securities, whether Treasury obligation or mortgage-backed issues. Nor does the list include funds investing in securities of intermediate or short maturities.

A few other observations:

- Top performers apparently tend to be small or medium size rather than large. Only two of the 25 have assets well in excess of $1 billion.
- No-load funds are well represented. The total return rates shown for the load funds, remember, do *not* reflect the loads. After adjustment for these charges, the returns actually earned by their investors are reduced.
- Operating expenses in excess of 1 percent of average net assets did not keep funds off the list. It is reasonable to assume that, all other things remaining equal, their returns would have been greater if expenses had been lower.

THE LARGEST BOND FUNDS

When bond funds are ranked according to size, as of September 30, 1989, differences emerge. Among the largest taxable funds (Table 5–6a), only one of which made the top performer list for 1984–89, 18 of 25 were invested in government or government-related securities. Six are high-yield bond funds. Only nine have been in operation for as many as ten years (seven in their current category), only eight more for as many as five years.

The Franklin U.S. Government Securities Series, which has invested primarily in Ginnie Maes since early 1983, remained by far the largest bond fund—indeed, the second largest non-money-market mutual fund. (The largest equity fund, Fidelity's Magellan, had assets of $12.4 billion.) Franklin is one of the funds that imposes a sales charge on the reinvestment of dividends as well as on ordinary sales of shares. Despite the charge, shareholders in 1988 reinvested about one-third of the $1.2 billion of dividends that Franklin distributed.

Not surprisingly, the list is dominated by load funds. Whatever the merits of these funds, it took salesmanship—and the linkage to the U.S. government—to attract enough money to build them to such size. And the sales people had to be compensated from the sales charge, whether front-end or deferred, or from the 12b-1 distribution expenses (included among operating expenses by funds that have 12b-1 plans).

Two of the five no-load funds on the list are not typical. The AARP GNMA and U.S. Treasury Fund, whose investment management is provided by Scudder, Stevens & Clark, has the support of the huge American Association of Retired Persons. Federated Short-Intermediate Government Trust, which requires a minimum initial investment of $100,000, is intended more for institutions than individuals (as are other Federated funds with similar requirements).

Table 5-6a   The Largest Taxable Bond Funds as of September 30, 1989

Fund	Assets in Billions	Fund Type	Compound Annual Rates of Return For Period Ended September 1989			Maximum Sales Charge *	Operating Expense Ratio **
			3 Yr	5 Yr	10 Yr		
Franklin U.S. Government Securities	$11.3	GNMA	8.0%	11.7%	9.2%#	4.00%***	0.53%
Dean Witter U.S. Government Securities	10.0	GNMA	7.0	9.3	—	5.00 D	1.18
Putnam High Income Government	7.9	USG	5.6	—	—	6.75	0.75****
(Kemper) Investment Portfolios							
Government Plus	6.0	USG	5.6	—	—	5.00 D	1.98
American Capital Government Securities	4.7	USG	6.3	9.7	—	6.75	0.69
Kemper U.S. Government Securities	4.4	GNMA	7.5	12.5	10.2#	4.50	0.50
Prudential-Bache Government Plus	3.8	USG	6.4	—	—	5.00 D	1.60
Van Kampen Merritt U.S. Government	3.6	USM	7.4	11.9	—	4.90	0.71
MFS Lifetime Government Income Plus	3.5	USG	—	—	—	6.00 D	2.01
Prudential-Bache High Yield	2.8	HY	6.5	11.2	10.8	5.00 D	1.30
Merrill Lynch Federal Securities	2.7	GNMA	7.5	11.4	—	4.00	0.69
Colonial Government Securities Plus	2.6	USG	7.0	11.4	—	6.75	1.13
AARP GNMA & U.S. Treasury	2.5	GNMA	6.9	—	—	None	0.81
Putnam High-Yield Trust	2.3	HY	8.5	11.7	12.0	6.75	0.61
(Franklin) AGE High Income	2.2	HY	6.4	10.8	10.6	4.00***	0.56
SLH Government Securities	2.2	USG	5.0	9.6	—	5.00 D	1.47
Vanguard GNMA	2.0	GNMA	8.4	12.3	—	None	0.35
Dean Witter Government Securities Plus	1.9	USG	—	—	—	5.00 D	1.49
Federated Short-Intermediate							
Government	1.9	SUS	6.7	9.2	—	None	0.47****
IDS Bond Fund	1.8	GB	8.1	13.0	11.8	5.00	0.77
Merrill Lynch Retirement Inc.	1.7	USM	6.6	—	—	4.00 D	1.37
Fidelity High Income	1.6	HY	6.5	12.4	12.6	None	0.77
Dreyfus GNMA	1.6	GNMA	6.7	—	—	None	1.01
Kemper High Yield Fund	1.6	HY	10.7	14.5	13.3	4.50	0.72
Dean Witter High Yield	1.6	HY	2.3	8.6	10.6	5.50	0.49

Investment objective/policy changed to the present one during the period.

GB	= General bond	SUS	= Short U.S. government
GNMA	= GNMA	USG	= U.S. government
HY	= High yield	USM	= U.S. mortgage

Note: See Table 5-4a for asterisked references.

Sources: Assets and returns, Lipper—Fixed Income Fund Performance Analysis (rates of return annualized by author); sales charges and expense ratios, fund prospectuses and reports.

The only no-load funds for unaffiliated individual investors that made the list of the largest 25 taxable funds are Vanguard's GNMA Portfolio, with around $2 billion in net assets, and Fidelity High Income and Dreyfus GNMA, with around $1.6 billion each.

Of the 14 largest tax-exempt bond funds (Table 5-6b), Franklin and Dreyfus each took three slots with their California, New York and national funds. Dreyfus and Merrill Lynch each placed two. Five are gen-

Table 5–6b   The Largest Tax-Exempt Bond Funds as of September 30, 1989

Fund	Assets in Billions	Fund Type	Compound Annual Rates of Return For Period Ended September 1989			Maximum Sales Charge *	Operating Expense Ratio **
			3 Yr	5 Yr	10 Yr		
Franklin California Tax-Free Income	$9.8	SSM	7.0%	10.9%	6.3%	4.00***	0.49
IDS High Yield Tax-Exempt	4.4	HYM	7.4	12.7	8.8	5.00	0.61
Franklin Federal Tax-Free Income	3.8	GM	7.0	12.2	—	4.00***	0.51
Dreyfus Tax Exempt Bond Fund	3.5	GM	6.8	11.4	7.1	None	0.71
Franklin New York Tax-Free Income	2.8	SSM	7.1	12.1	—	4.00***	0.51
Merrill Lynch Municipal Insured A	2.0	Ins	7.1	11.6	—	4.00	0.52
Kemper Municipal Bond Fund	1.8	GM	7.7	12.9	8.6	4.50	0.51
Fidelity High Yield Municipals	1.7	HYM	6.6	12.2	8.3	None	0.60
Dreyfus New York Tax Exempt Bond	1.7	SSM	5.7	10.7	—	None	0.69
Putnam California Tax Exempt Income	1.5	SSM	7.7	12.4	—	4.75	0.51
Colonial Tax Exempt High Yield	1.5	GM	6.5	11.3	10.9#	4.75	1.06
SLH Managed Municipals	1.5	GM	7.3	12.3	—	5.00	0.57
Dreyfus California Tax Exempt	1.4	SSM	5.9	10.6	—	None	0.70
Merrill Lynch Municipal High Yield A	1.4	HYM	6.8	12.0	—	4.00	0.55

Note: See Table 5–4a for asterisked references.

GM = General municipal   Ins = Insured municipal
HYM = High-yield municipal   SSM = Single-state municipal

Sources: Assets and returns, Lipper—Fixed Income Fund Performance Analysis (rates of return annualized by author); sales charges and expense ratios, fund prospectuses and reports.

eral municipal funds invested nationally, one an insured fund, and three high-yield funds. The other five are single-state funds, indicating the strength of the appeal of double or triple tax exemption to taxpayers of California and New York.

INCOME VS. TOTAL RETURN

The emphasis in this chapter has been almost exclusively on bond funds' total return, not yield or current income. As you'll recall, there is a good reason for this: total return provides the best measure of bond fund performance.

Although bond fund marketers may promote yield—which, they say, is what sells bond fund shares—it is the total return that matters, or should matter, most to bond fund investors—whether they take the dividends in cash or reinvest them in additional shares. (To minimize the chance that advertisements of funds maximizing yields—but excessively risking principal—may mislead investors, the SEC in 1988 adopted new rules requiring funds to state 1-, 5-, and 10-year average total return data in their ads along with yields—and to standardize yield calculations.)

Superior funds, such as those ranked within their classifications in this chapter, are managed with total return in mind. They may say so explicitly in prospectuses. Or they may imply it, saying that a fund's goal is to produce maximum current income consistent with stability (or preservation) of principal.

There may be years when even prudently managed funds can suffer negative total returns because their portfolio securities dropped more in market value than could be offset by higher income resulting from higher interest rates. Before long, returns should again turn positive, thanks to the combined effects of recovery in securities' values, increases in interest income and purchases of bonds at lower prices.

To see what funds' portfolio managers have had to contend with in trying to maintain stability of principal, look at Table 5-7, which shows how principal and interest have figured in the total return of Salomon Brothers' Broad Investment-Grade Bond Index and its components since the index was introduced in 1980. Note, for instance, that in 1982, when bonds had their best year of the decade, mortgage-backed securities (such as Ginnie Maes) and investment-grade corporate securities had interest income of 17 percent and 16 percent, respectively, and their principal rose by even more. Note also that in 1980 the drop in principal of the corporates exceeded their interest payments by a hair, resulting in a net *decrease.*

The data illustrate the volatility of the principal—and, therefore, the total return—of U.S. Treasury securities, whose safety is undeniable but whose fluctuations have not been addressed candidly in the rosy promotion materials of some bond funds that invest in them. In five of the nine years covered, the principal of Treasuries fell, shrinking total return. In 1987, their worst year of the decade, the total return fell to less than two percent, even though Treasuries generated interest at a rate of nearly nine percent.

Drops in principal such as shown in the table are not a critical concern for those who will hold until maturity and are confident of the issuer's creditworthiness, as in the case of Treasury securities. But bond fund managers must manage their portfolios—that is, continually make decisions as to what and when to buy, sell and hold—so that the combined principal of their securities does not swing as widely as that of individual bonds. They also must be mindful of the possible cost consequences of options and futures strategies.

No one can guarantee that a person investing in a bond fund and taking distributions in cash ever will get his or her investment back because no one can predict where interest rates will be tomorrow, next

Table 5–7 Rate of Return Components for Investment-Grade Securities 1980–1988

Year	Principal	Interest	Total Return
		Salomon Brothers Broad Investment-Grade Bond Index	
1980	(7.24)%	10.06%	2.82%
1981	(5.70)	12.18	6.48
1982	16.62	15.16	31.78
1983	(3.24)	11.45	8.21
1984	2.31	12.67	14.98
1985	9.78	12.48	22.26
1986	5.17	10.28	15.45
1987	(6.26)	8.86	2.60
1988	(1.33)	9.31	7.98
		Treasury Securities	
1980	(4.63)%	9.80%	5.17%
1981	(2.62)	12.14	9.52
1982	12.92	14.58	27.50
1983	(4.48)	11.17	6.69
1984	2.12	12.33	14.45
1985	8.79	12.14	20.93
1986	5.84	9.88	15.72
1987	(6.50)	8.45	1.95
1988	(1.88)	8.92	7.04
		Agency Securities	
1980	(3.98)%	9.55%	5.57%
1981	(1.18)	11.21	10.03
1982	12.58	13.49	26.07
1983	(2.98)	11.47	8.49
1984	1.94	12.46	14.40
1985	5.92	11.94	17.86
1986	4.18	10.13	14.31
1987	(5.45)	8.78	3.33
1988	(1.56)	8.93	7.37
		Mortgage Securities	
1980	(10.13)%	10.62%	0.49%
1981	(11.58)	12.76	1.18
1982	24.23	17.11	41.34
1983	(1.28)	12.11	10.83
1984	2.48	13.29	15.77
1985	12.45	13.22	25.67
1986	2.62	10.82	13.44
1987	(5.41)	9.47	4.06
1988	(1.01)	9.81	8.80

	Corporate Securities		
			Total
Year	Principal	Interest	Return
1980	(10.61)%	10.29%	(0.32)%
1981	(9.53)	12.27	2.74
1982	21.07	16.10	37.17
1983	(2.58)	11.50	8.92
1984	3.00	13.08	16.08
1985	12.07	12.93	25.00
1986	6.41	10.62	17.03
1987	(7.06)	9.12	2.06
1988	(0.31)	9.76	9.45

Source: Salomon Brothers, Inc. Reprinted with permission.

month, next year or any time. But the least that fund managers can do is try to keep their NAV as stable as feasible within the constraints of their duration/maturity policies.

MAINTAINING PRINCIPAL

For both investors who take dividends in cash and those who may one day do so, it's important to know how much fund managements try to maintain their principal. Table 5-8 shows how well the various bond fund categories have done in the three, five and ten years ended in 1988. The first three columns show the groups' average annual total returns after reinvestment of dividend and capital gains distributions—data calculated similarly to those used earlier in this chapter. The last three columns show what happened to principal after dividends were taken out in cash (but any capital gains distributions were reinvested).

The groups are ranked in order of return on principal for the three years ended in 1988. You'll quickly realize that virtually all fund groups, except those linked to common stocks or those having shorter maturities, lose some principal, on the average, over time. The larger losses apparently were experienced by funds invested in government-guaranteed or government-related mortgage securities and by high-yield funds. Municipal bond funds, on the whole, fared better than taxable funds.

Within each group, of course, there were better-than-average as well as worse-than-average performers. Groups that showed a reduction in principal, such as the corporate, general, high-yield, GNMA and U.S. government securities funds, included some funds whose principal rose. Fund groups whose average principal went up included funds whose principal went up by appreciably more than the averages.

The case for maintaining principal stability takes on even greater significance when the figures are compared with the behavior of the con-

Table 5–8   Annual Rates of Return with and Without Reinvested Dividends for Periods Ended in 1988 by Fund Categories

Category	Total Reinvestment			Principal Only		
	3 Years	5 Years	10 Years	3 Years	5 Years	10 Years
Convertible	7.3%	10.1%	14.9%	1.2%	3.5%	7.4%
Short-Intermediate	7.0	9.7	—	0.5	1.7	—
Flexible	9.1	12.5	11.9	0.0	2.1	1.4
Corporate BBB	8.2	11.6	10.3	(0.8)	1.2	(0.8)
Intermediate	7.1	10.4	10.4	(1.0)	0.6	(0.2)
U.S. Government	6.9	10.0	10.5	(1.4)	(0.5)	(0.5)
Corporate A	7.3	11.3	10.4	(1.6)	1.3	(0.8)
General Bond	7.4	11.4	10.4	(2.2)	0.5	(0.9)
U.S. Mortgage	6.8	10.1	9.4	(2.3)	(0.8)	(1.0)
GNMA	6.7	10.4	8.5	(2.8)	(0.4)	(2.6)
High-Yield	8.8	10.6	11.5	(3.4)	(1.8)	(1.5)
World Income	NA	17.6	—	NA	NA	—
Balanced	NA	13.1	14.5	NA	NA	NA
General Municipal	9.3	11.6	7.9	1.7	3.2	(0.7)
Insured Municipal	9.0	10.8	8.0	1.6	2.6	(0.4)
High-Yield Municipal	9.4	10.7	9.0	1.1	2.1	2.3
Intermediate	7.2	8.5	7.1	0.7	1.3	(0.5)
Short-Intermediate	5.7	6.6	6.4	0.1	0.4	0.4
CPI	3.3	3.5	5.9	3.3	3.5	5.9

Source: Lipper Analytical Services.

sumer price index (bottom line). When all distributions were reinvested, each group average had a positive real (i.e., inflation-adjusted) return for each of three periods. But when income distributions were taken in cash, even the groups with positive average returns didn't have positive real returns.

To point this out is not to suggest that only bond funds were, or are, vulnerable to inflation's bite. Even the highest quality debt securities are not immune, as anyone who has bought a Treasury note or bond realizes. No review of the performance of fixed-income investments during the 1980s—whether bond funds or any other—is complete without mentally, if not literally, adjusting for the inflation that was so debilitating. Given the realities of our time, no planning for the 1990s is complete without bearing the ever-present potential of inflation in mind.

ENDNOTES

1. Duration is the weighted-average life of a portfolio, calculated on the basis of the present value of future interest payments and principal repayments. Because it is based on the timing of these cash flows, many regard duration as a more significant measure than weighted-average maturity of a portfolio's potential volatility in response to changes in interest rates.
2. Until mid-1989, Lipper had combined these government and investment-grade funds into two groups: short-intermediate and intermediate taxable bond funds.
3. A fund that was primarily invested in them, Municipal Lease Securities Fund, outperformed all other short municipal funds with an average total return of 7.1 percent for the three years ended September 1989. Two months later, the SEC ordered it to suspend redemptions "because it appeared to the Commission that it was not reasonably practicable for the Fund to determine the value of its net assets." Prospects for the fund and its shareholders were uncertain at year's end.

CHAPTER 6

Do Bond Funds Belong in Your Portfolio?

Having reviewed the increase in the volume of government and corporate debt securities being issued, as well as the growth and performance of the various types of mutual funds that invest in them, you're probably wondering whether you should buy shares in bond funds. If you already own such shares, you may be wondering whether you should hold them or switch to other funds.

Before you can answer either question, you really need to ask yourself whether *any* type of debt securities is appropriate for you. And that question can't be properly answered before you ask yourself a more fundamental one: can debt securities contribute to your investment strategy?

DEVELOPING AN INVESTMENT STRATEGY

Since bond funds are simply an indirect—and usually desirable—way of owning marketable debt securities, it's critical to determine whether you should be buying these instruments in the first place. As we've seen in earlier chapters, marketable debt instruments—whether those of the United States Treasury, a multi-billion-dollar corporation, or your city or school district—have basic elements in common. They're all essentially IOU notes, promising to pay a stated rate of interest (known as the coupon rate) at regular intervals and to repay the principal on a stated maturity date. Further, they can be bought or sold at any time.

Debt securities have fixed face values, called par, but not fixed market values. As their market values fluctuate with market interest rates in the period between their issuance and maturity, so do their yields. That's because the constant amount of interest they pay annually rises and falls as a percent of market values. Their market values can, and do, swing from discount to premium, or vice versa, until they are eventually redeemed at par—unless, of course, they're called before maturity.

Marketable debt securities are very different from interest-bearing financial assets, such as banks' certificates of deposit (CDs), whose principal value and yields remain fixed and whose redemption before maturity may result in a penalty.

CDs, savings accounts and savings bonds that are insured or backed by the U.S. government are suitable for savings, and savings come first. Before you think of investing in any marketable securities (other than Treasury bills) whose value can fall below your cost, you'll want to be sure that you have enough money in savings with *no doubt* about its access and safety. How much is enough? That's up to you. It should suffice to tide you over an emergency—such as job loss or a costly illness—by providing living expenses for whatever period seems appropriate.

In considering how much of your money should be in savings and where you ought to have it, there are at least two points you'll want to keep in mind:

1. You pay a price for safety, whether provided by federal deposit insurance or the federal government's promise to pay its own obligations: the types of financial assets that involve the lowest risk tend to offer the lowest interest rates.

2. The safest assets may free you from worry about loss of principal (although the failure of a bank or savings and loan association may cause you inconvenience) but not from worry about inflation. The principal you salt away in a CD or savings account will lose purchasing power (just as will the principal of a marketable security). So will the interest payments: the $550 you get for putting $10,000 in a 5.5 percent account will not buy in the second year what it will in the first.

There's little you can do about these relatively low yields and inflation concerns other than to choose the highest-yielding but *safe* vehicle(s) for your savings. Even if their rates do fluctuate, taxable or tax-exempt money market mutual funds provide a highly desirable means of earning interest close to market levels—and thus higher than inflation—but they are not *absolutely* risk-free. Their record has been solid, however, and they generally involve so little risk that you may wish to use a prudently managed one for a portion of your savings.

If you're still working, have money left over after you've taken care of your savings requirements and are going to be able regularly to put money aside after providing for living expenses, you can think about investing in securities. You may want to use the money to accumulate a lump sum by some future year to (1) enable you to finance a major expenditure, (2) generate additional retirement income to supplement your expected pension and Social Security checks or (3) satisfy some other goal. Or you may want to supplement your income.

If you're in or close to retirement, you may want to invest a sum you already have available, or will be getting, to produce additional income at a rate that is stable or, ideally, will grow with inflation.

You can achieve either goal—the accumulation of capital or the production of income, or both—by investing in a diversified portfolio of securities. How much of it should consist of debt securities and how much of equities depends on the goal you choose and, for accumulation, the time you have to attain it.

If you're building capital, you'll want to invest in a mix of financial assets whose combined rate of total return (i.e., including reinvestment of income) can be expected to provide the growth you require. While you should be able to rely on common stocks to supply most of the growth over time, their short-run volatility makes it prudent not to rely on them exclusively—especially if your plan is for too short a period. The stock market could be down just when you had planned to use the money.

To reduce your exposure to the risks inherent even in a diversified list of blue chip stocks, portions of your assets should be allocated to debt securities and cash equivalents. How you allocate the assets is a function not only of their and your expected returns but also of your ability and willingness to accept market risk. The more time—and patience—you have for your money to work for you, the more you should be able to accept the volatility inherent in a growth-oriented portfolio.

If you have any doubt about the desirability of asset allocation, look at Tables 6–1 and 6–2, which illustrate the range of annual returns for

Table 6–1   High and Low Rates of Total Return for Principal Financial Assets, 1979–1988

Asset Category	Highest Rate	Year	Lowest Rate	Year
Common stocks	32.4%	1980	(4.9)%	1981
High-yield bonds*	36.6	1982	6.5	1987
Long-term corporate bonds	43.8	1982	(4.2)	1979
Long-term government bonds	40.3	1982	(4.0)	1980
Intermediate government bonds	29.1	1982	2.9	1987
Treasury bills	14.7	1981	5.5	1987
Consumer Price Index	*13.3*	*1979*	*1.1*	*1986*

*Not available for 1979–80.

Sources: Common stocks, corporate bonds, government bonds and Treasury bills, Ibbotson and Sinquefield, *op. cit.;* high-yield bonds, *First Boston High-Yield Handbook,* First Boston Corporation; December to December changes in CPI, Bureau of Labor Statistics, U.S. Department of Labor.

Table 6–2   Leading and Lagging Financial Assets, Annual Total Returns by Years, 1979–1988

Year	Best Performing Category		Worst Performing Category		Increase in Consumer Price Index
1979	Common stocks	18.4%	Long-term corp. bonds	(4.2)%	13.3%
1980	Common stocks	32.4	Long-term govt. bonds	(4.0)	12.5
1981	Treasury bills	14.7	Common stocks	(4.9)	8.9
1982	Long-term corp. bonds	43.8	Treasury bills	10.5	3.8
1983	Common stocks	22.5	Long-term govt. bonds	0.7	3.8
1984	Long-term corp. bonds	16.4	Common stocks	6.3	3.9
1985	Common stocks	32.2	Treasury bills	7.7	3.8
1986	Long-term govt. bonds	24.4	Treasury bills	6.2	1.1
1987	High-yield bonds	6.5	Long-term govt. bonds	(2.7)	4.4
1988	Common stocks	16.8	Intermediate govt. bonds	6.1	4.4

Sources: Common stocks, Treasury bills, corporate bonds and government bonds, Ibbotson and Sinquefield, *op. cit.;* high-yield bonds (1981–88), First Boston Corporation, *op. cit.;* December to December changes in consumer price index, Bureau of Labor Statistics, U.S. Department of Labor.

major asset categories and their oscillation from being top performers to bottom performers and back again.

If you have any doubt about your ability to allocate your assets, be sure to look for the next appearance in *The Wall Street Journal* of the periodic table comparing the variety of asset allocation strategies of the nation's largest brokerage firms and the range of results they achieved. Seeing how their well-known money managers have disagreed—and how poorly some of them fared—you should feel less reluctant to try your hand. If necessary or desirable, you're always able to change your allocation.

If generation of income is your objective, you'll want to invest in financial assets that can be relied on to provide the level of income you're aiming at. In all likelihood this will mean debt securities but, even if you're retired, not necessarily debt securities alone. Given their vulnerability to inflation's bite and the fluctuation of interest rates, some allocation to equities may also be called for. Since dividends grow over time with corporate earnings, dividend-paying stocks of strong corporations should help your portfolio's income to grow—and provide some appreciation besides.

Whatever your goal, try to figure out how you can attain it, given your age, employment/income situation, the amount of money you have (or will have) for investing, and your ability or willingness to tolerate risks. A pocket calculator or compound interest table may be necessary. Until you get your hands on one, Tables 6–3 through 6–5 may provide some general guidance. They'll give you an idea of how many years of compounding at various rates it can take to develop a one-time investment or annual investments into a targeted amount or how much has to be invested at various rates of return to earn a specific amount annually.

When you reckon what rate of return or total return (including reinvestment of interest and dividends) it would take to realize your goals, you'll see whether your goals are realistic and, if so, what investment mix is called for.

We know from data, such as those calculated by Ibbotson Associates, that Treasury bills (a form of cash equivalent) have produced an average annual total return of 3.5 percent since 1926 but around 9 percent in the ten years ended with 1988. Long-term U.S. government bonds have provided returns of 4.4 percent and 10.6 percent, respectively, for the same periods. Stocks, as measured by the S&P 500 index, have grown at around 10 percent per year over the long period, but at around 16 percent in more recent years.

No one—not the chairman of the Federal Reserve, a brokerage firm economist, a newsletter editor or a radio/TV personality—can tell you what rates of return will be provided by these financial assets during the period you want your money to work for you. Perhaps the most practical thing you can do is formulate a strategy based on what seem to be reasonable rates. If, for example, you can achieve your objective with a long-run pre-tax return rate of around five percent, you may want to take little or no risk and stay with CDs, money market funds, Treasury bills (the latter require a minimum investment of $10,000) or short-term Treasury notes (which require a minimum of $5,000). For a total return of up to 7.5 percent or so, you'll also want debt securities with longer maturities, such as intermediate-term Treasury notes, plus a dash of high-yield, high-grade stocks. Beyond that, you should consider more common stocks and long-term government or investment-grade corporate fixed-

---

Table 6–3   Years Required To Accumulate $100,000

Investment	Years Compounding at				
	5%	7.5%	10%	12.5%	15%
$ 2,500	75.6	51.0	44.6	31.3	26.4
5,000	61.4	41.4	31.4	25.4	21.4
7,500	53.1	35.8	27.2	22.0	18.5
10,000	47.2	31.8	24.2	19.6	16.5
12,500	42.6	28.8	21.8	17.7	14.9
15,000	38.9	26.2	19.9	16.1	13.6

Note: No provision is made for income taxes.

Table 6–4 Years of Annual Investments Required To Accumulate $100,000

Annual Amount	5%	7.5%	Compounded at 10%	12.5%	15%
$ 2,500	22.5	19.2	16.9	15.2	13.9
5,000	14.2	12.7	11.5	10.6	9.9
7,500	10.5	9.6	8.9	8.3	7.9
10,000	8.3	7.7	7.3	6.9	6.6
12,500	6.9	6.5	6.2	5.9	5.6
15,000	5.9	5.6	5.4	5.2	5.0

Note: No provision is made for income taxes.

income securities, and plan to reinvest at least a portion of your income so that you can benefit from compounding.

Although significantly higher total returns were achieved on stocks and bonds during periods in the 1980s, the odds are against earning such amounts over a long period. Therefore, if your plan calls for a high return, you may want to think of moderating your goal, stretching the time to its realization, and/or investing more money. Reaching for a high return could involve taking more risk than is wise.

These are obviously only broad suggestions; they need to be adapted to your situation. Among other things, income tax rates need to be taken into consideration, unless you're planning to invest only in an IRA or other tax-sheltered program. Thus, to actually earn five percent in annual income, you may need to think in terms of tax-exempt securities yielding in that range. To build capital at an average annual rate of ten percent, you need a rate of total return, reflecting reinvestment of taxable income, that's a bit higher. If your accumulation of a large lump sum depends in part on the realization of capital gains, you must also remember your potential capital gains tax liability.

Table 6–5 Investment Required To Earn $1,000 Annually

Interest Rate	Investment
5%	$20,000
6%	16,667
7%	14,286
8%	12,500
9%	11,111
10%	10,000

Note: No provision is made for income taxes.

THE REWARDS OF OWNING DEBT SECURITIES

If it appears that you should invest mostly or partly in debt securities, you'll first want to be aware of their principal disadvantages as well as their advantages. The potential rewards follow first.

Reliable Income Flow.   You invest in a debt security—bond, note, debenture or other—primarily to obtain a predictable flow of income that you can rely on for a certain number of years. Frequency of payments—semiannual, quarterly, monthly—may be important, but reliability is crucial. You are most likely to obtain this by confining yourself to securities issued by governments or corporations that can be expected to maintain interest payments without fail.

Higher Income.   The rate of income—that is, the yield, or return on investment—is normally higher for marketable debt securities having (1) longer maturities or (2) lower credit ratings. There may be exceptions to (1) in periods when the yield curve is not normal. There are *no* exceptions to (2).

In theory, common stocks, which, after all, are riskier investments, should offer higher yields than bonds. Not many people can remember when they last did.[1]

Tax Exemption.   Income from certain governmental bonds is exempt from certain income taxes. Interest on state and local government bonds is exempt from federal income tax; it also may be exempt from state and local income taxes. (Tax-exempt interest is not always lower than the after-tax interest on taxable securities of comparable maturity and quality. It depends on yield spreads and a taxpayer's bracket.) Interest on federal securities is exempt from state and local taxes (but not from federal tax).

Potential for Capital Gains.   Because prices of outstanding bonds rise when interest rates fall, it is possible that you could sell bonds for more than you paid for them—that is, realize capital gains instead of holding them to maturity. Of course, you won't be able to generate the same amount of income by replacing what you sold with new bonds because lower rates will prevail. Opportunities to realize sizable capital gains from the sale of bonds do occur from time to time and can be very profitable, but they are not frequent enough to permit you to make long-range plans based on their regular occurrence.

Lower Volatility. Bonds do not consistently fluctuate in step with stocks—at times they move in opposite directions—and tend to be less volatile than stocks. Therefore, the allocation of some assets to bonds should make a growth-oriented portfolio less volatile than if it were invested only in stocks. Of course, it also is likely to moderate the portfolio's rate of growth.

THE RISKS OF OWNING DEBT SECURITIES

Owning debt securities isn't all reward. It also entails risks, as mentioned in earlier chapters and recapped here.

Interest Rate Risk. The flip side of the potential for capital gains is the potential for capital losses. When interest rates rise, bond prices fall. If you buy a bond at par and intend to hold it until maturity, this shouldn't make any difference. If you buy a bond at a premium, however, there's no assurance you can avoid a loss.

An actual example, using U.S. Treasury notes, will illustrate the interest rate risk that is common to all debt securities. In November, 1978, the Treasury issued ten-year notes bearing 8 3/4 percent coupons. In November, 1988, when they matured, the Treasury issued new ten-year notes bearing 8⁷/₈ percent coupons. The coincidental similarity in coupon rates could indicate to a neophyte that interest rates were essentially stable over the decade. Anyone who bought one of the notes for $1,000 in 1978 and cashed it in for $1,000 at maturity, however, will recall that rates were anything but stable. The price of the notes slumped to $708.75 in September, 1981, and soared to $1,055.63 in August, 1986, according to DRI/McGraw-Hill, before drifting back to par in 1988.

Clearly, careful planning is essential. To reduce the risk of loss that may be incurred when one has to sell before maturity to raise cash, one shouldn't buy a bond with a longer maturity than is appropriate to one's circumstances.

Credit Risk. The risk that an issuer will default on payment of interest or principal is accepted when buying any domestic debt security other than those backed by the full faith and credit of the U.S. government. Credit risk is minimized with issues of corporations, state and local governments whose expected ability to make payments on schedule has been checked by Moody's, Standard & Poor's or other competent analysts, or with issues that are covered by insurance. Risk is maximized with issues that have been given a low credit rating and with a number of obligations that are not rated. (Some issuers, for one reason or another, don't apply for ratings.)

Inflation Risk. Even if the interest rate for a newly issued marketable security is above the current inflation rate—and provides you a real rate of return—the purchasing power of your future interest payments drops over the life of the bond, as will the purchasing power of your bond's principal. Table 6–6 shows what would happen to the purchasing power of a ten-year bond in the case of a 4 percent inflation rate that is (unrealistically) assumed to remain constant. Regardless of actual interim fluctuations in inflation and the bond's market value, a compound average inflation rate of 4 percent would result in a 33.5 percent fall in purchasing power by the end of the tenth year. A 5 percent inflation rate would result in a 40.1 percent drop. And so on.

Event Risk. This risk, widespread in the latter 1980s, is that the creditworthiness of a corporation would be jeopardized by an event that raises doubts about its ability to service debt out of earnings. Whether an acquisition, leveraged buyout (LBO), disaster, court award of damages or some other event, the consequences are similar: debt expands sharply, earnings are slashed or both. The company's outstanding bonds are downgraded, their prices fall—but their yields rise—and they may be disqualified as investments for certain investors (such as investment-grade bond funds).

Reinvestment Risk. The right of corporations and state and local governments to call their securities after certain periods obliges investors to reinvest at lower yields. This, of course, necessitates a downward revision of expected current income for the years until a called issue's maturity.

Table 6–6   Impact of Constant Four Percent Inflation Rate on a Ten-Year Bond

End of	Face Value	Constant Dollar Value	Fall in Purchasing Power
Year 1	$10,000	$9,600	(4.0)%
Year 2	10,000	9,216	(7.8)
Year 3	10,000	8,847	(11.5)
Year 4	10,000	8,494	(15.1)
Year 5	10,000	8,154	(18.5)
Year 6	10,000	7,828	(21.7)
Year 7	10,000	7,515	(24.9)
Year 8	10,000	7,214	(27.9)
Year 9	10,000	6,925	(30.8)
Year 10	10,000	6,648	(33.5)

Similar circumstances can arise with investments in Ginnie Mae or other mortgage-backed securities. When interest rates fall, homeowners are more likely to prepay mortgages, lifting the rate at which monthly principal repayments are passed through to securities holders. When this money is reinvested, it also has to be put to work at lower rates, which again can upset income expectations.

ADVANTAGES OF BOND FUNDS

If, after looking at the pros and cons, you conclude that your investment portfolio ought to include debt securities, you have to decide whether to own them directly, indirectly or both ways. Each approach has its advantages and disadvantages.

While indirect ownership is feasible through interests in three major types of investment companies—mutual funds, closed-end funds (sometimes called publicly traded funds) and unit investment trusts (UITs)— we'll concentrate on mutual funds. As many people have realized, they provide investors benefits that are not duplicated by closed-end funds or UITs and don't have some of their drawbacks.

The advantages of owning debt securities via bond mutual funds, instead of owning them directly, may be familiar to you because they're similar to those offered by money market and stock mutual funds, but we'll review them briefly to make sure you're aware of all that funds offer.

Diversification. No attribute of mutual funds is more important than the diversification they conveniently afford individual investors, regardless of how much or how little they're investing. Diversification to help reduce the risk of a sharp drop in a bond's price in the event of an issue's downgrading, or possibly of total loss in case of default, is crucial to anyone who invests in non-guaranteed or non-insured securities.

Even when buying U.S. government bonds or notes and not having to worry about credit risks, it still is desirable—if not essential—to reduce market risk by investing in diverse maturities (unless, of course, you know when you want your money and are able to select the appropriate maturity in an ordinary Treasury issue or zero coupon obligation.)

Since most people cannot invest enough money to buy a diversified list of debt securities on their own, mutual funds make a lot of sense. For as little as $1,000—the same amount as the minimum denomination of many (but not all) individual bonds—a bond fund provides instant diversification among issuers or, in the case of the U.S. government, among issues. Some funds have even lower minimum initial investment requirements—especially for IRAs—or none at all; few have minimums exceeding $3,000. And once an account is opened, subsequent investments, maintaining the same diversification, can usually be made for $100 or less.

Professional Management.   If, like most investors, you're occupied with work and other activities, you probably don't have the time it takes to acquire and properly manage a diversified portfolio of bonds. Even if you could spare the time, it is unlikely that you would have the requisite knowledge and be able to command the statistical and analytical resources available to portfolio managers of bond funds.

Proper management of a bond portfolio requires: knowing which issues of which issuers to buy or sell; when to buy or sell; how to buy or sell at the most favorable prices; how to adjust a portfolio's weighted average maturity or duration; how to adjust its average credit quality; how to hedge prudently against interest rate changes; how to maximize protection against calls and how to conduct research to check the credit quality of both rated and unrated bonds—to name a few of a manager's responsibilities.

Surely there can be little doubt that these requirements indicate the need for competent professionals who can discern opportunities in the undulation of yield curves or yield spreads. You can better devote your time and talent to choosing the professionals and monitoring their performance as they manage their (your) portfolios. (The same could be said of closed-end bond funds but not of UITs, which are invested in relatively fixed portfolios that are supervised but not really managed.)

Ease of Entry and Exit.   Given the generally low minimum initial and subsequent investments, it is more feasible for most individual investors to acquire an indirect interest in a diversified portfolio of debt securities via a bond fund than to buy the securities directly. You also can get out of funds quickly when you want, in contrast with some bonds for which markets may be illiquid. Whether dealing directly with a fund organization through its toll-free 800 telephone number and the mail or indirectly through a broker or other sales person, it's usually easy to obtain the necessary prospectuses, shareholder reports and other information you need to decide which bond fund(s) to choose. If you're dealing directly, it's also easy to buy shares by mail or wire or to exchange for shares from another fund within a fund family (thereby possibly incurring taxable capital gains on shares being disposed of). A number of funds provide automatic investment plans, in which your bank account is debited directly, making it convenient to pursue dollar cost averaging. When you're dealing directly with a fund and you want to redeem shares, all it takes is a phone call if you've requested the telephone redemption option ahead of time. You can get your money by mail or by wire. You also may be able to establish automatic withdrawal, whereby money is regularly credited to your bank account, or to take advantage of a fund's free check writing option. No matter how you redeem, you'll always want to remember the possible tax consequences.

Transaction Costs. There are many bond mutual funds whose shares you can buy directly from the fund organizations—and can redeem when the time comes—without paying anyone a sales charge, or load. These no-load funds put *all* of your money to work. When they buy and sell bonds in your behalf, they usually are able to negotiate very low brokerage commissions or dealer's markups. On the other hand, when you buy individual debt securities, you always have to pay commissions, markups or fees at higher individual rates—unless you're buying Treasury securities from the Treasury's Bureau of Public Debt or a Federal Reserve Bank. (Load funds, of course, involve front-end charges at rates as high as 8.5 percent or deferred sales charges up to 5 percent when redeeming—in addition to the transaction costs incurred by the funds. Closed-ends and UITs involve commissions, too.)

Ease of Receiving and Reinvesting Income. When you own bonds directly, you typically receive interest payments every six months. Many bond funds, however, offer income distributions every month or every three months, frequencies that many investors seem to prefer.

Investors who want to reinvest their income from bonds can do so much more easily with bond mutual funds. Unlike bonds, whose denominations of $1,000 or more make reinvestment difficult for all but the largest holders, bond funds have no minimum for reinvesting the income distributions. And the funds take care of reinvestment for you, automatically, if you've advised them that's what you want them to do. Even fractional shares can be purchased—and usually are, inasmuch as distributions rarely equal the exact prices of whole fund shares.

DISADVANTAGES OF BOND FUNDS

There are some disadvantages to owning debt securities via bond mutual funds instead of directly, but for many people they are far outweighed by the advantages. You must form your own judgment.

No Specific Maturity. Bond funds have no specific maturity, except for the handful of target funds. This means that in planning your financial strategy, you cannot count on a fund's shares to have a certain value by a specified date in some future year.

A fund with a policy of maintaining a weighted average maturity of five years or 25 years will still be maintaining such average five or 25 years from now unless (1) it changes its investment policy—something you'd be informed about and might have to vote on—or (2) market conditions at the time call for a temporary adjustment. It does so simply by turning over its portfolio.

Transaction Costs.   Sales charges on purchases of shares in front-end load funds may run as high as 8.5 percent and contingent deferred sales charges on other funds may run as much as 5 percent if you don't hold the shares long enough. Thus, they may be higher than the commissions imposed on purchases of individual debt securities. But that alone should not persuade you to bypass funds; go for no-load funds that meet your criteria.

Annual Fees.   Unless you use an investment adviser or other consultant, you don't pay anyone an annual fee to manage your portfolio when you buy and sell your own securities.

When you buy shares in a mutual fund, however, you have to pay a fee for the professional management that attracted you to the fund in the first place. There also are other, minor costs for such items as record-keeping, accounting and custody. You don't actually mail in a check for these services. The amount is simply subtracted from income prior to the mailing or crediting of income distributions. A number of funds also impose so-called 12b-1 distribution charges, but you don't have to invest in them; there are plenty of good funds that don't.

The total annual fee doesn't have to be high. For very fine funds, it can run from as little as 0.5 percent (or less) to around 1.0 percent of average net assets. You need not even consider funds whose expenses run as high as 2 percent or more. (Closed-end funds' expenses also run around 1 percent or less. Being unmanaged, UITs involve no management fees; sponsor, trustee and evaluator fees, however, total around 0.2 percent per year.)

Largely because of the management and other operating expenses, even well-managed bond funds that are essentially invested in one class of securities are inclined to have slightly lower total returns over time than unmanaged indices for such securities (assuming reinvestment of distributions in both cases). As noted by Dr. Jacob S. Dreyer, chief economist of the Investment Company Institute, the lag is exacerbated by the cash balances that funds maintain to accommodate redemptions and which, when the yield curve is normal, may earn interest that's one percent (or more) less than what bonds earn. (Investors in funds with front-end or back-end loads, of course, experience even greater lags than investors in no-load funds, all other things being equal. So do those with high expenses.)

On the other hand, total returns of the better-managed, homogeneous bond funds tend to be less volatile than the unmanaged indices for the classes of securities in which they're concentrated. That's because their managers try to achieve reasonable stability of principal by taking defensive measures when bond prices are falling and by engaging in tactics to enhance total return when bond prices are rising. In some periods, they may even offset operating expenses and match the performance of the indices.

Considering what you can get for your money, therefore, you may regard 0.5 percent to 1.0 percent of assets as a reasonable price to pay each year for good mutual fund management.

ENDNOTES

1. Moody's Aaa corporate bond yield average went ahead of the yield on Standard & Poor's 500 Stock Index in 1959 (4.38 percent vs. 3.23 percent).

C H A P T E R   7

Finding and Investing in the Fund(s) Right for You

By now, you know the pros and cons of bonds and bond funds. Your financial strategy indicates the need to invest in, say, one or two bond funds. How do you decide *which* one or two would be right for you, and, having decided, how do you go about investing? We'll try to provide answers in this chapter.

You *won't* find recommendations of specific funds. A fund that's right for you may not be right for another reader with different requirements. Moreover, a fund that might have been recommendable when this book went to press could have changed its investment objective, investment adviser or portfolio manager by the time you read this. Such change might have made it inadvisable to invest in the fund.

What you *will* find are the major criteria that you can apply, on your own, for selecting (1) fund categories and (2) funds within the categories. You'll see that this need not be difficult. You can do it with a modest amount of effort at little or no cost. The better you master fund selection, the less surprised you'll be by fund performance when your money is at risk.

To be your own bond fund adviser you have to understand, remember and act on the basis of some simple, fundamental principles. Perhaps the two most important ones are:

1. Whether you plan to take income dividends in cash or to reinvest them, a bond fund should be chosen on the basis of its expected rate of *total return*, calculated to reflect increases (decreases) in net asset value (NAV) plus reinvestment of dividends and any capital gains distributions—*not on the basis of the dividend rate*. Funds managed to maximize income instead of total return may take excessive risks,

jeopardizing principal. Table 7-1 shows the negative or low rates of total return suffered in the 12 months ended in September 1989, by all of the funds that had the highest rates of income distribution that year (excluding special situations). For those in operation at least five years, the table also shows their average annual rates of total return for that period.

Table 7-1   Leaders in Current Yield*

Fund	Yield for 12 Months Ended Sept. 1989	Total Return 12 Months Ended Sept. 1989	1984–1989 Avg. Annual Total Return
Dean Witter High Yield	18.1%	(4.22)%	8.6%
American Capital High Yield	15.7	(4.00)	9.2
Venture Income (+) Plus	15.5	0.77	7.9
MacKay-Shields High Yield	15.0	3.04	—
Security Income High Yield	15.0	1.59	—
Kemper Diversified Income**	14.7	13.75	7.5
Alliance Bond High-Yield	14.7	(1.97)	—
First Investors Bond Appreciation	14.7	(8.04)	5.3
AIM High Yield	14.4	2.64	8.0
Keystone B-4	14.4	1.05	7.7
Executive Investors High Yield	14.3	5.13	—
Maxus Fund	14.2***	10.57	—
(Franklin) AGE High Income	14.2	4.96	10.8
Pacific Horizon High Yield	14.2	4.01	11.2
Federated High Yield	14.1	6.40	12.0
Putnam High Yield	14.1	5.96	11.7
(Kemper) Investment Portfolios Diversified Income**	14.0	11.25	—
First Investors Fund for Income	14.0	2.98	8.7
United High Income	14.0	2.22	10.8
PaineWebber High Yield	13.9	3.67	10.1
SLH High Yield	13.9	2.27	10.6
Northeast Investors Trust	13.8	4.82	13.8
Van Kampen Merritt High Yield	13.8	2.79	—
Transamerica High Yield	13.8	(0.71)	—
National Bond	13.8	(1.45)	6.6

*Yields reflect income distributions divided by September 30, 1989, net asset values per share (adjusted for any capital gains distributions) and may differ from 30-day annualized yields calculated in compliance with SEC definition.
**Changed investment objective from option income to high yield in February 1989.
***Non-representative yield, attributable to change in dividend distribution policy during the 12 months.

Source: Lipper—Fixed Income Fund Performance Analysis, published by Lipper Analytical Services, Inc.; 1984–89 rates of return annualized by author.

2. Your expectation of targeted rates of total return over time should be based—as in the case of equity investments—on realistic targets and on probabilities of attainment, not certainty.

We'll first run through the three major factors involved in choosing the fund classification(s) that seem most suitable for you: exposure to income taxes; exposure to default, or credit quality; and exposure to interest rate risk, or maturity. Then we'll discuss the criteria for selecting one or more funds within the group(s).

Because you'll be considering fund categories in terms of the investment objective classifications used by Lipper Analytical Services, you'll want to scan Table 7–2 to become familiar with them. You may even want to insert a bookmark here so that you can easily refer to the table again.

TAX CONSIDERATIONS

The first thing to decide is whether federal, state and/or local income taxes are to be determining factors in your planning. Are you, or should you be, interested in a bond fund whose current income is taxable by one or more layers of government or in a fund whose income is partially or totally tax-exempt?

If you are thinking of a bond fund for an IRA or other tax-sheltered retirement account, you'll *only* want a taxable bond fund because the yields on taxable debt securities are higher for comparable credit quality and maturity than those on tax-exempts. While you should be concerned about the consistent superiority of a fund's total return, you can be indifferent about its absolute level of current income and its occasional realization and distribution of short-term or long-term capital gains. You won't have to worry about paying federal, state or local taxes until you take money out of the account. Then you'll pay on everything you take out (except for contributions you could not deduct), as you take it out, regardless of whether it's your principal, reinvested dividends or capital gains distributions, or net capital gains you've earned on your redemption of fund shares.

If you are investing outside a tax-sheltered context, you'll probably need to calculate whether you could earn a higher return on your investment in a taxable fund, after allowing for federal, state and local income taxes, or in a tax-exempt fund. Fund marketing executives say that many prospective investors who inquire about funds fail to think of the possibility that tax-exempt funds could be more profitable for them; they have the impression that tax-exempts are only for wealthier people. Others are attracted to tax-exempts, perhaps by ads pushing "triple tax-free

Table 7–2   Key Attributes of Lipper Bond Fund Classifications

TAXABLE	Credit Quality	Maturity	Other Factors
Short-Term U.S. Government	Highest	Short	
Short-Term Investment Grade	High	Short	
Intermediate U.S. Government	Highest	Intermediate	
Intermediate Investment Grade	High	Intermediate	
U.S. Government	Highest	Intermediate to long	
GNMA	Highest	Intermediate to long	Prepayment risk
U.S. Mortgage	High	Intermediate to long	Prepayment risk
Corporate A-Rated	High	Intermediate to long	
Corporate BBB-Rated	High	Intermediate to long	
General Bond	Varies	Intermediate to long	
High-Yield	Low	Intermediate	Vulnerability to recession
Convertible Securities	Varies	Intermediate	Link to Stocks
Flexible Income	—	—	Link to stocks
Balanced*	—	—	Link to stocks
World Income	Varies	Varies	Foreign yields, currencies
TAX-EXEMPT			
Short-Term Municipal	High	Short	
Intermediate Municipal	High	Intermediate	
General Municipal	High	Long	
Insured Municipal	Highest	Long	
High-Yield Municipal	Low	Intermediate	Vulnerability to economic weakness

*At least partly invested in bonds, but not regarded as bond funds.

income," when simple analysis would show that they'd be better off in taxable funds.

Because the relationships between taxable and tax-exempt securities' yields are continually changing, the only way to be sure which is more advantageous for you is to do the arithmetic. Although the focus in fund selection will be on total return, the calculation is based on the yield, reflecting distribution of fund income from interest-paying securities, regardless of whether the dividends are taken in cash or reinvested. Occasional capital gains distributions need not complicate the calculation because they are taxable whether made by taxable or tax-exempt funds.

One way to estimate the after-tax rate of current income is to take the average yield of a taxable fund group that you might be interested in and subtract the income tax you'd have to pay to the federal, state and local governments. (You may not have to pay state and local taxes on income distributions attributable to U.S. government securities. It depends largely on your state's tax law.) Then check whether a tax-exempt fund group of comparable credit quality and maturity would provide an equal, higher or lower income. Remember that your state and local governments may tax income distributions of municipal bond funds attributable to interest from securities of other states.

To illustrate, note that, according to Lipper, funds in the General Bond category had an average income distribution rate of 9.3 percent for the 12 months ended September 1989. This would leave someone in the 15 percent bracket with a return of 7.9 percent after federal taxes; 28 percent bracket, 6.7 percent; and 33 percent bracket, 6.2 percent. General Municipal bond funds had an average income distribution rate of 6.9 percent for the same period. Clearly, those in the 15 percent bracket would have more income by investing in the taxable group and paying the taxes. To calculate whether in the long run their total return would be higher, requires predicting the unpredictable: relative price fluctuations of taxable and tax-exempt securities.

Alternatively, you might be in the 28 percent bracket, see that General Municipal bond funds yield an average of 6.9 percent and wonder what would be the taxable equivalent yield that a taxable fund would have to pay to match that. You subtract .028 from 1.00 to obtain 0.72, then divide the 6.9 percent by 0.72. The result: 9.6 percent. For the 15 percent and 33 percent brackets, the taxable equivalent yields would be 8.1 percent and 10.3 percent, respectively.

Such rough comparison only gets you started, however (you'd also have to figure out the state and local taxes to have a more meaningful comparison), since you can't invest in a fund group average. You eventually will want to repeat the calculation with actual funds that appeal to you. If there are one or more single-state municipal bond funds available to you, you may want to include it (them) in your analysis.

CREDIT QUALITY CONSIDERATIONS

Knowing the approximate long-run rate of total return you expect of your bond fund(s), you can surmise the level of credit risk you'd have to accept to achieve it and aim at a fund category accordingly.

If you are concerned about credit risk and your required return is relatively low—that is, close to money market fund rates—you should be able to concentrate on funds invested in securities having the highest credit quality: U.S. Treasury issues, highest-grade corporates or insured municipals. Unless you only would be able to sleep at night if you were invested in a government bond fund—even though you know the government *does not guarantee* the fund's shares—you may wish to consider funds principally invested in high-quality corporates. Over time, you should be able to earn a slightly higher return without incurring great additional risk.

If your required return is 1–2 percent higher, you should be able to rely on funds invested in GNMA and other government agency securities, investment-grade corporates, a mix of governments and investment-grade corporates or highly rated municipals.

If your required return is still higher, and if you're considering taxable funds, you might also look to funds linked to the stock market as well as the bond market: flexible income, convertible securities or balanced funds. Investment in the taxable or tax-exempt high-yield fund categories may be indicated—but only for a portion of your bond fund assets.

Before checking on high-yield bond funds, you will want to ask yourself whether you are really able, and willing, to assume the risks incurred when investing (indirectly) in securities of lower than investment grade.

Remember, there is usually a reason for the lower credit ratings assigned to bonds in the high-yield category. Financial analysts, scrutinizing the issuers' financial statements and other pertinent information, have concluded that there is a reasonable doubt that the corporations or state or local governments will be able to pay interest and repay principal when scheduled. That doesn't mean that no investor should ever buy a low-grade bond, as investors have been doing since John Moody began to rate low-quality bonds many years ago. It does mean that only investors who understand the risks of default and can tolerate them should buy the bonds—and then only in batches large enough to provide some protection through diversification.

In no areas of investment do mutual funds epitomize the benefits of diversification more than in high-yield corporate and municipal bonds. One or two issues in a fund's portfolio can go into default, which, of course, will affect a fund's total return, but the consequences are not necessarily disastrous. If the portfolio is managed proficiently, it probably can absorb one or two defaults and still provide a higher return than would have been available from a higher-quality fund of the same fund family (i.e., one having similar operating expenses).

If you are uncomfortable with the risks inherent in high-yield bonds and bond funds, you may be well advised to stay with those that are concentrated in investment-grade debt securities and include a flexible income or balanced fund to boost your total return.

MATURITY CONSIDERATIONS

Given a normal credit market environment in which interest rates are higher for debt securities of long maturities than for short maturities—the relationship depicted by a yield curve with an upward slope (Figure 7-1)—you invest in long maturities to earn a higher current income and, consequently, higher total return. Interest rates—and the spreads among

Figure 7-1   Treasury Yield Curve

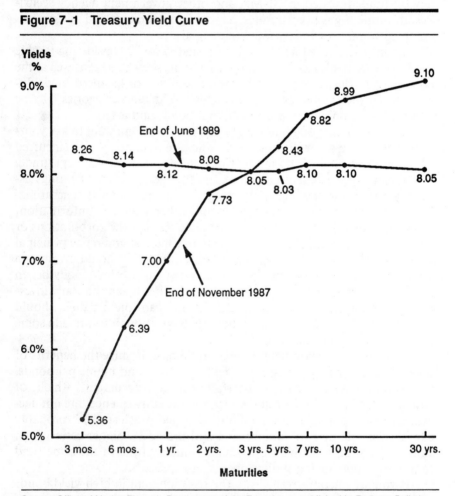

Source: Office of Market Finance, Department of the Treasury, as published in *Treasury Bulletin*.

yields of various maturities—are continually changing, however. Because longer durations cause prices of long bonds to rise or fall more in response to an identical rate change than those of short maturities, the longer bonds involve greater opportunity for capital gains when rates fall and greater risk of loss when rates rise.

While bond funds with longer average maturities may normally be expected to provide higher current income than funds of shorter maturities but identical credit quality, they also are normally more volatile. That's why it's prudent to base your bond fund investment decision on the number of years to expected redemption and your tolerance of volatility—and refrain from buying funds invested in maturities longer than appropriate. It should not matter whether you are accumulating capital and reinvesting distributions or investing for current income. In the latter case, given that there is always the possibility of having to invade principal to supplement income, you'd want to minimize the chance that you'll have to sell some shares while prices are in a cyclical decline.

Older individuals—especially those who are retired and rely on investments as primary or supplementary sources of cash—need to be aware of the risks of long maturities more than younger persons. People who are still employed are better able to cope with a drop in portfolio values because they can more easily afford to wait for bond prices to recover. Their wages or salaries tend to rise with inflation, just at the time that higher interest rates are likely to cause bond prices to drop. Moreover, if they're reinvesting and/or continuing to invest fresh money, they are picking up more shares at lower prices.

If you can't decide among short-,[1] intermediate- and long-term funds, you may find the intermediate group an acceptable compromise, at least for your first bond fund investment. Given a normal yield curve, intermediate-term funds may offer nearly as high a total return as long-term funds but with less volatility.

Or you may want to cull out for study funds that have no maturity restrictions and, instead, permit their managers to adjust weighted average maturities or duration targets as they see fit. Their performance records (see below) should indicate how well the managers have used their discretion.

Of course, if you prefer a fund that will mature in a specific year and want to avoid the risk of reinvesting interest income at lower rates, you could choose one of the zero coupon funds whose target maturity comes closest to your goal. Unlike investors in other bond funds, you could know roughly what your shares would be worth upon redemption in a specific future year and, thus, the rate of total return you could expect. Most likely, there will be volatility along the way, but it shouldn't matter; it's the ultimate value that counts. On the other hand, unless the fund is in an IRA or is a tax-exempt zero bond fund, you'd have to pay taxes on credited—but unreceived—income each year until maturity.

CHOOSING A CATEGORY

You're now ready to choose a category (Table 7–2) from which you'll be able to pick a fund that will reflect tax, credit quality, and maturity considerations in a way consistent with your investment goals. You may wish to study funds in a couple of categories having common denominators (e.g., GNMA and U.S. Mortgage, Corporate A-Rated and Corporate BBB-Rated).

The decisions you make—between taxable and tax-exempt, high and low credit risk, short-term and long-term maturity—should be based more on your expected return and risk tolerance than on current bond market conditions. The easiest way to compare your expectations with actual total return and yield data for the various taxable and tax-exempt categories is to look up the table "Lipper Fixed-Income Fund Performance Analysis," which appears in the quarterly mutual fund section of *Barron's*. (It appears in February, May, August and November.)

As you can see in Table 7–3, the table provides total return data (reflecting reinvestment of distributions) for the most recent quarter, year and five years—in this case, for periods ended September 1989—as well as the average 12-month rates of income dividends. (Total returns for the same five-year period for balanced and world income funds, which appeared in another table, were 109.27 percent and 127.53 percent, respectively.)

To make the five-year data more useful to you, you'll want to convert them to compound annual rates. If such conversions are not among your favorite pastimes, you may find Table 7–4 helpful. Annualized five-year rates not only will give you an idea as to how realistic your expectations are but they also will provide a benchmark against which the most recent year's numbers can be compared. A lower rate in the most recent year may raise a question as to whether the longer-run rate is sustainable; a higher recent rate may provide modest cause for encouragement but should not lead to undue optimism.

Table 7–5 illustrates why it's useful to go beyond a comparison of a five-year average and recent-year total return. The five-year average annual rate conceals the fluctuation to which bond funds are subject and which underscores the importance of knowing your risk tolerance and of investing for a number of years. Note, for example, the volatility of the averages for U.S. government and government-related funds, including a *negative* total return for USG funds in 1987, indicating a drop in principal exceeding the year's income. Note also how competitive the returns of

Table 7–3   Lipper Fixed-Income Fund Performance Analysis

Performance of Fixed-Income Fund Averages	9/30/89 Total Net Assets ($ Bil.)	Number of Funds	Total Reinvestment			Avg. 12 Mo. Yield
			% Chg. 6/30/89– 9/30/89	% Chg. 9/30/88– 9/30/89	% Chg. 9/30/84– 9/30/89	
Short-Term						
Money Market Instrument	238.61	267	2.10	8.75	42.18	8.4
Institutional Money Market	39.85	34	2.22	9.19	45.08	8.8
Short-Term U.S. Government	39.93	120	2.07	8.50	40.19	8.2
Institutional U.S. Government	33.91	36	2.16	8.90	43.41	8.6
Adjustable Rate Preferred	0.91	17	3.30	5.95	34.84	9.1
General S-T Tax-Exempt	53.87	138	1.39	5.86	26.75	5.7
California S-T Tax-Exempt	8.58	29	1.34	5.72	26.63	5.6
New York S-T Tax-Exempt	4.32	27	1.31	5.36	25.32	5.2
Other States S-T Tax-Exempt	3.43	18	1.44	5.94	25.78	5.8
	423.43	**686**				
Taxable						
Short U.S. Government	4.56	25	1.22	8.27	56.98	8.1
Short Inv Grade Debt	3.41	32	1.61	8.76	53.48	8.7
Intmdt. U.S. Government	1.65	24	0.81	8.42	66.70	7.9
Intmdt Inv Grade Debt	2.62	30	1.18	9.14	72.23	8.2
U.S. Government	49.23	138	0.58	9.92	67.39	8.5
GNMA	43.10	45	1.08	9.26	66.06	9.0
U.S. Mortgage	9.12	20	0.97	8.70	65.95	8.7
Corp. Bond—A Rated	8.46	42	0.73	10.32	78.15	8.7
Corp. Bond—BBB Rated	6.33	48	0.73	9.71	77.10	8.3
General Bond	6.17	19	0.39	8.72	74.43	9.3
High Current Yield Fds	32.76	88	–1.21	5.25	67.18	12.9
Convertible Securities	3.23	33	5.13	16.66	87.44	6.0
Flexible Income	2.46	20	2.12	11.63	88.83	8.9
Miscellaneous	0.17	4	1.44	7.08	88.03	9.5
	173.28	**568**				
Tax-Exempt						
Short Municipal	2.64	19	1.30	5.99	40.50	6.2
Intmdt Municipal	4.07	30	0.55	6.37	52.58	6.2
General Municipal	32.78	107	–0.38	8.60	75.73	6.9
Insured Municipal	7.73	24	–0.30	8.89	71.01	6.7
Hi-Yield Municipal	16.64	28	0.14	9.29	71.63	7.5
Single State Municipal	39.41	267				
	103.28	**475**				
Total	**699.99**	**1729**				

Source: *Lipper—Fixed Income Fund Performance Analysis,* as reported in *Barron's* Nov. 13, 1989 edition.

Table 7–4   Five-Year Performance Reckoner*

Cumulative Total Return for 5 Years	Value of $10,000 Invested 5 Years Ago	Compound Annual Return
25%	$12,500	4.56%
30	13,000	5.39
35	13,500	6.19
40	14,000	6.96
45	14,500	7.71
50	15,000	8.45
55	15,500	9.16
60	16,000	9.86
65	16,500	10.53
70	17,000	11.20
75	17,500	11.84
80	18,000	12.47
85	18,500	13.09
90	19,000	13.70
95	19,500	14.29
100	20,000	14.87

*Author's calculations.

tax-exempt funds can be and how often World Income funds are out of step with funds concentrated in domestic debt securities.

The current outlook for interest rates and the yield curve are less important in determining your category choice than your circumstances and your long-run strategy's requirements. That is because rates and curve shapes surely will fluctuate during the years that you plan to be invested. (If you're not planning to stay in for several years, you probably should stay with a money market fund. Remember Table 7–5!)

SCREENING FUNDS FOR HISTORIC PERFORMANCE

Once you've chosen a category (or two), you'll want to make your search manageable by screening the group, on the basis of historic performance, to identify five or six promising funds from which you ultimately may pick one.

A bond fund's historic performance does not guarantee future performance, whether good or bad. *No one* can predict or guarantee consistently superior future performance. But if historic performance data cover enough years to include periods of high and low interest rates, they provide an easily available gauge for measuring how well a fund has been managed through both favorable and unfavorable market conditions.

Table 7–5   The Volatility of Bond Funds: Annual Average Total Returns by Categories, 1984–1988

Investment Objective	1984	1985	1986	1987	1988	5-Year Annual Average
TAXABLE						
Convertible Securities	2.07%	23.72%	15.33%	(5.87)%	13.23%	11.46%
Corporate A-Rated	13.20	21.53	13.74	0.66	7.84	11.64
Corporate BBB-Rated	12.14	21.89	13.90	1.97	8.07	11.76
Flexible Income	12.18	23.07	15.79	(0.10)	11.67	13.06
GNMA	13.08	18.25	11.05	2.33	7.27	10.41
General Bond	12.67	20.75	13.26	1.71	8.61	11.49
High-Yield	7.77	21.25	12.46	1.47	12.54	11.25
Intermediate*	13.17	18.41	13.39	1.79	6.28	10.58
Short-Intermediate*	12.58	13.04	9.72	4.39	6.55	9.34
U.S. Government	11.76	17.15	14.55	(0.32)	6.88	9.79
U.S. Mortgage	12.76	18.68	10.82	2.21	7.33	10.53
World Income	2.34	29.67	30.17	20.94	4.78	16.90
Balanced	7.16	27.52	16.34	2.66	11.08	14.08
TAX-EXEMPT						
General Municipal	8.86	19.86	18.06	(1.04)	11.07	11.24
High-Yield Municipal	10.76	18.99	16.96	0.04	11.33	10.60
Insured Municipal	NA	NA	NA	NA	11.02	10.48
Intermediate Municipal	7.82	10.89	11.40	2.14	6.77	8.01
Short-Intermediate**	NA	NA	NA	NA	5.80	6.33

Sources: Taxable funds, Standard & Poor's/Lipper *Mutual Fund Profiles;* tax-exempts, *Lipper—Fixed-Income Fund Performance Analysis,* published by Lipper Analytical Services, Inc.

*Categories were split in 1989 into funds concentrated in U.S. government securities and those concentrated in investment-grade issues. "Short-intermediate" was changed to "Short-Term."
**Category renamed Short Municipal Bond Funds in 1989.

They tell you whether a fund has been a consistent performer or has had good years alternating with poor ones.

When you look at a fund's historic rate of total return together with a measure of its volatility, you can judge whether apparently strong performance was due more to skillful portfolio management or to excessive risk-taking combined with good luck. Funds that have had consistently above-average total returns over time while incurring moderate risk are worth a closer look. They are more likely to perform satisfactorily in the future, given the same management and policy, than funds that have had below-average total returns and have been inconsistent performers.

Thus, whether you're planning to take income distributions in cash or to reinvest them, your next step is to compile a list of funds that led your category in total return for the latest five years. You might list all the funds whose rates of return exceeded the group's average for the period or, if that would be too many, take the top five or six.

Be sure to look at performance over enough years to take in both favorable and unfavorable bond market conditions. Five years are widely regarded as sufficient for that purpose, and, for the same reason, data for five years are easily available. In the event that you're looking at a category in which only one or two funds have been in operation for five years, you may want to reduce the period to three. But don't be tempted to consider funds with shorter records, unless there's a compelling reason—such as the record of the portfolio manager at another fund. You don't want to risk your money on funds that haven't proven themselves.

When you've identified performance leaders for the period, you've only begun. You'll also want to determine whether the funds performed with reasonable consistency, year after year, in good markets and bad, or whether they took shareholders for greater-than-average roller coaster rides. Mathematically inclined investors check on the volatility of funds' returns by looking at their standard deviations. You may simply want to compare the yearly total returns of each leader with the Lipper average for the category for each of the five years, as listed in Table 7–5. If a fund matches or exceeds the group average for four out of five years, it deserves further scrutiny.

If while going through the data, you come across something unusual, such as a fund whose performance has been far ahead of its peers, it may be worthwhile to look into the situation. It could be, for example, that the fund has changed its investment objective or policy and has been reclassified by Lipper. The total return that drew your attention may be largely due to performance while aiming at a different objective, and, consequently, you should pass over the fund until it proves itself anew.

GETTING INFORMATION ON PERFORMANCE

Now that you know what to look for, how do you go about getting a list of top fund performers for the category(ies) in which you're interested? The easiest way to get the names would be to look them up in the most recent quarterly issue of *Lipper—Fixed Income Fund Performance Analysis* (LFIFPA). It may not be available to you, however, because its subscribers are primarily professional money managers.

Fortunately, there are alternatives. Lipper fund data also are disseminated at regular intervals in other publications[2] (at least four as this book went to press). Other media use data, grouped into fewer categories, from other services. You may find most or all of them in your library or, of course, you can always buy them.

Some sources make it easy for you to compile your list. They not only identify the top-performing bond funds for five-year periods but they also provide total returns on an annualized basis. Others rank them according to their cumulative five-year return, necessitating your conversion of the figures to annual rates for your analysis. Or they show how a $10,000 investment in a fund would have grown in five years, which is another way of saying the same thing. You can get an approximate—perhaps sufficient—idea of annual rates by referring to Table 7-4.

The following four major publications regularly include comprehensive Lipper data:[3] Standard & Poor's/Lipper *Mutual Fund Profiles,* a quarterly guide published jointly by Standard & Poor's and Lipper, conveniently ranks the top performers for five-year (and other) periods for each Lipper taxable bond fund category. It contains annualized average five-year returns, as well as total returns for individual years, in profiles of around 750 taxable bond and stock funds. It gives the same information for each Lipper category so that you can easily make comparisons. The guide also offers five-year data in tables listing an additional 550 taxable and tax-exempt funds, each one appropriately tagged with its category.

Barron's publishes a quarterly survey of mutual fund performance, "Barron's/Lipper Gauge," which presents comprehensive Lipper data for around 1,750 taxable bond and stock funds in alphabetical sequence but does not categorize most bond funds; except for Convertible Securities, Flexible or Mixed Income and World Fixed-Income, they simply carry "fixed income" as their investment objective. Thus, you have to know what funds you're looking for in the category that interests you. If you do, it's easy to find them, ascertain their five-year performance, and compare the figure with the category average that's in the same issue's "Lipper Fixed-Income Fund Performance Analysis" table. If you don't have the names, the work might be a bit of a challenge. Investors looking for leaders among more than 450 national or single-state municipal bond funds are much better off: they not only can easily find the funds' five-year performance data by classification but also their ranks.

The Wall Street Journal each day on the next-to-last page of Section C carries a table, "Mutual Fund Scorecard," listing the top 15 (and bottom 10) performers for a stock or bond fund category for the latest 12 months. It also provides their total returns for five years (plus other data) and the Lipper averages for the group. For major categories, it carries the table once a month. Inasmuch as the funds are ranked according to performance for the most recent 12 months, a table may not include all top performers for the latest 5 years. On the other hand, some of those that are omitted may have slipped significantly in performance during the recent period, and you would not wish to consider them anyway.

Money, in connection with its semiannual rankings of over 900 mutual funds, which include five-year compound annual returns, ranks the top performers for five years in eight taxable and three tax-exempt bond fund categories. While also providing Lipper data, its presentation involves fewer categories, reflecting the consolidation of categories with similar objectives. The publication also offers five top performers every month, ranked by one-year returns; thus, the lists also may exclude some that have been superior long-run performers but did not do so well in the short run.

If you are unable to get your hands on the foregoing publications, other sources, using different categories—or no categories at all—also may help you to find the bond fund you're looking for. The other sources include the following:

Annuals.   Yearly publications, such as *The Individual Investor's Guide to No-Load Mutual Funds,* published by the American Association of Individual Investors, and *The Handbook for No-Load Fund Investors,* published by *The No-Load Fund Investor,* contain five-year and annual performance data and rankings for no-load funds. The *Handbook* also includes low-loads. Both group bond funds into two categories: taxable and tax-exempt. The *Handbook* combines convertible, flexible income and balanced funds with equity income funds in another category, simply called income.

Wiesenberger Investment Companies Service, started in 1940 and the oldest annual, provides total return data for five-year and other periods, as well as for individual years, for both load and no-load funds. Organized still differently, its categories include income funds with flexible policies; those invested in senior securities; specialized funds invested in international issues (including world income funds); funds focused on U.S. government securities; those in tax-exempt bonds; and balanced funds.

Data Services.   Morningstar, publisher of the biweekly *Mutual Fund Values,* provides total return data for five-year and other periods for over 1,000 funds, including bond funds grouped into these categories: corporate bond—general; corporate bond—high quality; corporate bond—high yield; government bond—general; government bond—mortgage backed; government bond—Treasury; international bond; convertible; balanced; municipal bond—general; municipal bond—high quality; and municipal bond—high yield. All are ranked according to percentiles both within their objective groups and the total Morningstar universe.

Performance data for taxable and municipal bond funds are provided monthly for five-year and other periods in *CDA Mutual Fund Re-*

port, published by CDA Investment Technologies. The taxable bond funds are divided into four categories: corporate, government/agency, high yield and international debt issues. All are ranked—but not separately—according to percentiles among the 1,500 stock and bond funds in the CDA universe.

Periodicals. In its annual mutual fund ranking feature, *Changing Times* provides Investment Company Data's five-year (and other) total return figures for over 1,500 funds, including bond funds in eight categories: high-quality bond; high-yield bond; global bond; Ginnie Mae/mortgage bond; government security; international bond; high-quality muni; and high-yield muni. It also ranks the top 25 bond funds for the period. In its monthly issues, it provides top performers for the latest year, but these do not necessarily include the top performers for five years.

Forbes' annual fund survey divides around 500 bond fund listings (including closed-end funds) into foreign bond, taxable bond, municipal bond and adds 100 balanced funds. For a long-term perspective of taxable bond funds, it offers CDA's annual average total return data for a span that takes in three full bond market cycles—close to ten years in the 1989 edition; these numbers are combined with figures for the most recent twelve months. For the other categories, the periods for total return data vary.

Using Morningstar data, *Business Week* provides annual ratings of nearly 600 fixed-income funds, but it includes total returns for no longer than three years. The funds are divided into corporate, government, municipal, international and convertible.

U.S. News & World Report's annual mutual fund roundup includes lists of ten leading long-run performers among corporate, government, high-yield and tax-free bond funds. The rankings are based on an index that reflects results for several periods, including five years, as calculated by Kanon Bloch Carré & Company. Five-year data for the top-ranked funds are also given.

Newsletters. Examples of newsletters that regularly provide comprehensive performance data, including five-year returns, are *The No-Load Fund Investor,* a monthly; *United Mutual Fund Selector,* a semimonthly; and Wiesenberger's *Management Results,* a quarterly. The *Investor* and *Management Results* organize bond funds in the same way as their organizations' annuals. In the *Selector,* taxable funds are listed alphabetically, grouped according to load levels, and include five types of bond funds: convertible, high yield, fixed income, income and balanced. The list of municipal bond funds, published separately, combines the various types.

SELECTING THE FUNDS

The next step is to check top performers on your list according to a number of criteria to see which fund is likely to be best for you. To do this, you will need the current prospectus and most recent annual or semiannual shareholder report for each fund. Both can easily be obtained by telephoning the funds. Since most have "800" telephone numbers—which you can find in fund annuals, periodicals or data service listings—it usually won't cost you a cent.

The criteria to investigate are as follows:

1. Investment objectives/policies
2. Investment adviser
3. Portfolio manager
4. Shareholder transaction expenses
5. Annual fund operating expenses
6. Fund size
7. Other considerations

Investment Objectives/Policies

First and foremost, you'll want to make sure that a fund's investment objectives and policies are consonant with your strategy, that it had the same objectives for the entire period for which you have performance data, and that it continues to have them.

The Investment Company Act of 1940 requires each mutual fund to state its objectives and policies, concisely and clearly, in the front of its prospectus. A brief statement of the objectives must be on the cover page. Elaboration and description of the policies must follow immediately. (For an example of how objectives and policies are worded on a prospectus cover, see Figure 7-2.)

Prospectuses must describe the types of securities in which the fund invests, any special investment practices and techniques it employs (including their probable effects, such as high portfolio turnover), and the principal risk factors associated with investment in the fund (whether it invests in bonds rated Baa/BBB or lower, in securities denominated in foreign currencies, in other mutual funds; whether it writes put and call options, borrows money, has a short operating history, and so on). The prospectus also must state whether the fund's objectives may be changed without a vote of the majority of its shareholders.

If a fund invests in U.S. government securities, the prospectus must not only describe the types of securities but also state whether they are

---

Figure 7–2   Example of Statement of Investment Objectives/Policies

---

Dreyfus A Bonds Plus, Inc. (the "Fund") is an open-end, diversified, management investment company, known as a mutual fund. Its goal is to provide you with the maximum amount of current income to the extent consistent with the preservation of capital and the maintenance of liquidity.

The Fund invests principally in debt obligations of corporations, the U.S. Government and its agencies and instrumentalities, and major banking institutions.

At least 80% of the Fund's portfolio is invested in bonds rated at least A by Moody's Investors Service, Inc. or Standard & Poor's Corporation.

Source: Dreyfus A Bonds Plus, Inc.

---

supported by the full faith and credit of the United States, whether the issuing agencies have the ability to borrow from the Treasury or only on their own credit, and so on.

You will want to ensure that the fund is managed for maximum total return consistent with the level of risk you're prepared to accept.

Whether you're investing for current income or for capital accumulation, *avoid* any fund that states or implies that it is investing for a constant level of distributions. Since you know that interest rates fluctuate and that income dividends can be expected to fluctuate accordingly, you know that speculative techniques such as option writing, return of your capital or both may be required to supplement dividends to maintain distributions at a constant level. (You'll find thoughts on how to receive a flat stream of cash from a fund later in this chapter.) Moderate use of certain techniques, such as engaging in futures contracts to hedge against interest rate fluctuations, may be appropriate, but excessive use of others, such as writing options to maintain a flat payout, can result in missed opportunities for capital appreciation or the risk of losses.

A fund that returns your capital on the installment plan to maintain a flat level of distributions is, in effect, buying your loyalty with your own money (and throwing off data services that sometimes erroneously treat return of capital as capital gains distributions). Needless to say, the part of a distribution that's a return of capital is non-taxable, but that isn't the point (even if funds try to give it a positive spin); a fund that makes this a policy fails to provide you a return on a part of your investment—after charging you a fee for management.

When scanning a prospectus or annual report, be alert to the possibility that a fund may have changed its investment objectives or policies during the five-year (or other) period for which you are examining performance data. Funds may not disclose it in years following the change, and data services and periodicals may not indicate it in their tables.

Investment Adviser

The investment adviser, whose name appears in the prospectus, is the firm responsible for managing a fund's portfolio—under the overall supervision of its board of directors (trustees). The 1940 act requires that all investment advisory services must be provided pursuant to a written contract approved by a fund's shareholders. Renewals—their terms can't exceed two years—or changes must be voted on by a fund's shareholders or board. The contract can be terminated at any time.

You'll want to be sure that the fund's current investment adviser is the same one it has had over the period for which you are relying on the performance data. While a fund is required to indicate any adviser change in a footnote to the 10-year table of financial information at the front of the prospectus, the requirement may be overlooked. Fund data services may not show the change either. Therefore, it's a good idea to question the fund. If there has been a change, you may want to disregard the fund unless you are aware of the new adviser's investment record.

You may wish to read what the prospectus says about the investment adviser. It must describe the adviser's experience, state who controls the firm, and divulge the nature of the business of the controlling company or individual(s). (A large number of advisers are units of insurance companies, manufacturing companies and broker-dealers.) The prospectus also must report the services that are provided by the investment adviser and the compensation paid (including terms other than the simple percentage of average net assets).

Portfolio Manager

You'll also want to be sure that the portfolio manager who achieved the record that attracts you—an employee of the investment adviser or perhaps its sole shareholder—is still in the job. Mutual funds have not been required to identify their portfolio managers, the people with day-to-day responsibilities for managing portfolios, or to announce news of changes, as they have been required to identify their investment advisers and to report changes in them.

Having proposed such disclosure as recently as 1982 and 1984 only to back away in the face of industry opposition, the SEC made a similar proposal in December 1989. It would require disclosure of the name, title, business experience and tenure of everyone making significant contributions to the investment advice provided a fund.

If the proposal is adopted, you still may have to check by phone to see whether the portfolio manager listed in the prospectus remains the same. If you learn that a manager has been in the job fewer than five years, you know that he/she is not responsible for the entire five years' performance for which you have data. If, on the other hand, you learn that the manager of a superior fund has had the job longer than five years, you probably have a good prospect.

If the proposal is not adopted, you may get the names of portfolio managers, if not always their length of service, from the increasing number of funds that are including signed comments by portfolio managers in their shareholder reports. Annuals, magazines and newsletters also increasingly are providing this information. But telephone checks may still be required.

Shareholder Transaction Expenses

It is extremely important to determine whether or not and to what degree you would be subject to charges for buying or selling a fund's shares.

At the front of a prospectus, funds are required by the SEC to disclose clearly in a table (see Figures 7–3a–c) whether they impose sales loads (charges) on the purchase of shares and on the reinvestment of dividends; deferred sales loads or redemption fees, on the sale of shares; and/or exchange fees—and, if so, how much the charges are. The best known is the "front-end" sales load; the maximum rate permitted under a rule of the National Association of Securities Dealers is 8.5 percent.

It is easy to understand why a broker or other salesperson would *want* a commission for selling mutual fund shares, just as he/she would want a commission for selling anything else. It is also easy to understand why many funds are structured to *charge* sales loads, front-end or deferred: to give an incentive to salespeople to sell the shares, thereby help-

---

Figure 7–3a Example of Shareholder Transaction Expenses for No-Load Funds

Shareholder Transaction Expenses

Sales load "charge" on purchases	None
Sales load "charge" on reinvested dividends	None
Redemption fees	None
Exchange fees	None

Source: T. Rowe Price GNMA Fund prospectus.

Figure 7–3b   Example of Shareholder Transaction Expenses for Funds with Sales Loads on both Purchases and Reinvested Dividends

Shareholder Transaction Expenses

Maximum Sales Load Imposed on Purchases (as a percentage of offering price)	4.00%
Maximum Sales Load Imposed on Reinvested Dividends (as a percentage of offering price)	4.00%
Deferred Sales Charge	NONE
Redemption Fees	NONE
Exchange Fee (per transaction)	$5.00

Source: Franklin U.S. Government Securities prospectus.

Figure 7–3c   Example of Shareholder Transaction Expenses for Funds that have no Front-End Load but impose a Deferred Sales Load

FUND EXPENSES

Shareholder Transaction Expenses

Maximum Sales Load Imposed on Purchases	None
Maximum Sales Load Imposed on Reinvested Dividends	None

Deferred Sales Load (as a percentage of the original purchase price):

Year Since Purchase Payment Made	Contingent Deferred Sales Charge as a Percentage of the Original Purchase Price
First	5.0%
Second	4.0%
Third	3.0%
Fourth	2.0%
Fifth	1.0%
Sixth and thereafter	None
Redemption Fees	None
Exchange Fee	None

Source: Prudential-Bache GNMA Fund prospectus.

ing the funds' assets to grow and the investment advisers to earn larger management fees.

It is not easy to understand why so many bond fund investors, capable of doing their own research, of dialing an "800" telephone number to get information, of making decisions and of doing business by mail, would want to *pay* a load.

Anyone paying a load to a broker or other salesperson—as much as $850 for an investment of $10,000—should expect to receive something for the money. That something has to be useful financial planning or investment advice and/or other services.

Anyone agreeing to pay a load on the reinvestment of dividends has got to wonder what possible service could justify it, inasmuch as the work is probably done by a computer in a second or two and the fund has managed to sell additional shares at less overhead cost than it takes to sell shares to new investors. (Whether investors know they've agreed to reinvestment charges is another matter. The prospectus of the Franklin U.S. Government Securities Series clearly states: "...income dividends will be automatically credited to your account in the form of additional shares at the public offering price, which includes the (4%) sales charge....")

Anyone agreeing to pay a deferred sales load, which is scaled down over five or six years until it is eliminated altogether, must consider whether the possibility of such a charge could inhibit his/her willingness to get out of a fund in the event that becomes necessary or desirable. Five or six years is a long time, during which anything can happen. Deterrents to frequent trading are understandable, but why should an investor be shackled with a deterrent to redemptions for so many years? And, anyway, what does an investor get for the money?

Front-end or back-end, a sales load cannot be regarded as an incentive to, or reward for, fund performance because it is *not* paid to the portfolio manager(s) but rather to securities dealers and other organizations and the salespersons they employ. Performance, good or bad, is independent of the presence or absence of a load. And performance is what matters.

Since it is self-evident that the investor who has his/her money at work in a no-load will have a higher return than the investor in a load fund, other factors being equal, checking on whether or not a fund imposes a load is essential in screening prospects. In looking at funds' total returns, you will want to see whether the data reflect loads. Unless you get the data from the funds' own literature and it is clearly stated that allowance has been made, they usually don't. Thus, returns published by others may overstate the actual return on investment that an investor would have experienced.

There are two ways to deal with this. One is to obtain the total return
data for the load funds that are calculated on the basis of an actual investment and, therefore, are comparable with the no-load funds you're
considering. Make sure that they are for the same periods. (The severity
of the impact of a load on an investor's return is, of course, a function of
how long the shares are held. Even an 8.5 percent front-end load matters
less when shares are held many years. But it still reduces an investor's
profit.) The other way is simply to look only at no-load funds that meet
your requirements.

Annual Fund Operating Expenses

Mutual funds are required to report annual operating expenses in two
places at the front of their prospectuses (as well, of course, as in semiannual and annual reports). One is a simple table (Figure 7–4), which item-
izes management fees, 12b-1 fees, other expenses and their total as a
percentage of average net assets. The other is the ten-year table of condensed financial information (Figure 7–5), showing expenses expressed
as cents per fund share and as a percentage of average net assets (commonly referred to as the expense ratio) as well as other important data.

Since funds' total return data reflect deductions for their annual operating expenses, why should you bother to check the expense ratios of
the funds you're considering? Given two funds with identical portfolios
and equally proficient portfolio managers producing identical investment income per share, the fund with the lower annual operating expenses will have the higher *net* investment income per share and the

Figure 7–4   Example of Annual Fund Operating Expenses

Annual Fund Operating Expenses	Short-Term Government Bond Portfolio	Short-Term Bond Portfolio	GNMA Portfolio	U.S. Treasury Bond Portfolio	Investment Grade Bond Portfolio	High Yield Bond Portfolio
Management Expenses	0.12%	0.14%	0.13%	0.17%	0.12%	0.13%
Investment Advisory Fees	0.01	0.02	0.03	0.02	0.06	0.09
Shareholder Accounting Costs	0.12	0.11	0.12	0.10	0.13	0.12
12b-1 Fees	None	None	None	None	None	None
Distribution Costs	0.03	0.04	0.04	0.04	0.04	0.04
Other Expenses	0.04	0.03	0.03	0.03	0.03	0.03
Total Operating Expenses	0.32%	0.34%	0.35%	0.36%	0.38%	0.41%

Source: Vanguard Fixed Income Securities Fund prospectus.

Figure 7–5   Example of 10-Year Table of Condensed Financial Information

Selected data (for a share outstanding throughout each year) and ratios are as follows (audited):

	1988	1987	1986	1985	1984	1983	1982	1981	1980	1979
Income and Expenses										
Income	$ 1.19	$ 1.20	$ 1.34	$ 1.41	$ 1.37	$ 1.38	$ 1.36	$ 1.43	$ 1.39	$ 1.25
Operating expenses	(.12)	(.12)	(.12)	(.12)	(.12)	(.12)	(.09)	(.09)	(.10)	(.11)
Net investment income	1.07	1.08	1.22	1.29	1.25	1.26	1.27	1.34	1.29	1.14
Dividends from net investment income	(1.07)	(1.10)	(1.22)	(1.29)	(1.25)	(1.25)	(1.27)	(1.36)	(1.30)	(1.15)
Capital Changes										
Net realized and unrealized gains (losses) from investments, futures and options	.01	(.99)	.59	1.12	.06	(.04)	1.55	(.94)	(1.04)	(1.03)
Net increase (decrease) in net asset value	.01	(1.01)	.59	1.12	.06	(.03)	1.55	(.96)	(1.05)	(1.04)
Net asset value:										
Beginning of year	12.40	13.41	12.82	11.70	11.64	11.67	10.12	11.08	12.13	13.17
End of year	$12.41	$12.40	$13.41	$12.82	$11.70	$11.64	$11.67	$10.12	$11.08	$12.13
Ratio of operating expenses to average net assets (%)	.94	.94	.88	.91	1.02	.97	.93	.83	.83	.84
Ratio of net investment income to average net assets (%)	8.53	8.37	9.12	10.57	11.04	10.61	11.96	13.08	11.24	9.07
Portfolio turnover rate (%)†	19.6	33.7	24.1	29.9	40.3	39.8	40.5	58.7	61.6	48.1
Number of shares outstanding at end of year (000 omitted)	19,722	19,497	18,532	13,394	10,507	9,492	7,819	5,746	4,930	4,649

†The ratios after 1984 include U.S. Government long-term securities, which were excluded from the ratio calculation in prior years.

Source: Scudder Income Fund prospectus.

higher income dividend. All other things remaining equal, its total return has to increase its edge over time.

Management and "other" fees combined should average no more than 1 percent of average net assets, and you can find well-managed bond funds with expense ratios of 0.50 percent or less. Expenses in this range allow for an adequate fee to compensate an investment adviser so it can suitably reward the portfolio manager and staff. Expenses also should cover the other costs of serving shareholders, including account maintenance, postage, administration, printing costs, legal fees, custodian's fees, accounting fees, telephone charges (including those for calls to the "800" number) and so on. Shareholders derive benefits from all of these types of expenses and presumably would not question them.

Shareholders derive no material benefit from the 12b-1 fees, which provide for distribution or other expenses incurred under a plan adopted pursuant to the SEC rule for which they are named. Ranging from around 0.25 percent to around 1.25 percent of average net assets, they may be used to compensate brokers or underwriters or to pay for promotion and advertising to attract new shareholders. Any resulting increase in assets would directly benefit the investment adviser, whose compensation is usually based on a fund's assets, or the salespeople, who also may get a share of the sales load. If there are benefits to shareholders, they're not perceptible.

If the expense ratio of a fund is too low to seem true, it might be. You may have run into a case in which the investment adviser has waived or agreed to reimburse part of the fee, thereby reducing the expense ratio and raising return. A footnote to the expense table and condensed financial information table should say so. In these cases, you need to look at what the fee would have been before the waiver or reimbursement, which amount should also be stated, because that could be what you will pay sooner or later when the adviser's offer is terminated.

No-load funds, usually sold directly by their management companies, are caught in a paradox as far as operating expenses are concerned. On the one hand, they have the incentive to keep their costs low so that they can strengthen their appeal to investors who do their own research. But if they try too hard to keep costs down, they may not spend enough to draw attention to themselves and attract new investors—unless their performance is so strong that media coverage would make self-promotion superfluous. Not paying brokers a commission to stimulate sales, they can't expect anyone else to do their selling for them.

At the risk of stating the obvious, let it be noted here that no matter how much fund costs may be emphasized, attention should not be diverted from the return on investment that a fund can provide you.

Fund Size

Whether a bond fund is large or small should not matter very much to a shareholder, once it is large enough to have its shares' prices listed in the newspapers. There are good and poor performers among large as well as among small funds. Because of the default risk inherent in low-grade investments, a larger high-yield bond fund would appear preferable because its portfolio is likely to contain more issues, providing greater diversification. Yet size is no guarantee of performance. Of the 11 high-yield funds with assets of over $1 billion that had been in operation for five years in September 1989, only three—those of Kemper, Vanguard and Fidelity—were among the top ten performers.

Otherwise, the benefits of size should be felt more predictably in the fixed costs among annual operating expenses than in other aspects. Fixed costs—those that are the same regardless of fund size—can cause a small fund to have higher operating expenses in relation to assets because they are spread across a smaller base. As a fund grows and fixed costs are spread across a larger base, the expense ratio should subside. Yet the economies of scale are not very noticeable when fixed costs are a small fraction of total operating expenses.

Other Considerations

Other factors also require consideration, although they are not as critical in meeting your investment objectives as consistently superior performance.

Registration. Make sure the fund is registered to be able to sell its shares in your state.

Minimum Investment. Each fund you choose should have a minimum initial investment within your reach. Most requirements range from $250 to $3,000. If you don't have enough to open an account with a fund you want, simply save your money in a money market fund or savings account until you've got it.

IRAs and Other Plans. If you're investing in an IRA or other retirement plan, find out whether the fund offers such plans and, if so, whether the minimum initial investment is lower. There may be a $10 annual fee. Sales loads may be waived if your employer has an arrangement for investing in an IRA via payroll withholding.

Good Service. Mutual fund investing is a long-term proposition. If you're going to live with the fund(s) you choose, you're going to want good service: prompt handling of your purchase or redemption instructions, availability of distribution options to meet your needs, redemption by checkwriting, prompt response to your requests for information or literature, patient explanations on the telephone, accurate recordkeeping, prompt and clear statements and forthright periodic reports on performance. (SEC has proposed the latter be required.)

Telephone Exchange Privileges. Your first consideration should be to choose a fund that will help you realize your investment goals. If a bond fund is a member of a fund group that gives you the opportunity to switch by telephone to or from a money market or other fund, so much the better. Remember, though, that in a taxable account the switch out of a bond fund is a transaction that may result in a taxable capital gain or a capital loss. To discourage those who want to engage in frequent trades for short-term gains, thereby increasing fund costs and interfering with portfolio management, funds have increasingly imposed limits on exchange frequency. These should not bother long-term investors, whose interests they are to serve.

Automatic Investment/Withdrawal Plans.   A number of funds make it convenient for investors to invest their money, or take it out, by arranging to debit or credit their bank accounts automatically at intervals. These arrangements facilitate investment by dollar-cost averaging and receipt of cash distributions on a regular basis.

INVESTING IN A FUND

If one fund survives your screening as the most promising prospect for you—compatible investment objective, continuing management by person who achieved record of high total return with low volatility, reasonably stable income, low cost, good service—you're ready to invest. If two seem to be equally attractive on the basis of performance and costs, you may want to lean toward the one that appears to provide better service. If none seems attractive, and your candidates included all above-average performers in a category for the last five years, you may want to look at three-year data or, perhaps, to try another category with similar objectives.

Dollar-Cost Averaging.   If you're planning to invest money from time to time, try to schedule a certain amount at regular intervals, perhaps taking advantage of an automatic investment scheme that's linked to your bank account. This practice, called dollar-cost averaging, is a disciplined way to invest regardless of whether the market is up or down. It avoids the possibility of your responding emotionally to current market conditions or forecasts of interest rates. When share prices are higher, your dollars will buy fewer shares; when they're lower, they'll buy more. If you made a good fund choice, dollar-cost averaging should help you hold down the average cost of your shares in the long run and, thus, result in your owning more shares than the same total investment might have bought otherwise.

Lump Sum Investing.   If you have a lump sum to invest, you might consider putting it to work in increments to minimize the risk of buying a lot of shares just before interest rates rise, causing prices to fall. You might divide the money into four or five equal amounts (depending on the size of the lump sum), invest one portion and put the balance into a money market fund for later transfer at regular intervals. This would be appropriate, for example, if you are getting a lump sum from an employer's qualified profit-sharing or pension plan and want to roll it over, tax free, into one or more IRAs within the 60 days permitted by the Internal Revenue Service.

Cash Distributions vs. Reinvestment.   When filling out a fund's application form, you have to check a box indicating whether you want dividends and/or any capital gains distributions to be reinvested or paid in cash. If you're investing in a bond fund as part of your strategy to build capital, the decision is easy: you indicate that you want to reinvest.

If you need the income, you can ask for dividends to be paid to you at the monthly or quarterly intervals offered by the fund. Be prepared for the dividends to fluctuate as interest rates fluctuate and for the possibility that your principal may slip.

Steady Cash Plus Growth.   On the other hand, if you want current income, you may wish to refrain from requesting distributions in cash and take a different approach that could let you participate in a fund's growth to a limited extent. Given that you've not fallen for a fund that keeps distributions flat by pursuing risky option techniques and/or returning some of your capital to supplement interest income, but want flat-amount monthly or quarterly checks nonetheless, there is a technique you can use.

Ask to have dividends (and any capital gains) reinvested when they are distributed. To obtain cash, have the fund sell enough shares to provide what you need, and let the rest continue to earn interest for you. Except for the recordkeeping for tax purposes involved in a taxable account, this should not be difficult to do. As a first step, you would determine how much cash you could get regularly if you took an amount a bit less than the fund's recent income distribution rate. If, for example, the fund has been distributing a net investment income at a rate of nine percent and you're investing $15,000, you could decide to take eight percent, or $1,200 a year. You'd ask for monthly checks of $100, and the fund would sell the requisite number of shares to provide the money. When prices are higher, fewer shares would have to be sold, of course, than when prices are lower.

To the extent that the fund's monthly dividend distributions exceed $100, you would have more money from interest remaining invested; and the additional shares you'd have as a result would earn interest themselves. You might have to supplement your withdrawal occasionally by selling more shares than the dividend distribution had just bought. If it became too frequent, you might want to revise your withdrawal rate.

Using this approach, as illustrated in Table 7-6, you ought to have a stable payout—a bit less than you would have by receiving all income in cash—and, over time, a growing principal. The additional bookkeeping—to keep track of small capital gains or losses resulting from sales—should be worthwhile.

Statements.   After you send in your new account application form and check, you'll get a statement advising you how many shares you bought at what price. The same will happen each time you invest additional money, and your statement also will report how much income has been credited to your account.

Table 7-6   Hypothetical 10-Year Results of a Strategy for Constant Cash Withdrawals—and Possible Growth of Principal

Assumptions:

Investment: $10,000 in 1,121* shares of Vanguard Investment Grade Bond Portfolio @ $8.92
Purchase date: December 31, 1978
Dividends: Reinvested
Capital gains distributions: Reinvested
Cash withdrawals: $200 per quarter

Year	Dividends	Capital Gains Distributions	Cash Withdrawn	Number of Shares Held	NAV	Year-end Value of Shares
1979	$897	0	$800	1,133	$8.09	$9,174
1980	945	0	800	1,152	7.62	8,785
1981	1,067	0	800	1,190	7.32	8,713
1982	1,178	0	800	1,243	8.28	10,298
1983	1,229	0	800	1,297	7.86	10,195
1984	1,348	0	800	1,368	7.86	10,756
1985	1,422	0	800	1,447	8.46	12,246
1986	1,307	0	800	1,506	8.73	13,154
1987	1,198	$185	800	1,576	7.84	12,363
1988	1,188	0	800	1,626	7.83	12,732
Total	$11,779	$185	$8,000			

*Except for NAVs, shares and dollars are rounded to whole numbers.

Source: The Vanguard Group.

Table 7-6 illustrates how someone who invested $10,000 in Vanguard Investment Grade Bond Portfolio at the end of 1978 might have fared in ten years of dividend and capital gains reinvestment and of cash withdrawals in constant amounts that were a bit below the fund's yield.

Noting that the fund's yield had been close to nine percent, one could have decided to take cash payments at an annual rate of eight percent of the initial investment—or $200 per quarter. In ten years, one would have received and reinvested $3,964 in dividends and capital gains beyond the $8,000 of cash withdrawals and wound up with over 500 additional shares. By the end of 1988 total holdings would have been worth $12,732—27 percent more than the original investment.

If instead one would have taken all dividends in cash and reinvested capital gains, yearly withdrawals would have fluctuated between $1,127 and $845. One would have received a total of $9,942—$1,942 more—but emerged with only an additional 15 shares (attributable to reinvestment of the 1987 capital gains distribution) and had holdings valued at $8,901, $1,099, or 11 percent, below the original investment.

Applying a similar strategy to another fund—whether invested in securities of similar or different maturities and credit quality—or applying the same strategy to the Vanguard fund for a different period might have had different results. Whether such a strategy would be as rewarding under future market conditions as it would have been during the ten years of the hypothetical case, no one can predict. It seems worth a try.

It's important to keep your statements. You'll need them both to calculate income tax liabilities for income and capital gains (unless yours is an IRA account), to report tax-exempt income and to calculate your investments' performance.

MONITORING YOUR FUND

There should be no need for you to race for the morning paper each day to see how your bond fund did the previous day—unless the bond market had an exceptional up or down day and you wish to see how your fund was affected.

It ought to be sufficient to monitor your fund every three months, when you should get a report from the fund on its performance and when new Lipper and other data are issued. The report should include an explanation by the portfolio manager as to why the fund performed as it did in the previous quarter and why any significant portfolio changes may have been made—including adjustments in credit quality or maturity/duration. Unless you're curious, you don't need to take time to study the portfolio; its characteristics should be summarized in the manager's report and its merit should be reflected in the performance data. The Lipper or other data services' figures will enable you to see how the fund's performance compared with others in its group and the group average, and how the group's performance compared with other groups. Your fund's report may highlight such comparisons—especially when favorable—or a comparison with a bond index that's used as a benchmark.

If you find the fund report and data reassuring, affirming the wisdom of your choice, rejoice. There is no need to do anything.

If your fund's total return slipped but not as much as other leaders in its group or the group average, your fund probably is being managed as well as possible, given its investment objective and bond market conditions. On the assumption that the objective remains a proper one for you, there probably is no cause for alarm. If your fund slipped more than the group's other leaders or average, you ought to look for an explanation in the fund report. If it's acceptable, accept it. If the report is too vague, phone the fund for an explanation. If it seems that the portfolio manager has not appeared as able to deal with adverse market conditions as his/her peers, you'll want to be on the alert for a possible move.

Should you find that your fund is underperforming its group average for two or three quarters, you'll definitely want to judge whether improvement is likely and, if not, consider switching. Go through the process that led you to choose the fund and see whether another leader in the group seems a stronger candidate now, provided the group's investment objective remains your objective. If so, it might be a good idea to switch. If both are no-load funds, the switch shouldn't cost anything more than a couple of stamps and a little time.

Should your fund group underperform other groups for two or three quarters, you might question whether the group's investment objective is right for you—especially if there is a greater likelihood that you could fall short of your target. You might consider whether a group with another investment objective would be more appropriate. On the other hand, looking at the long term, you may conclude that the situation will correct itself as market conditions change and that the credit quality and maturity/duration characteristics of your group are consistent with your goals. Staying put may be better for you after all.

Between reports, it's important to keep your eyes peeled for announcements of possible significance by your fund such as changes in investment objective, investment policy, investment adviser, or portfolio manager, which might lead you to switch. Any other changes that indicate the fund could become less desirable might also give you cause to consider switching.

In managing your own money, it is, of course, useful to be aware of conditions in the U.S. (or world) credit market—to observe whether long-term or short-term interest rates are rising or falling, whether investors are sufficiently confident in the economic outlook to bid up medium-quality bonds, or whether there is "a flight to safety." But it's probably more prudent to use your awareness to understand why your bond fund performs as it does than to let it lead you into trying to "time the market" by frequent switching. If your fund is in the hands of a capable portfolio manager, you should be able to be confident in his/her skill to cope with kaleidoscopic changes.

INVESTING IN ADDITIONAL FUNDS

If you're investing enough money to warrant it, and if it's consistent with your investment strategy, you may wish to invest in a second or even a third bond fund. Aside from the likelihood that you'd want a taxable and tax-exempt fund for different purposes, it could make sense, for example, to diversify among credit qualities (e.g., a government securities fund and a high-yield fund) or maturities (e.g., a long-term fund and a short-term fund).

Just select the categories that you feel are suitable and apply the criteria, allocating money in proportions that seem right. You can always change them.

If you want to invest in two or more bond funds, it would be convenient, of course, to be able to choose funds within the same fund family. But it isn't very often that one family has funds among the leaders in the categories you're interested in. When it doesn't occur, and you have to choose between performance and convenience, give the nod to performance.

May you have the results you're hoping for, and may you enjoy them in good health.

ENDNOTES

1. The phrases *short-term funds* and *short-term maturities* often are applied to money market funds, thereby causing confusion. Money market funds are

defined by the SEC as mutual funds that maintain a stable price per share and invest at least 80 percent of their net assets in securities maturing in 13 months or less. Short-term bond funds, in the context used here, are those fitting the Lipper definition.

2. The suggestion that you turn to certain periodicals, annual guides or other sources for five-year total return data should not, of course, be interpreted to mean that you ignore whatever else they have to offer. Competing fiercely with one another to serve you, the investor, they pack in a rich—and expanding—variety of additional performance information that you may find of interest, such as ratings reflecting levels of risk or historic performance in up and down markets.

3. Presentations of fund data by publications change from time to time and, therefore, may differ from the descriptions in this chapter, which are based on those available when this book went to press.

GLOSSARY

Definitions generally are phrased in a mutual fund context, although many of the terms have wider application.

Adviser. *See* Investment adviser.

Average net assets. The average of a fund's net assets at the beginning and end of a year (or other period). When used as the divisor for calculating yearly expense and net investment income ratios for a prospectus' 10-year table of condensed financial information, the SEC requires the average of a year's monthly averages. It permits funds simply to add the NAV at the beginning of the first month and end-of-month NAVs for the 12 months, then divide the sum by 13.

Balanced fund. One that has multiple objectives of income, stability of capital and possible growth of capital. A fund that calls itself balanced is required by the SEC to maintain at least 25 percent of the value of its assets in debt securities and/or preferred stock.

Bond. A popular term for a debt security (more properly called note, debenture or something else) that is issued by a unit of government or a corporation to an investor from whom it borrows money. The bond obligates the issuer to repay the loan on a stated maturity date, which may be as many as 30 or more years away, and to pay interest at a fixed rate at regular—usually six-month—intervals until then. *Also see* Convertible bond, Corporate bond, Federal agency securities, Mortgage-backed securities, Municipal bond and Treasury bill, Treasury bond and Treasury note.

Bond market. The diffuse, electronically connected network of trading rooms, securities exchanges, brokers and dealers in which new bond issues are bought/sold (primary market) and outstanding issues are traded (secondary market). While a number of bond issues are listed and traded on stock exchanges, by far the larger share of transactions take place in the over-the-counter market. Bond funds buy in both the primary and secondary markets, depending on their needs and opportunities.

Bond market risk. *See* Interest rate risk.

Bond rating. The rating of corporate and municipal bonds according to their relative investment qualities, performed by rating services such as Moody's Investors Service and Standard & Poor's Corporation. Ratings are designed to provide investors a simple way of selecting bonds that have acceptable levels of credit risk.

The two principal rating firms use similar symbols to indicate gradations of quality: Aaa, Aa, A, Baa, Ba, B, Caa, Ca and C (Moody's); and AAA, AA, A, BBB, BB, B, CCC, CC, C and D (Standard & Poor's). Moody's also applies numerical modifiers (e.g., Aa1, Aa2, etc.) while Standard & Poor's uses a plus (+) or minus (-) sign (e.g., AA+, AA-, etc.).

When mutual funds state the quality levels of bonds they seek to buy, or to avoid, their investment objectives or policies often mention the ratings of bonds that are preferred, acceptable or unacceptable. Unrated bonds, some of which are held by bond funds, do not necessarily lack quality; it could be that the corporations or governmental units that issued them did not apply for ratings for one reason or another. *Also see* High-grade bond, High-yield bond and Investment-grade bond.

Broker. A person or firm engaged in the business of purchasing and selling securities for the accounts of others. If a broker is an affiliate of a fund, the fund must say so.

Broker-dealer. A firm or individual engaged in the business of buying or selling securities on its/one's own behalf or on behalf of others.

Call. The provision in a bond indenture by which the issuer reserves the right to repay the principal of all or part of an issue prior to maturity. Borrowers find it advantageous or necessary to exercise this option when market interest rates fall below coupon rates; when excess cash flow enables them to cut their debt and borrowing costs; when they wish to sell assets pledged as collateral; when sinking fund provisions require gradual retirement of an issue or when other circumstances warrant. The call clause specifies the price that the issuer will pay holders. Usually, the call price exceeds the face value, inasmuch as it includes a call premium—which declines as a bond approaches maturity—to partially compensate bondholders for depriving them of income they had counted on. When interest rates have fallen and an issuer calls a bond issue to replace it with a new one at a lower yield, the action is referred to as a refunding.

Call protection. The provision assuring bondholders that a bond cannot be called during a specified period of its life. Refunding protection is a similar provision to assure holders that a bond is non-refundable for a certain period.

Call risk. The risk that a bond will be called.

Capital gains distribution. The distribution to a mutual fund's shareholders of net long-term capital gains realized on the sale of portfolio securities. A 1970 amendment to the Investment Company Act prohibits funds from making them more than once a year except by SEC rule.

Certificate of deposit (CD). A form of time deposit at a commercial or savings bank or savings and loan institution that has a specific maturity, which may range from three months to five years. If withdrawn before the maturity date, a CD is subject to an interest penalty. CDs issued in very large denominations may be sold or transferred prior to maturity. Negotiable CDs are commonly held by money market mutual funds.

Collateral. The property that a borrower pledges to secure a loan. It becomes subject to a lender's seizure if the borrower defaults.

Contingent deferred sales load. *See* Deferred sales load.

Convertible bond. A corporate debt obligation that may be exchanged for a specified number of shares of a company's common stock. (Terms are usually expressed as a ratio of shares per $1,000 bond or as a price per share.) When the market value of the stock rises above the price at which conversion would be advantageous, the bond's price rises accordingly. When the price of the stock falls, the value of the bond is increasingly determined by the interest it pays, so its drop is cushioned by the yield.

Corporate bond. A bond issued by a corporation. Unlike a share of common stock, which represents ownership in a corporation and, therefore, a proportionate share of its profits, a bond represents its debt. A corporation must pay interest to its bondholders before paying dividends to its stockholders. In the event of a company's failure, bondholders are accorded preferential status over stockholders in the division of assets. A corporate bond may be secured by assets (for example, a mortgage bond is secured by property) or unsecured (known as a debenture). To owners of secured bonds, a corporation's expected earning power matters even more than collateral because it assures them of timely interest and principal payments. To owners of unsecured bonds, of course, earning power is everything.

Coupon rate. The annual rate of interest that a bond pays (usually in semiannual installments), as specified on the bond.

Credit quality. The level of risk that a bond's issuer will default, which may or may not be acceptable to a given bond fund or other investor. While a rating assigned by a rating service may correctly indicate a bond's credit quality, the investment adviser of a well-managed bond fund will go beyond the rating and do its own research to ascertain a bond's investment merit—and to assess whether a bond is fairly priced. *Also see* Bond rating.

Credit risk.   The risk that a bond's issuer will default.

Custodian.   A company—usually a commercial bank—that is qualified to keep custody of a fund's securities and other assets, as required by the Investment Company Act.

Dealer.   A person or firm engaged in the business of buying and selling securities for his/her or its own account. If a dealer is an affiliate of a fund, the fund must say so.

Default.   The failure of a bond's issuer to pay interest or repay principal when scheduled.

Deferred sales load.   A sales charge deducted from the proceeds when shareholders of some funds sell (redeem) their shares within a specific period of years following purchase. It is calculated as a percentage of the original purchase price or of redemption proceeds. Funds imposing this load must report to the SEC how much they collect and, if they share the revenue with underwriters, dealers or others, how much they retain.

Diversification.   The policy of reducing one's vulnerability to loss by investing in a variety of financial and non-financial assets, having different characteristics and involving different risks. More narrowly, the policy of having one's own or a mutual fund's financial assets divided among different securities types, issuers, industries and/or geographic regions to reduce investment risk.

For mutual (and closed-end) funds, the Investment Company Act has a specific definition: it regards a fund as diversified if no single issuer of securities (excluding the U.S. government) included among 75 percent of its total assets accounts for over five percent of the total, and the securities of no single issuer account for more than ten percent of that company's outstanding voting securities. If a fund does not meet this definition, it's "non-diversified" in the eyes of the law. Every fund must state whether it is diversified or non-diversified at the front of its prospectus. In addition, every fund must meet certain diversification requirements under Subchapter M of the Internal Revenue Code to qualify as a regulated investment company so that it won't be subject to income tax.

Dividend.   The payment to a fund's shareholders of the net investment income earned from interest and dividends on the money market instruments, bonds and stocks in its portfolio. It excludes profits from the sale of securities or the distribution of money from any other source, such as option income or the return of a shareholder's capital. The Investment Company Act requires a fund to disclose if a distribution includes anything other than net investment income. Although bonds' issuers typically pay interest semiannually, bond funds commonly distribute dividends monthly. *Also see* Capital gains distribution.

Dollar-cost averaging. The practice of investing a fixed amount of money in a fund at regular intervals (such as monthly or quarterly) regardless of market conditions. It is intended to thwart the temptation to invest too much during the euphoria of a booming market or to sell in panic during a market slide. On the assumption that a fund is well chosen, buying (for the same number of dollars) more shares when prices are lower and fewer shares when prices are higher should result in a lower average cost per share if the discipline is maintained over time.

Duration. Duration is widely regarded as more meaningful than maturity as an indicator of a bond's (portfolio's) sensitivity to interest rate changes because it reflects interest rates and timing of all payments including interest to a holder, not the timing of the principal repayment alone. The duration of a bond is the sum of the number of years until each cash flow is received, weighted by the present value of each year's cash flow relative to the bond's total market value. The duration of a bond portfolio is the market value-weighted average of the durations of the bonds it holds.

For securities such as zero coupon obligations, which involve no payments of any kind until maturity, duration equals maturity. For all others, duration will always be shorter than maturity. A low-yield bond has a longer duration than a high-yield bond of identical maturity because interest payments account for a smaller percentage of the total of its expected cash flows. Prices of bonds of longer duration are more sensitive to changes in interest rates than those of bonds of shorter duration.

Event risk. The risk that the issuer of an outstanding bond issue may become unable to pay interest or to repay principal because of an event, such as a leveraged buyout (LBO) of the company's common stock, a merger or an acquisition, that encumbers the corporation with additional debt.

Exchange fee. A fee imposed by some funds for exercise of the exchange privilege (*See* Exchange privilege).

Exchange privilege. The option that a number of mutual fund families accord their shareholders, enabling them to sell shares of one of their funds and invest the proceeds in another. Such a transaction, except for tax-sheltered accounts, may result in a taxable capital gain. The privilege may be limited to a stated number per year to prevent excessive trading, which can interfere with portfolio management and add to a fund's expenses—events inconsistent with the long-term nature of mutual fund investing.

Expense ratio.   A fund's total expenses per share—a management fee, possibly a 12b-1 fee, and other expenses—divided by average net assets per share. The figure, which should not run higher than 1 percent and could be lower than 0.5 percent, must be prominently shown in a fund's prospectus and also stated in annual and semiannual reports. If a ratio has been reduced because some fees are being temporarily waived or reimbursed by the investment adviser, a footnote should say so.

FHA-insured mortgages.   Mortgages insured by the Federal Housing Administration, established in 1934 and now a unit of the Department of Housing and Urban Development.

Face value.   The principal amount an issuer will repay when redeeming a bond at maturity. Also known as par.

Family of funds.   Two or more mutual funds that share the same investment adviser or principal underwriter and hold themselves out to investors as being related.

Fannie Mae.   *See* Federal National Mortgage Association.

Federal agency securities.   The collective term for securities issued by the two broad categories of federal agencies—those owned by the federal government and those sponsored by it but owned privately—to raise capital for specific sectors of the economy such as housing, agriculture and education.

Federal Home Loan Banks.   Twelve regional banks, owned by savings and loan institutions that are members of the Federal Home Loan Bank System. These banks provide reserve credit to member institutions. They raise funds through the sale of debt securities.

Federal Home Loan Mortgage Corporation (FHLMC, or Freddie Mac). Established by Congress in 1970 to increase the availability of mortgage money for home buyers. It does this by buying mortgages from a variety of lenders—primarily conventional mortgages but also loans insured or guaranteed by the FHA or VA, respectively—so that those lenders can use the funds to make new mortgages. FHLMC replenishes its cash by issuing mortgage-backed securities, called Mortgage Participation Certificates, or PCs, which it guarantees.

Freddie Mac's senior participating preferred stock could be owned only by the savings and loan industry until January 1989, when the stock began trading publicly. With enactment of the Financial Institutions Reform, Recovery and Enforcement Act of 1989—the "thrift industry bailout bill"—Freddie Mac's preferred stock was converted to voting common stock. *Also see* Mortgage-backed securities.

Federal National Mortgage Association (FNMA, or Fannie Mae). Chartered by the federal government in 1938 but a stockholder-owned corporation since 1970, it has helped to provide credit for low-income, moderate-income and middle-income home buyers by raising funds in securities markets. FNMA buys conventional as well as FHA-insured and VA-guaranteed mortgages from savings and loan associations, mortgage companies and other institutions that originate them. To finance the acquisition of those loans for its portfolio, FNMA borrows money by issuing unsecured bonds. Fannie Mae provides liquidity to the mortgage market through its mortgage-backed securities guaranty business. Loans are originated by local lenders that then combine the mortgages into pools. FNMA reviews the underwriting of the loans and issues the securities with its guaranty of timely interest and principal payments. *Also see* Mortgage-backed securities.

Federal Open Market Committee (FOMC). The committee that sets the objectives for the Federal Reserve System's conduct of open market operations. Its 12 members include the 7 members of the System's Board of Governors, the president of the Federal Reserve Bank of New York, and, on a rotating basis, the presidents of 4 of the remaining 11 Federal Reserve Banks.

Fiscal policy. Federal government policy regarding taxation and expenditure. The deficits it has produced have led to an increase in the volume of federal debt securities available for purchase by individual and institutional investors, including bond funds.

Fixed-income securities. Bonds and preferred stocks. Although the interest and dividends they pay, respectively, are fixed in amounts, their market values are not. They fluctuate and, therefore, so do their yields.

Freddie Mac. *See* Federal Home Loan Mortgage Corporation.

Fundamental policy. Any investment or other policy that a mutual fund deems to be fundamental is one that may not be changed without approval of a majority of the fund's outstanding voting securities.

General obligation bond.   A class of municipal bonds that is supported by the taxing power of the state or local government issuer.

Ginnie Mae.   *See* Government National Mortgage Association.

Government National Mortgage Association (GNMA, or Ginnie Mae).   Established in 1968 as a government corporation within the Department of Housing and Urban Development to increase liquidity in the secondary market for government-backed residential mortgages by attracting new, non-traditional sources of capital for such loans. Since 1970, when it originated mortgage-backed securities (MBS), its principal activity has been its MBS guaranty program. Issued by some 1,200 approved private lending institutions, collateralized by FHA-insured and VA-guaranteed mortgages, and given the backing of the full faith and credit of the United States upon receiving Ginnie Mae's approval, its certificates are the most widely held and most widely traded MBS in the world. At times, the GNMA program provides more than 90 percent of all the money going into FHA-backed and VA-backed home loans. *Also see* Mortgage-backed securities.

High-grade bond.   A bond receiving one of the two highest ratings: Moody's Aaa or Aa, or Standard & Poor's AAA or AA.

High-yield bond.   Common term for a speculative bond, sometimes called a junk bond. Its purchasers demand a *relatively* high rate of interest—sometimes as much as four to five percent above that of Treasury securities of comparable maturity—to compensate for the higher probability of default that such a bond entails. (During periods of tight money, even Treasury securities' yields are *absolutely* high.) The low credit quality of these bonds is indicated in the below–investment-grade ratings they are given by rating services: Ba or lower by Moody's, BB or lower by Standard & Poor's. Low ratings may be assigned at the time issues are new or, in cases of older issues—including "fallen angels" that once were of high quality—when companies' financial problems or restructuring lead the services to downgrade their securities. Funds invested in high-yield bonds have performed well at times, poorly at other times.

IRA.   Individual retirement account, a vehicle that enables an employee to save or invest for retirement in an eligible institution (such as a mutual fund) on a tax-deferred basis, supplementing an employer's plan in which he/she may participate. Depending on current law and one's circumstances, annual contributions to an IRA may be totally or partially deductible from taxable income. Deducted contributions and investment gains are taxed when distributed.

Income fund.   A mutual fund (usually a bond fund) that has as its principal objective the production of current income gained primarily through investment in debt obligations.

Indenture.   The contract between the issuer of a bond issue and its purchasers. It covers interest and principal payments, maturity, call provisions and other terms.

Interest rate risk.   The risk that the prices of outstanding bonds or bond fund shares will fall when interest rates rise. It is greater for bonds of long duration than for those of short duration.

Intermediate term.   Definitions vary. A period of five to ten years is a common one.

Investment adviser.   A firm (or person) that, pursuant to a written contract mandated by the Investment Company Act and approved by a fund's shareholders, regularly furnishes advice to a mutual fund with respect to buying or selling portfolio securities or is empowered to determine what securities should be purchased or sold. A fund's prospectus must identify the adviser, state the basis of compensation (around 0.5 percent of average net assets is average), and note any changes. The adviser may be an autonomous corporation or the direct or indirect subsidiary of such a company. If the latter, the prospectus must disclose who controls the adviser. Some funds have sub-advisers, largely to supplement the principal adviser's expertise.

Investment Advisers Act of 1940.   The act of Congress that provides for regulation of investment advisers by the Securities and Exchange Commission.

Investment company.   An issuer of securities, organized as a corporation, trust or partnership, which is primarily in the business of pooling investors' money for the purpose of investing, reinvesting and trading in corporate and government securities. The Investment Company Act of 1940 divided investment companies into three principal classes: face-amount certificate companies, unit investment trusts and management companies. It further divided management companies into two types: open-end, also known as mutual funds, and closed-end.

Investment Company Act of 1940.   The act of Congress that provides for the registration and regulation of investment companies by the Securities and Exchange Commission. It was intended to correct conditions, illuminated in an SEC study ordered by Congress in 1935, "which adversely affect the national public interest and the interest of investors." Conditions that needed correction included inadequate or inaccurate information regarding investment companies' securities and policies, management of investment companies in the self-interest of insiders, concentration of control through pyramiding, unsound or misleading accounting methods, excessive borrowing and inadequate reserves.

Investment-grade bond.   A bond receiving one of the top four ratings from the rating services (i.e., Baa or higher from Moody's; BBB or higher from Standard & Poor's).

Investment income.   The interest and dividend income received by a fund from issuers of the securities in its portfolio. It does not include gains realized from sales of securities. *Also see* Net Investment income.

Investment objective.   The goal that an individual or institutional investor plans to achieve through investing in securities. It is usually expressed as current income, long-term capital appreciation, or both (total return); if the latter, one may be accorded a higher priority than the other. A mutual fund must declare its investment objective(s) at the front of its prospectus and state whether it (they) may be changed without a vote of a majority of the fund's shares.

Investment policy.   The policy pursued to attain an investment objective. Most important, the investment policy indicates type(s) of securities that are to be bought. A mutual fund must state its policies in its prospectus, including not only the types of securities to be bought but also, if appropriate, the proportions of assets to be invested in each and the risks associated with them. The prospectus must designate which policies are fundamental—and, therefore, not to be changed without approval of a majority of the fund's shares—and which may be changed by management on its own. In the latter case, enlightened managements usually report to shareholders what they're doing and explain why.

Issuer.   A corporation or government unit that issues or has issued securities.

Junk bond.   *See* High-yield bond.

Load.   *See* Deferred sales load and Sales charge.

Long term.   Definitions vary. A common one: ten years or more.

Management fee.   The annual fee that a fund pays its investment adviser for investment advice, portfolio management and any administrative fees not included in "other expenses." Whatever the basis for compensation, to be disclosed in the prospectus, the fee is reported both in dollars and as a percentage of average net assets. The average management fee paid by the mutual fund industry is about 0.5 percent.

Market risk.   *See* Interest rate risk.

Market timing.   A technique intended to enable an investor to buy securities before their prices go up and to sell securities before their prices fall. Those who sell market-timing services claim that it enables investors to earn higher returns than they could by merely buying securities and holding them. Some question whether anyone can consistently practice market timing successfully. Traders who use mutual funds for this purpose have caused fund organizations to limit the frequency of switching (*see* Exchange privilege) because their transactions have tended to increase fund costs for other shareholders and have made portfolio management more difficult.

Maturity.   The length of time until the date on which an issuer promises to repay the principal of a bond.

Medium-grade bond.   Bonds rated A or Baa by Moody's, or A or BBB by Standard & Poor's.

Minimum initial investment.   The lowest amount of money a fund will accept to open an account. Some funds have no minimum at all. Others range from $250 to $25,000 or more. A number of funds permit investors to reach the minimum level over a period of time. Minimum initial requirements to open IRAs and other tax-sheltered accounts often are lower than those for taxable accounts.

Monetary policy.   The policy of the Federal Reserve System to influence the availability and cost of money and credit in a way that should promote economic growth, high employment and price stability. It is implemented through the management of three tools: open market operations (the Fed's purchases and sales of government securities in the open market), discount policy (setting the interest rate at which eligible banks may borrow funds from the 12 Federal Reserve Banks) and reserve requirements (the reserves that commercial banks and other depository institutions must hold against deposits).

Money market fund.   A mutual fund whose policies require it to invest at least 80 percent of its assets in debt securities maturing in 13 months or less.

Mortgage-backed securities.   Securities conceived to tap additional capital resources for residential mortgages by expanding the secondary market for them. A typical MBS represents an interest in a pool of millions of dollars' worth of conventional or government-backed mortgages, sold in denominations as small as $25,000 or less. MBS investors receive monthly "pass-through" of principal and interest payments, as well as unscheduled principal payments from homeowners who prepay their mortgages, and the principal of foreclosed mortgages. Of greatest interest to bond funds—and bond fund investors—are MBS issued by lending institutions that originated the mortgages and guaranteed by Ginnie Mae, as well as those both issued and guaranteed by Freddie Mac and Fannie Mae. (Ginnie Mae doesn't issue its own MBS.) *Also see* Federal Home Loan Mortgage Corporation, Federal National Mortgage Association, Government National Mortgage Association and Prepayment risk.

Municipal bond.   A bond issued by a state or local government (city, county, school district, special district, etc.) or one of its agencies to provide revenues—usually for capital expenditures—supplementing money collected from taxes and other sources. Municipal bonds are classified into two broad categories: general obligation bonds and revenue bonds. With certain exceptions, their interest payments are exempt from federal income tax and may also be exempt from state and local taxes. *Also see* General obligation bond and Revenue bond.

Municipal bond fund.   A mutual fund invested in municipal bonds. The exemption from income taxes of the interest payments received from the bonds' issuers is passed through to owners of a fund's shares. To call itself a tax-exempt fund, the SEC stipulates that a fund must have a fundamental policy requiring that at least 80 percent of its income will be exempt from federal income tax or that at least 80 percent of its assets will be invested in tax-exempt securities.

Municipal bond insurance.   A form of insurance, introduced in 1971 and now written by several companies, that guarantees timely payment of principal and interest on municipal bonds in the event that issuers default. Policies may be bought by state and local governments to cover their new issues or by mutual funds to cover outstanding municipal bond issues in their portfolios.

Mutual fund.   The popular designation of an open-end investment company that provides a medium for public investors to pool their money for investment in a professionally managed portfolio of government and/or corporate securities. A mutual fund may issue an unlimited number of shares and must stand ready to redeem (buy back) any investor's shares at the current net asset value (NAV) per share at any time. *Also see* Investment company.

NASD.   *See* National Association of Securities Dealers.

NASDAQ.   NASD's electronic securities quotations system through which eligible mutual funds' NAVs, offering prices and other data (as well as national market system and other over-the-counter securities' quotations) are collected and disseminated daily to news media, quotation vendors such as Dow Jones and Quotron and brokers. To qualify for the mutual fund media list, a fund must have 1,000 shareholders or $25 million in net assets. To stay on the list, a fund must have 750 holders or $15 million in net assets.

NAV. *See* Net asset value per share.

National Association of Securities Dealers (NASD). A self-regulatory organization, recognized in statute, that has jurisdiction over member broker-dealers (who are also registered with the SEC) and prescribes rules governing their handling of transactions in mutual funds and over-the-counter securities. One of its rules established the maximum for sales loads its members may charge when selling mutual fund shares. *Also see* NASDAQ and Sales charge.

Net asset value (NAV) per share. The value of one share of a mutual fund's common stock. It is obtained by subtracting a fund's liabilities from the market value of its assets and dividing the result by the number of outstanding shares. NAV is the price at which a no-load fund's shares can be bought and at which all funds' shares must be redeemed. Funds imposing a front-end sales load add it to the NAV, reducing the amount of an investor's money at work. Those imposing a deferred sales charge subtract it from the proceeds of share sales.

Net investment income. The amount that remains of a fund's investment income after expenses are deducted, enabling it to distribute dividends to its shareholders.

No-load fund. A mutual fund that sells its shares directly to the public (by mail, telephone, bank wire or at its office) and does not charge a sales fee, whether of the "front-end" or "deferred" type, to compensate salespeople.

Offering price. The price (sometimes called the "asked" price) at which a fund's shares are sold to investors. For no-load funds, it is equivalent to the NAV per share. For other funds, it's the NAV plus the sales charge.

Open-end investment company. *See* Mutual fund.

Par. A bond's face value.

Portfolio. The financial assets—cash, money market instruments, bonds, preferred stocks and/or common stocks—owned by an individual or an institutional investor such as a mutual fund.

Portfolio manager. The employee of the investment adviser—or perhaps the principal owner—who handles the day-to-day management of the portfolio. Some funds have co-managers. Others manage their portfolios by committees.

Portfolio turnover rate.   The rate at which the assets in a portfolio are changed during a given period, usually one year. SEC requires that a fund disclose its rate in the condensed financial information table at the front of its prospectus. For this purpose, the rate must be calculated by dividing the lesser of purchases or sales of portfolio securities for a given year by the monthly average of the value of a fund's portfolio securities. For this figure, the numerator and denominator shall exclude all U.S. government securities and other securities, including options, whose maturities or expiration dates at the time of acquisition were one year or less. A high rate may indicate a fund incurs high brokerage commissions and/or dealer markups. These may—or may not—result in a drag on performance; it depends largely on what the turnover achieves in enhancing total return.

Prepayment risk.   The risk that the owner of a Ginnie Mae or other MBS will receive principal payments ahead of schedule, primarily because a drop in interest rates has led mortgagors to prepay their mortgages. Under the circumstances, investors won't realize the income they had expected for as long as they had expected it. Those reinvesting cash flows from MBS will have to invest the unexpected additional cash at the lower interest rates then prevailing.

Primary investment.   If a fund's name implies that it will invest in a particular type of security other than money market instruments or tax-exempt bonds, SEC requires that its investment policy calls for at least 65 percent of its total assets to be so invested. (For money market instruments and tax-exempts, the concentration requirement is 80 percent.)

Principal underwriter.   A mutual fund's principal underwriter is the firm that, pursuant to a written contract, acts as a principal in buying fund shares for distribution or acts as agent in selling fund shares to dealers and/or to the public.

Prospectus.   The pamphlet (part of the registration statement) that a mutual fund is required by the Securities Act of 1933 and the Investment Company Act of 1940 to provide investors when offering its securities for sale. Its purpose is to supply essential financial and other information about a fund in a way that will assist investors in making informed decisions about whether to buy the securities. It covers such things as the fund's investment objectives and policies, investment risks, management, costs and distributions. *Also see* Statement of additional information.

Rating.   *See* Bond rating.

Real interest rate.   The rate of interest after adjustment for inflation—a more meaningful measure for some investors or borrowers than the nominal interest rate. If, for example, a bond has a nine percent interest rate at a time when inflation is four percent, its real interest rate is five percent. A bond can have a negative real interest rate when inflation exceeds the nominal interest rate.

Redemption. An investor in a registered mutual fund has the right to redeem his/her shares, that is, to sell them back to the fund, at the NAV at any time. (This contrasts with closed-end funds, whose investors sell their shares to other investors, via brokers, at market value, which may be above or below NAV, depending on the shares' supply-demand balance.) No mutual fund can suspend the right of redemption or postpone the date of payment for more than seven days, except in an emergency or other unusual circumstances.

Redemption fee. A charge, other than a deferred sales charge, that is imposed by some funds on the redemption of shares.

Registration statement. The document that a mutual fund must file with the SEC, in accordance with the Investment Company Act and Securities Act, prior to making a public offering of its shares. The statement is divided into three parts: the prospectus (which investors must receive), a statement of additional information (which investors may receive on request) and other information (which is primarily for the SEC's scrutiny and retention).

Reinvestment privilege. In lieu of cash payments, dividend and/or capital gains distributions can be automatically reinvested in additional shares of a fund, when requested by a shareholder. Some of the funds that impose sales loads on ordinary share purchases also impose them on shares bought through reinvestment. Under the NASD's rule, fees may run as high as 7.25 percent.

Reinvestment risk. The risk that the owner of a debt security, reinvesting interest in another issue, will not be able to earn as much from the new investment because interest rates are lower. Investors eager to avoid this risk can buy zero coupon bonds. *Also see* Prepayment risk.

Revenue bond. A class of municipal bonds backed only by the tolls, user fees, rents and other revenues received from the activity (airport, turnpike, etc.) for which a government entity issued them. They generally are more risky than general obligation bonds.

Risk. The probability that an investment can cause one to lose money or to make less than one could reasonably expect. The term is applied to several concepts: the risk that a business or government unit will be unable to meet its obligations to securities holders or fail altogether; the risk that the principal of one's portfolio will decline in current dollars (instead of growing) or be totally lost; the risk that the purchasing power of one's principal will dwindle because of inflation; the risk that the market value of more volatile securities bought to earn a high return may be down when one must or wants to sell them.

Sales charge (front-end sales load).   The difference between the price at which a fund's shares are sold to the public and the portion of the proceeds that are invested by the fund (or NAV per share). The sales charge, or commission, is shared by underwriters, dealers, brokers and other salespeople. Under the Securities Exchange Act of 1934 and the Investment Company Act of 1940, the National Association of Securities Dealers has the authority to prohibit its members from selling a mutual fund's shares at a price that includes an excessive sales charge. An amendment to NASD's Rules of Fair Practice, effective in June 1976, set the maximum at 8.5 percent of the offering price (or about 9.3 percent of the NAV). It stipulated three conditions: dividends must be reinvested at the NAV, quantity discounts recognizing previous purchases had to be offered, and minimum quantity discounts had to be made available. If a charge is imposed on reinvested dividends, the maximum sales charge is reduced to 7.25 percent. If none of the conditions is met, the maximum load drops to 6.25 percent. *Also see* Deferred sales load and No-load fund.

Securities and Exchange Commission.   An independent agency of the U.S. government, created under the Securities Exchange Act of 1934, that administers the laws covering the issuance and trading of securities. Its Division of Investment Management has responsibility for overseeing the regulation of mutual funds, other investment companies and investment advisers.

Short term.   Definitions vary. Sometimes refers to maturities that coincide with those of money market funds, that is, as short as one year. In a bond fund context, the reference is usually to periods ranging from one to five years.

Statement of additional information.   Also known as Part B of the registration statement, the SAI elaborates on information provided in a prospectus and also provides additional information. SAIs must be made available to mutual fund investors on request at no charge.

Subchapter M.   The section of the Internal Revenue Code that exempts mutual funds that qualify as "regulated investment companies" from the obligation of paying income taxes on their otherwise taxable income. To qualify, they must distribute at least 90 percent of their income to their shareholders and meet certain other conditions, including one of adequate diversification. Thus, the tax liabilities flow through to the shareholders (unless they're invested in tax-deferred accounts such as IRAs).

Tax-exempt fund. *See* Municipal bond fund.

Taxable equivalent yield. The yield you'd have to earn on a taxable investment to equal that of a tax-exempt bond or bond fund.

Total return. The growth (or decline) in the value of an investment, calculated to include the assumed reinvestment of interest and/or dividends and, in the case of mutual funds, the reinvestment of capital gains distributions. It is the most comprehensive measure of the results obtained by an investor from an investment and the most meaningful benchmark for comparing the performance of various investments.

For a fund, total return for a given period is the sum of the appreciation or depreciation in its NAV per share, income paid in dividends, and distributions from realized net capital gains; the latter two are assumed to have been reinvested in additional shares. Total returns covering various periods of years are expressed as average annual compounded rates by some, as cumulative figures by others. An SEC rule, adopted in 1988 to prevent misleading advertising and to standardize performance data for easier comparison by investors, directs any fund using performance data in an advertisement or brochure to include average annual compounded total returns for the most recent one-year, five-year and ten-year periods. The data, which must reflect sales charges, were mandated for three periods to show investors how returns can vary. Results calculated and published for a fund by its management and by data services may differ, depending on when the distributions are assumed to have been reinvested and on whether, and how, the computation reflects a sales load that the fund may impose on share purchases.

Treasury bill. A U.S. Treasury security, issued in minimum denominations of $10,000, maturing in 3, 6, or 12 months. Purchased at prices below their face values, they do not involve interest payments. An investor's return is the difference between the price paid and the proceeds received when a bill is sold or matures.

Treasury bond. A U.S. Treasury security, issued in minimum denominations of $1,000, maturing in ten years or more. Interest is paid semiannually.

Treasury note. A U.S. Treasury security, maturing in from two to ten years. Minimum denominations are $5,000 for two-year and three-year notes and $1,000 for those maturing in four or more years. Interest is paid semiannually.

12b-1 fees.   Certain distribution costs incurred by a fund, such as advertising and compensation for underwriters, brokers or other sales personnel, that are passed on annually to its shareholders under a written plan that complies with the SEC's Rule 12b-1, adopted in 1980. If a fund imposes such a fee, it must say so in its prospectus and state the rate, which can be up to 1.25 percent of average net assets. Depending on how long one owns a fund, the cumulative annual cost of 12b-1 fees can exceed even the highest front-end sales load in not too many years. Many funds charge both.

VA-guaranteed mortgages.   Mortgage loans guaranteed by the Department of Veterans Affairs (formerly the Veterans Administration).

Withdrawal plan.   The option that some funds give shareholders to withdraw a fixed amount of cash at regular intervals, necessitating sales of shares when distributions fall short of the requested sum.

Yield.   Widely understood as the rate of income received annually from an investment, expressed as a percentage of its principal—appropriate as the measure of performance for an investment whose principal is fixed, such as a CD, but *inappropriate* for investments whose principal is not fixed, such as bonds and bond fund shares. When current yield is calculated by dividing a bond's annual interest payments by its market value, it fails to take into account whether the bond is selling above or below par. The figure that does that and is, therefore, more meaningful is "yield to maturity," which reflects the amortization of premiums or discounts as well as income.

As popularly defined, yield also is improperly used as the basis for buying shares of bond funds and, until the SEC stopped the practice in 1988, was improperly used as the basis for advertising them. Whether bond fund shares are still sold orally on this basis by brokers and others, beyond the eyes and ears of the SEC, you may know firsthand. For a bond fund, the figure comparable to a CD's yield—a year's net investment income distributions per share divided by a fund's NAV per share—is more appropriately referred to as the "distribution rate."

What bond funds now call yields (or "SEC 30-day annualized yields") must be calculated in a way that reflects the amortization of premiums or discounts of their portfolio securities as well as their sales loads, if any. The SEC however, maintained that even this newly defined yield tells the reader of a fund ad or booklet too little about the fund and can even be misleading: a fund with a high yield, which might be favorably perceived, could actually have been—and continue to be—losing value. Therefore, the commission stipulated that yield can only be cited together with a fund's average annual total returns for the most recent one-year, five-year and ten-year periods. *Also see* Net investment income, Total return and Yield to maturity.

Yield curve.   The graphic plotting of yields of homogeneous debt securities for a range of maturities. The most frequently and widely published is the yield curve of Treasury securities ranging from 3 months to 30 years. When the curve slopes up to the right—indicating that yields are higher as maturities become longer—it is said to have a normal shape.

Yield to maturity.   A more meaningful yield figure than current yield because it not only reflects the discounted present value of all future interest payments at the coupon rate but also provides for the appreciation (depreciation) that will bring a bond selling at a discount (premium) back to par by the time it matures. A variation is "yield to first call"—a similar calculation reflecting the call price that would be paid on the first call date. *Also see* Duration.

Yield spread.   The yield relationships of bonds having different quality, call provisions or other attributes.

Zero coupon securities.   Debt obligations of the U.S. Treasury and other issuers, which are sold at discount from face value and don't pay interest. The size of the discount depends on interest rates and maturities. Instead of periodic interest payments and ultimate principal repayment, zeros provide for a single payment of the face value on a specific date in the future. The difference between one's cost and the face value is the return earned when a zero is held to maturity. Zeros are popular with investors who wish to avoid reinvestment risk and who want specific sums available on a certain date. At times, they can be extremely volatile, but that should not concern anyone holding them to maturity.

Bond Funds in Operation for over 5 Years (Through September 1989) by Investment Objectives

The following list includes funds, as classified by Lipper Analytical Services, that are generally available to individual investors.

TAXABLE FUNDS

Convertible Securities Funds

Fund	Fund Family
AIM Convertible Securities, Inc.	AIM
American Capital Harbor Fund	American Capital
Dreyfus Convertible Securities Fund	Dreyfus
Phoenix Convertible Fund Series	Phoenix
Putnam Convertible Income-Growth Trust	Putnam

Corporate A-Rated

D.L. Babson Bond Trust Portfolio L	Babson
The Bond Fund of America	American Funds
Dreyfus A Bonds Plus, Inc.	Dreyfus
GIT Income Trust A-Rated Portfolio	GIT
John Hancock Bond Trust	Hancock
IAI Bond Fund, Inc.	IAI
Kemper Income and Capital Preservation Fund	Kemper
Keystone Custodian Fund, Series B-1	Keystone
Merrill Lynch Corporate Bond High Quality Port.	Merrill Lynch
Nationwide Bond Fund	Nationwide
Phoenix High Quality Bond Fund Series	Phoenix

Fund	Fund Family
Pioneer Bond Fund	Pioneer
Putnam Income Fund	Putnam
SLH Investment Grade Bond Portfolio	SLH
Scudder Income Fund	Scudder
Security Income Fund Corporate Bond Series	Security
Sentinel Bond Fund	Sentinel
Sigma Income Shares, Inc.	Sigma
SteinRoe Managed Bonds	Stein Roe
Transamerica Investment Quality Bond Fund	Transamerica
United Bond Fund	United
Vanguard Investment Grade Bond Portfolio	Vanguard

Corporate BBB-Rated Funds

Alliance Bond Fund Monthly Income Portfolio	Alliance
American Capital Corporate Bond Fund, Inc.	American Capital
Axe-Houghton Income Fund, Inc.	Axe-Houghton
Calvert Income Fund	Calvert
Columbia Fixed Income Securities Fund	Columbia
Fidelity Flexible Bond Portfolio	Fidelity
Financial Bond Shares Select Income Portfolio	Financial
IDS Selective Fund, Inc.	IDS
IDS Strategy Income Fund	IDS
Massachusetts Financial Bond Fund	MFS
New England Bond Income Fund	New England
Newton Income Fund	Newton
PaineWebber Investment Grade Bond Portfolio	PaineWebber
T. Rowe Price New Income Fund, Inc.	Price
Thomson McKinnon Income Fund	Thomson McKinnon

Flexible Income Funds

Investors Income Fund, Inc.	Capstone
JP Income Fund	Jefferson-Pilot
Mutual of Omaha Income Fund, Inc.	Mutual of Omaha
National Total Income Fund	National
Nicholas Income Fund, Inc.	Nicholas
Northeast Investors Trust	Northeast
Seligman Income Fund, Inc.	Seligman
USAA Mutual Income Fund	USAA
Unified Income Fund, Inc.	Unified

Fund	*Fund Family*
Wellesley Income Fund	Vanguard

GNMA Funds

Dean Witter U.S. Government Securities Trust	Dean Witter
Federated GNMA Trust	Federated
Franklin U.S. Government Securities Series	Franklin
Home Investors Govt. Guaranteed Income Fund	Integrated
Kemper U.S. Government Securities Fund	Kemper
Lexington GNMA Income Fund, Inc.	Lexington
MFS Government Guaranteed Securities Trust	MFS
Merrill Lynch Federal Securities Trust	Merrill Lynch
PaineWebber GNMA Portfolio	PaineWebber
Pilgrim GNMA	Pilgrim
Prudential-Bache GNMA Fund, Inc.	Prudential-Bache
Putnam U.S. Govt. Guaranteed Securities Income	Putnam
Retirement Planning Funds of America Bond Fund	Venture
Vanguard GNMA Portfolio	Vanguard

General Bond Funds

CIGNA Income Fund	CIGNA
Colonial Income Trust	Colonial
Composite Income Fund, Inc.	Composite
FPA New Income, Inc.	FPA
IDS Bond Fund, Inc.	IDS
Keystone Custodian Fund, Series B-2	Keystone

High-Yield Funds

AGE High Income Fund	Franklin
AIM High Yield Securities, Inc.	AIM
American Capital High Yield Investments, Inc.	American Capital
American Investors Income Fund, Inc.	American Investors
Bull & Bear High Yield Fund	Bull & Bear
CIGNA High Yield Fund	CIGNA
Colonial High Yield Securities Trust	Colonial
Colonial Income Plus Fund	Colonial
Dean Witter High Yield Securities Inc.	Dean Witter

Fund	*Fund Family*
Delaware Group Delchester High-Yield Bond Fund I	Delaware
Eaton Vance Income Fund of Boston	Eaton Vance
Federated High Income Securities, Inc.	Federated
Federated High Yield Trust	Federated
Fidelity High Income Fund	Fidelity
Financial Bond Shares High Yield Portfolio	Financial
First Investors Fund for Income, Inc.	First Investors
GIT Income Trust Maximum Income Portfolio	GIT
IDS Extra Income Fund, Inc.	IDS
Investment Portfolios High Yield Portfolio	Kemper
Investment Trust of Boston High Income Portfolio	ITB
Kemper Diversified Income Fund	Kemper
Kemper High Yield Fund	Kemper
Keystone Custodian Fund, Series B-4	Keystone
Lord Abbett Bond-Debenture Fund, Inc.	Lord Abbett
Mass. Financial High Income Trust—Series I	MFS
Merrill Lynch Corporate Bond High Income Port.	Merrill Lynch
National Bond Fund	National
Oppenheimer High Yield Fund	Oppenheimer
Pacific Horizon High Yield Bond Portfolio	Pacific Horizon
PaineWebber High Yield Bond Portfolio	PaineWebber
Phoenix High Yield Fund Series	Phoenix
Pilgrim High Yield Trust	Pilgrim
Prudential-Bache High Yield Fund, Inc.	Prudential-Bache
Putnam High Yield Trust	Putnam
SLH High Yield Fund, Inc.	SLH
United High Income Fund, Inc.	United
Vanguard High Yield Bond Portfolio	Vanguard
Venture Income (+) Plus, Inc.	Venture

Intermediate Investment-Grade Funds

Boston Company Managed Income Fund	Boston
Fidelity Intermediate Bond Fund	Fidelity
MassMutual Investment Grade Bond Fund	MassMutual
Merrill Lynch Corporate Bond Intermediate Term	Merrill Lynch
UMB Bond Fund, Inc.	UMB

Fund	*Fund Family*

Intermediate U.S. Government Funds

Benham Treasury Note Fund	Benham
Eaton Vance Government Obligations Trust	Eaton Vance
John Hancock U.S. Government Securities Trust	Hancock
Prudential-Bache Govt. Intermediate Term Series	Prudential-Bache

Short Investment-Grade Funds

DFA One-Year Fixed Income Portfolio	DFA
IDS Strategy Short-Term Income Fund	IDS
T. Rowe Price Short-Term Bond Fund, Inc.	Price
Scudder Short Term Bond Fund	Scudder
Vanguard Short Term Bond Portfolio	Vanguard

Short U.S. Government Funds

Federated Intermediate Government Trust	Federated
Federated Short-Intermediate Government Trust	Federated
Midwest Income Trust Intermediate Term Govt.	Midwest
Twentieth Century U.S. Governments	Twentieth Century

U.S. Government Funds

AMA Income Fund U.S. Government Income Plus	AMA
AMEV U.S. Government Securities Fund, Inc.	AMEV
American Capital Government Securities, Inc.	American Capital
Carnegie High Yield Government Series	Carnegie
Colonial Government Securities Plus Trust	Colonial
Composite U.S. Government Securities, Inc.	Composite
Federated Income Trust	Federated
Fidelity Government Securities Fund	Fidelity
Lord Abbett U.S. Government Securities Fund	Lord Abbett
Mutual of Omaha America Fund, Inc.	Mutual of Omaha
Oppenheimer U.S. Government Trust	Oppenheimer
SLH Government Securities Portfolio	SLH
United Government Securities Fund, Inc.	United
Value Line U.S. Government Securities Fund, Inc.	Value Line

Fund	*Fund Family*

U.S. Mortgage Funds

Alliance Mortgage Securities Income Fund	Alliance
Financial Independence U.S. Government Securities	Midwest
First Investors Government Fund, Inc.	First Investors
Fund for U.S. Government Securities, Inc.	Federated
SLH Managed Governments Fund	SLH
Van Kampen Merritt U.S. Government Fund	Van Kampen

World Income Funds

Mass. Financial International Trust—Bond Port.	MFS

TAX-EXEMPT FUNDS

General Municipal Bond Funds

American Capital Municipal Bond Fund	American Capital
Babson Tax-Free Income Fund Portfolio L	Babson
Benham National Tax-Free Trust Long-Term Port.	Benham
Bull & Bear Tax-Free Income Fund	Bull & Bear
CIGNA Municipal Bond Fund	CIGNA
Calvert Tax-Free Reserves Long-Term Portfolio	Calvert
Colonial Tax-Exempt High Yield Fund	Colonial
Composite Tax-Exempt Bond Fund, Inc.	Composite
Dean Witter Tax-Exempt Securities Trust	Dean Witter
Delaware Group Tax-Free Fund USA Series	Delaware
Dreyfus Tax Exempt Bond Fund, Inc.	Dreyfus
Eaton Vance Municipal Bond Fund L.P.	Eaton Vance
Federated Tax-Free Income Fund, Inc.	Federated
Fidelity Municipal Bond Portfolio	Fidelity
Financial Tax-Free Income Shares, Inc.	Financial
Franklin Federal Tax-Free Income Fund	Franklin
Fund for Tax-Free Investors Long-Term Portfolio	Rushmore
General Tax Exempt Bond Fund	Dreyfus
John Hancock Tax-Exempt Income Trust	Hancock
IDS Tax-Exempt Bond Fund, Inc.	IDS
Kemper Municipal Bond Fund	Kemper
Keystone Tax Free Fund	Keystone
Lord Abbett Tax-Free Income Fund National Series	Lord Abbett
MFS Managed Municipal Bond Trust	MFS
Mutual of Omaha Tax-Free Income Fund, Inc.	Mutual of Omaha
National Securities Tax Exempt Bonds, Inc.	National

Fund	Fund Family
New England Tax Exempt Income Fund	New England
Nuveen Municipal Bond Fund, Inc.	Nuveen
Oppenheimer Tax-Free Bond Fund	Oppenheimer
T. Rowe Price Tax Free Income Fund, Inc.	Price
Principal Preservation Tax-Exempt Plus Portfolio	Principal
Prudential-Bache National Municipals Fund, Inc.	Prudential-Bache
Putnam Tax Exempt Income Fund	Putnam
Safeco Municipal Bond Fund	Safeco
Scudder Managed Municipal Bonds	Scudder
Security Tax-Exempt Fund	Security
Seligman Tax-Exempt Fund National Series	Seligman
Shearson Lehman Managed Municipals, Inc.	SLH
Sigma Tax-Free Bond Fund, Inc.	Sigma
State Bond Tax Exempt Fund	State Bond
SteinRoe Managed Municipals	SteinRoe
The Tax-Exempt Bond Fund of America	American Funds
USAA Tax Exempt High Yield Fund	USAA
United Municipal Bond Fund	United
The Value Line Tax Exempt Fund High-Yield Port.	Value Line
Vanguard Municipal Bond Fund Long-Term Portfolio	Vanguard

High-Yield Municipal Bond Funds

Fidelity High Yield Municipals	Fidelity
GIT Tax-Free High Yield Portfolio	GIT
IDS High Yield Tax-Exempt Fund, Inc.	IDS
MFS Managed High Yield Municipal Bond Trust	MFS
Merrill Lynch Municipal Bond Fund High Yield	Merrill Lynch
SteinRoe High-Yield Municipals	SteinRoe
Vanguard Municipal Bond Fund High-Yield Port.	Vanguard
Venture Muni (+) Plus, Inc.	Venture

Insured Municipal Bond Funds

First Investors Insured Tax Exempt Fund, Inc.	First Investors
Merrill Lynch Municipal Bond Fund Insured Port.	Merrill Lynch
Transamerica Tax Free Income Fund	Transamerica
Vanguard Municipal Bond Fund Insured Long-Term	Vanguard

Fund	*Fund Family*

Intermediate Municipal Funds

Benham National Tax-Free Trust Intermediate-Term	Benham
Dreyfus Intermediate Tax Exempt Bond Fund, Inc.	Dreyfus
Fidelity Limited Term Municipals	Fidelity
Fund for Tax-Free Investors Intermediate-Term	Rushmore
USAA Tax Exempt Intermediate-Term Fund	USAA
Vanguard Municipal Bond Fund Intermediate-Term	Vanguard

Short Municipal Funds

Babson Tax-Free Income Fund Portfolio S	Babson
Calvert Tax-Free Reserves Limited-Term Portfolio	Calvert
Federated Short-Intermediate Municipal Trust	Federated
Limited Term Municipal Fund, Inc.	Thornburg
Merrill Lynch Municipal Bond Fund Ltd. Maturity	Merrill Lynch
Midwest Group Tax Free Trust Limited Term Port.	Midwest
T. Rowe Price Tax-Free Short-Intermediate Fund	Price
Scudder Tax Free Target 1990 and 1993 Portfolios	Scudder
USAA Tax Exempt Short-Term Fund	USAA
Vanguard Municipal Bond Fund Short-Term Port.	Vanguard

Single-State Municipal Bond Funds

California

Benham California Tax-Free Intermediate-Term	Benham
Benham California Tax-Free Long-Term Portfolio	Benham
California Muni Fund	Fundamental
California Tax Exempt Bonds, Inc.	National
Dean Witter California Tax-Free Income Fund	Dean Witter
Dreyfus California Tax Exempt Bond Fund	Dreyfus
Fidelity California Tax-Free Fund High Yield	Fidelity
Franklin California Tax-Free Income Fund, Inc.	Franklin
Kemper California Tax-Free Income Fund	Kemper
Pacific Horizon California Tax-Exempt Bond Port.	Pacific Horizon
Putnam California Tax Exempt Income Fund	Putnam
SLH California Municipals Fund Inc.	SLH
Safeco California Tax-Free Income Fund, Inc.	Safeco
Scudder California Tax Free Fund	Scudder

Kentucky

Dupree Kentucky Tax-Free Income Series	Dupree

Fund	*Fund Family*
Massachusetts	
Fidelity Massachusetts Tax-Free Fund High Yield	Fidelity
Investment Trust of Boston Mass. Tax Free Income Portfolio	ITB
Seligman Tax-Exempt Fund Massachusetts Series	Seligman
Michigan	
Seligman Tax-Exempt Fund Michigan Series	Seligman
Minnesota	
Seligman Tax-Exempt Fund Minnesota Series	Seligman
Voyageur Minnesota Tax Free Fund	Voyageur
New York	
Dreyfus New York Tax Exempt Bond Fund, Inc.	Dreyfus
Empire Builder Tax Free Bond Fund	Glickenhaus
Fidelity New York Tax-Free Fund High Yield	Fidelity
First Investors New York Insured Tax Free Fund	First Investors
Franklin New York Tax-Free Income Fund	Franklin
Lord Abbett Tax-Free Income Fund New York Series	Lord Abbett
New York Muni Fund	Fundamental
Oppenheimer New York Tax-Exempt Fund	Oppenheimer
Putnam New York Tax Exempt Income Fund	Putnam
Rochester Fund Municipals, Inc.	Rochester
SLH New York Municipals Fund Inc.	SLH
Scudder New York Tax Free Fund	Scudder
Seligman Tax-Exempt Fund New York Series	Seligman
Ohio	
Seligman Tax-Exempt Fund Ohio Series	Seligman
Oregon	
Columbia Municipal Bond Fund	Columbia
Pennsylvania	
DMC Tax-Free Income Trust—PA	Delaware

Fund Families

AIM Distributors
Eleven Greenway Plaza, Suite 1919
Houston, TX 77046
800-231-0803
800-392-9681 (Texas residents)

AMA Group
P.O. Box 641910
Chicago, IL 60664-9986
800-262-3863

AMEV Mutual Funds
P.O. Box 64284
St. Paul, MN 55164
800-872-2638
612-738-4000

Alliance Capital
P.O. Box 4089
Secaucus, NJ 07094
800-221-5672

American Capital
2800 Post Oak Blvd.
Houston, TX 77056
800-421-5666

American Funds Group
333 South Hope Street
Los Angeles, CA 90071
800-421-0180
213-486-9200

American Investors
P.O. Box 2500
Greenwich, CT 06836
800-243-5353
203-531-5000

Axe-Houghton
Axe Castle
Tarrytown, NY 10591
800-366-0444

Babson Group
Three Crown Center
2440 Pershing Road
Kansas City, MO 64108
800-4-BABSON
816-471-5200 (Missouri residents)

Benham Capital Management
  Group
1665 Charleston Road
Mountain View, CA 94043
800-321-8321
415-965-8300

Boston Company Family of Funds
20 Cabot Road
Medford, MA 02155
800-225-5267

Bull & Bear Group
11 Hanover Square
New York, NY 10005
800-847-4200
212-363-1100

CIGNA Family of Funds
One Financial Plaza
Springfield, MA 01103
800-56-CIGNA
413-784-0100

Calvert Group
1700 Pennsylvania Avenue, N.W.
Washington, DC 20006
800-368-2745
301-951-4810

Capstone Family of Mutual Funds
P.O. Box 3167
Houston, TX 77253-3167
800-441-9151

Carnegie Family of Funds
1100 Halle Building
1228 Euclid Avenue
Cleveland, OH 44115
800-321-2322

Colonial Group of Mutual Funds
One Financial Center
Boston, MA 02111
617-426-3750

Columbia Funds
Columbia Financial Center
1301 SW Fifth Avenue
P.O. Box 1350
Portland, OR 97207-1350
800-547-1707
800-452-4512 (Oregon residents)

Composite Group of Funds
Ninth Floor
West 601 Riverside Avenue
Spokane, WA 99201
800-544-6093
800-543-8072 (Washington State
  residents)

DFA Investment Dimensions
  Group
1299 Ocean Avenue
Suite 650
Santa Monica, CA 90401
213-395-8005

Dean Witter
Two World Trade Center
New York, NY 10048
212-938-4554

Delaware Group
Ten Penn Center Plaza
Philadelphia, PA 19103
800-523-4640
215-988-1333 (Philadelphia area)

Dreyfus Corporation
666 Old Country Road
Garden City, NY 11530
800-645-6561
516-895-1206 (New York City
  residents)
516-794-5200 (Long Island
  residents)

Dupree Mutual Funds
P.O. Box 1149
Lexington, KY 40589
800-432-9518 (Kentucky residents)
606-254-7741

Eaton Vance Funds
24 Federal Street
Boston, MA 02110
617-482-8260

FPA Funds
10301 West Pico Boulevard
Los Angeles, CA 90064
800-421-4374
213-277-4900

Federated Investors
Federated Investors Tower
Pittsburgh, PA 15222-3779
800-245-0242

Fidelity Investments
82 Devonshire Street
Boston, MA 02109
800-544-6666

Financial Programs, Inc.
P.O. Box 2040
Denver, CO 80201
800-525-8085
303-779-1233 (Denver area)

First Investors
120 Wall Street
New York, NY 10005
212-208-6000

Franklin Distributors
777 Mariners Island Blvd.
San Mateo, CA 94404
800-DIAL BEN

Fundamental Portfolio Advisors
Suite 1107
111 Broadway
New York, NY 10006
800-225-6864
212-608-6864

GIT Investment Funds
1655 Fort Myer Drive
Arlington, VA 22209-9950
800-336-3063
703-528-6500 (Washington, D.C.
  area)

Glickenhaus & Co.
13th Floor
230 Park Avenue
New York, NY 10169
800-845-8406
212-309-8400

John Hancock Distributors
John Hancock Place
P.O. Box 21
Boston, MA 02117
800-225-5291

IAI Funds
1100 Dain Tower
P.O. Box 357
Minneapolis, MN 55440
612-371-2884

IDS Mutual Fund Group
IDS Tower 10
Minneapolis, MN 55440
612-372-3733

Integrated Resources
10 Union Square East
New York, NY 10003
800-821-5100

Investment Trust of Boston Group
P.O. Box 26070
Kansas City, MO 64196
800-634-0002

Jefferson-Pilot Investor Services
P.O. Box 22086
Greensboro, NC 27420
617-654-6054

Kemper Financial Services
120 South LaSalle Street
Chicago, IL 60603
800-621-1048

Keystone Distributors
99 High Street
Boston, MA 02110
800-225-2618
617-338-3400

Lexington Family of
    Mutual Funds
P.O. Box 1515
Park 80 West Plaza Two
Saddle Brook, NJ 07662
800-526-0056

Lord Abbett Group of Funds
General Motors Building
767 Fifth Avenue
New York, NY 10153-0203
800-821-5129

MFS Family of Funds
500 Boylston Street
Boston, MA 02116
617-954-5000

MassMutual Integrity Funds
1295 State Street
Springfield, MA 01111
800-542-6767
800-854-9100 (Massachusetts
    residents)

Merrill Lynch Funds
Box 9011
Princeton, NJ 08543-9011
609-282-2000

Midwest Group
700 Dixie Terminal Building
Cincinnati, OH 45202-3874
800-543-0407
800-582-1898 (Ohio residents)

Mutual of Omaha
10235 Regency Circle
Omaha, NE 68114
800-228-9596
800-642-8112 (Nebraska residents)

National Funds
600 Third Avenue
New York, NY 10016
800-331-3420

Nationwide Family of Funds
One Nationwide Plaza
Columbus, OH 43216
800-848-0920

The New England Funds
399 Boylston Street
Boston, MA 02117
800-343-7104

Newton Income Fund
330 East Kilbourn Avenue
Two Plaza East, Suite 1150
Milwaukee, WI 53202
800-247-7039
800-242-7229 (Wisconsin residents)

Nicholas Company
700 North Water Street
Milwaukee, WI 53202
414-272-6133

Northeast Investors Trust
50 Congress Street
Boston, MA 02109
800-225-6704
617-523-3588

John Nuveen & Co.
333 West Wacker Drive
Chicago, IL 60606
800-621-7227
312-917-7844

Oppenheimer Family of Funds
P.O. Box 300
Denver, CO 80201
800-525-7048

Pacific Horizon Funds
156 West 56 Street
19th Floor
New York, NY 10019
800-332-3863

PaineWebber
1285 Avenue of the Americas
New York, NY 10019
800-544-9300

Phoenix Equity Planning
   Corporation
100 Bright Meadow Boulevard
Enfield, CT 06082-1989
800-243-4361

Pilgrim Group
10100 Santa Monica Boulevard
Los Angeles, CA 90067
800-331-1080

Pioneer Group
60 State Street
Boston, MA 02109
617-742-7825

T. Rowe Price
100 East Pratt Street
Baltimore, MD 21202
800-638-5660

Principal Preservation Portfolios
215 North Main Street
West Bend, WI 53095-3317
414-334-5521

Prudential-Bache
One Seaport Plaza
New York, NY 10292
800-225-1852

Putnam Management Company
One Post Office Square
Boston, MA 02109
800-225-1581

Rochester Family of Funds
379 Park Avenue
Rochester, NY 14607-2894
716-442-5500

Rushmore Group
4922 Fairmont Avenue
Bethesda, MD 20814
800-343-3355
301-657-1500

SLH Investment Portfolios Inc.
31 West 52nd Street
New York, NY 10019
212-528-2744

Safeco Mutual Funds
P.O. Box 34890
Seattle, WA 98124-1890
800-426-6730
206-545-5530 (Seattle area)

Scudder Funds
160 Federal Street
Boston, MA 02110-1706
800-225-2470

Security Funds
700 Harrison
Topeka, KS 66636-0001
800-888-2461
913-295-3127

Seligman Family of Funds
130 Liberty Street
New York, NY 10006
800-221-2450
800-522-6869 (New York State
    residents)

Sentinel Group Funds
National Life Drive
Montpelier, VT 05604
800-282-FUND
802-229-3900

Sigma Group
Greenville Center
C-200
3801 Kennett Pike
Wilmington, DE 19807
302-652-3091

State Bond Group
Suite 1650
8500 Normandale Lake Blvd.
Minneapolis, MN 55437
800-333-3952
612-921-8833

Stein Roe Mutual Funds
P.O. Box 1143
Chicago, IL 60690
800-338-2550

Thomson McKinnon
1 State Street Plaza
New York, NY 10312
800-628-1237
212-482-5894

Thornburg Management
119 East Marcy Street
Suite 202
Santa Fe, NM 87501
505-984-0200

Transamerica Group
1000 Louisiana
Houston, TX 77002
800-999-3863
713-751-2400

Twentieth Century Investors
P.O. Box 419200
Kansas City, MO 64141-6200
800-345-2021
816-531-5575

UMB Funds
Three Crown Center
2440 Pershing Road
Kansas City, MO 64108
800-4-BABSON
816-471-5200 (Missouri residents)

USAA Investment Management
    Company
USAA Building
San Antonio, TX 78288
800-531-8000

Unified Management
429 N. Pennsylvania Street
P.O. Box 6110
Indianapolis, IN 46206-6100
800-862-7283
317-634-3300

United Group of Mutual Funds
2400 Pershing Road
P.O. Box 418343
Kansas City, MO 64141-9343
816-283-4000

Value Line Family of Funds
711 Third Avenue
New York, NY 10017
800-223-0818
212-687-3965

Van Kampen Merritt
1001 Warrenville Rd.
Lisle, IL 60532-1394
800-225-2222

Vanguard Group
Vanguard Financial Center
Valley Forge, PA 19482
800-662-7447

Venture Advisers
124 East Marcy Street
Santa Fe, NM 87501
800-545-2098

Voyageur Funds
Suite 2200
100 South 5th Street
Minneapolis, MN 55402
800-553-2143
800-247-1576 (Minnesota residents)

INDEX